ADVANCE PRAISE FOR
the culture of classroom silence

"Most educators are accustomed to thinking of classrooms as discourse communities, and much of the literature reflects that interest. There are over 22,000 entries on Amazon.com for books dealing with classroom discourse. The other side of discourse is silence. Understanding its sources and functions is equally important. In her far ranging book, Sandra Bosacki has tackled the complex issue of classroom silence with insight and sensitivity. She draws from recent work on Theory of Mind (ToM) to address the developmental meaning and course of silence in children and adolescents. In doing so, she artfully integrates a wide range of issues from academic achievement, to person perception, sexuality, and spirituality as facets of one's life impacted by the positive effects of silent introspection, and negative effects of silence engendered by ostracism, humiliation, and psychic withdrawal. With respect to the latter, Bosacki reaches into her own personal history as well as recent work on adolescent development to shed light on the ways in which reflective adolescents oftentimes silence themselves. Finally, she provides the educator with a psychocultural approach to structuring classrooms to make use of the positive sides of silence, while minimizing the factors that contribute to the negative impact of being silenced. *The Culture of Classroom Silence* is a breathtaking act of scholarship that makes a substantive contribution to our understanding of development and classroom life."

Prof. Larry Nucci, College of Education, University of Illinois at Chicago

the

culture

of

classroom

silence

AC / SS Adolescent Cultures, School & Society

Joseph L. DeVitis & Linda Irwin-DeVitis
General Editors

Vol. 31

PETER LANG
New York • Washington, D.C./Baltimore • Bern
Frankfurt am Main • Berlin • Brussels • Vienna • Oxford

sandra leanne bosacki

the

culture

of

classroom

silence

PETER LANG
New York • Washington, D.C./Baltimore • Bern
Frankfurt am Main • Berlin • Brussels • Vienna • Oxford

Library of Congress Cataloging-in-Publication Data

Bosacki, Sandra Leanne.
The culture of classroom silence / Sandra Leanne Bosacki.
p. cm. — (Adolescent cultures, school, and society, vol. 31)
Includes bibliographical references and index.
1. Interpersonal communication in adolescence. 2. Silence—
Psychological aspects. 3. Educational psychology. I. Title.
II. Series: Adolescent cultures, school, and society; v. 31.
BF724.3.I55B69   155.5'18—dc22   2004010425
ISBN 0-8204-6783-9
ISSN 1091-1464

Bibliographic information published by **Die Deutsche Bibliothek**.
Die Deutsche Bibliothek lists this publication in the "Deutsche
Nationalbibliografie"; detailed bibliographic data is available
on the Internet at http://dnb.ddb.de/.

Cover design by Joni Holst

The paper in this book meets the guidelines for permanence and durability
of the Committee on Production Guidelines for Book Longevity
of the Council of Library Resources.

© 2005 Peter Lang Publishing, Inc., New York
275 Seventh Avenue, 28th Floor, New York, NY 10001
www.peterlangusa.com

Printed in the United States of America

To question my father, John Michael Bosacki,
who claims that all silence is good.

CONTENTS

TABLES

PREFACE

The mental seeds of this book were planted years ago. I believe the topic of silence chose me and that I was meant to write on the topic of silence, to address how our society values and prioritizes verbal skills over all other skills to reflect one's heart and mind. As a child, I was always enthralled with the power of silence, the effect it seemed to have on others, regardless of context. In the classroom, walking on a beach, or at home, it appeared the lack of conversation or human speech unnerved most people in that they often would try to disrupt the silence, or "fill the void." I remember wondering why people looked uncomfortable in the midst of silence. Is it that we cannot read each other's minds? When people choose not speak or to withdraw from conversation, we are denied access to a window of their mental state; we have no idea what they are thinking. Although we could attempt to read the nonverbal language signals emitted, we really have no way of telling if the nonverbal messages are genuine either. People can feign interest, emotional expressions, and so forth. In general, silence often reflects ambiguity on the part of the listener as the observer wishes to understand the other's experience.

Two experiential strands within the educational system, academic and social, further fueled my fascination with silence. My adolescent years at school left me wondering about the mixed and ambiguous messages that educators would send regarding silence and speech. Although teachers encouraged us to respond verbally to questions in class or as contributions to group discussions, speaking out was not encouraged outside of the learning context, or only certain questions were allowed. Although never explicit, critical questions of the educational system were not encouraged. By the end of my elementary school years, I had learned that as a student, you did not question school authorities. Thus, student speech was valued only contingent upon the teachers' agenda.

Socially, my experiences as both a child and adolescent were that of being considered a "quiet, shy, sensitive girl." Always eager to please authority figures, from an early age I became frustrated by the fact that my voice did not do my thoughts justice. Thus, by early adolescence, I had learned to prefer writing to speaking. The process of writing allowed me to sort out my thoughts before I communicated them and, more importantly, before I was to be judged by others. I learned that speaking made you vulnerable to criticism and judgment, so across most contexts, it was safest to remain silent and to listen to others. As a child, I derived exquisite pleasure from the belief that no one could read my mind. My thoughts were my own; my imagination was private. I loved to read because each book provided me with another world to escape to. And the best thing was, no one knew what I was thinking! I savored the notion that you could appear to look engaged and make people think that you were psychologically present, but in reality, your mind could be worlds away.

My fascination with silence, the mind, and emotions increased as I approached puberty. I distinctly remember the month of May in fifth grade. As I sat on my front porch in total silence amidst the freshly cut grass on a warm spring day in southern Ontario, I reflected on the quality of my life as a 10-year-old. Amidst the peace and tranquility, I experienced an inner storm. I recall thinking about my social position within the classroom, my role within my family as the responsible, older sister, and the expectations weighted upon me to maintain my "straight-A report card." On the eve of my eleventh birthday, despite the fact that I had a loving, middle-class family, supportive teachers, and a couple of best girlfriends, I felt enormous pressure and stress. I had to be perfect. How was I going to achieve this perfection—and more importantly, how was I supposed to maintain it throughout my entire life? I remember thinking I could not speak to anyone about this, that I had to remain silent about my inner chaos, as it would destroy the façade I presented to others.

Something significant occurred during that summer between grades five and six, which in my mind provided the impetus for my ongoing fascination as a researcher with the transition from middle childhood to adolescence. Within the span of three or four months, I had changed from a confident, courageous, almost "bossy" 10-year-old to an often silent, unhappy 11-year-old who was very worried about receiving the highest grades, being the perfect daughter, and the most popular in school. I started to worry about everything, including my physical appearance and voice. I became extremely self-conscious of how others perceived me, why the boys did not find me attractive, why my parents kept saying I was intelligent and attractive. As I now read my sixth-grade diary, some of my entries during this time appear contrived and forced, as if I was fighting my own voice, or trying to hide my real voice, of how I felt at the time. Although I was extremely unhappy, I did not want anyone to know, so I hid my feelings from everyone, including myself.

Those diary excerpts resonate with me to this day. During sixth grade, I learned to silence my feelings and thoughts. For some unknown reason, I needed to protect myself from the stares and judgments of others. Failure and rejection terrified me. But as I continued to remain silent and act as if everything was normal on the surface, I failed to develop my ability to read my own emotions. I began to focus my energies on becoming an expert in reading the emotions and thoughts of others, not my own. How could I have failed to develop my own "emotional literacy" when I had excelled academically?

During adolescence, I became fascinated with the power and simplicity of the act of silencing others. Although I have had my own personal experiences of social ostracism, I remember feeling nauseous as I watched some of my high school classmates ostracize or deliberately ignore particular students. I remember seeing the pain in the girl's or boy's face as a group of adolescents would purposely leave her or him out, or ignore the classmate as if she or he were invisible. No one wishes to feel invisible, and I was entranced by the power of the "silent treatment" as a means of control in the social world at school. In my view, particularly as an adolescent, the "silent treatment" or ostracism reigned above confrontation as a tool of power and control.

During my research conversations with sixth-grade girls and boys in their classrooms concerning issues of self-worth, emotions, social popularity, and similar topics, their stories often reminded me of my own school experiences as a sixth-grade student. As I listened to their self-descriptions and their reasons for why they chose to describe themselves in such a way, many of their statements resonated within me. As they shared their thoughts, I could see the worry and the emotional turmoil in their eyes around the urgency to excel socially and academically. I often imagined how these children would look when they approached 30, if the seemingly confident ones would remain confident and pleased with themselves. I wondered what or who would determine how they would develop as individuals. Would it be their teachers, their friends, their family, or a combination of all three? How did their language and cultural background affect their self-cognitions and emotion? How did their personal growth in general affect their relationships and their subjective of the preadolescent within the school milieu?

From my perspective now as a white, middle-class, 36-year-old Canadian female researcher and educator with Polish-Ukrainian heritage, I was surprised not to find the word *silence* in the index of Blackwell's new text on adolescence (Adams & Berzonsky, 2003). Although the terms *voice* and *silence* have been explored by researchers and writers such as Carol Gilligan, Susan Harter, and many others, they have mainly explored the issues of silence from a more developmental psychological approach, and have focused on the experiences of female adolescents. The experience of silence affects us all, and given the importance of the teen years with respect to overall development, I believe that silence plays a special role in adolescence.

We need to explore the issue of silence experienced by adolescents within the school system. Both educators and researchers need to focus on the inner world of the adolescent, which includes the experience of silence and how this connects to experiences of emotion, spirituality, and so on. It is my hope that this book will encourage educators and researchers to think further about, and to continue to question, issues of language, identity, and emotion in their work with youth.

Furthermore, I remain puzzled by North America's fascination with the importance of speech, and the overvaluation of confrontation and argumentation in the school system. What do we do with those students who cannot speak or with those who have the ability but choose to remain silent? Why do we often assume that verbal expression represents understanding? Given that we cannot experience another person's subjective experience, how can we ever "really know" if people truly know what they are talking about—or if they really understand what they are saying?

I realize that this book touches on the broad questions surrounding the inner life and school experience of the adolescent. It is impossible to relive one's own experiences as a sixth-grade student and thus impossible to read the mind of an 11-year-old. This book developed from my own writing, research, conference presentations, teaching, and personal experiences during childhood, adolescence, and as an adult. I currently teach various graduate courses in education, including developmental issues in childhood and adolescence, educational research methods, and gender issues in education. Throughout the past ten years, the questions and comments from my previous research participants, students, and colleagues have influenced my thinking around the topic of adolescents' inner worlds. Accordingly, these multiple voices have been integrated throughout this book, as they have inspired me to think further on the concept of silence and the implications it has for the classroom.

It is my hope that this book adds to the growing literature on the emotional lives and silences of adolescents, and how silence plays a critical role in the adolescent school experience. On a more personal note, this book has helped me to try to understand my own inner life, and to realize that personal development needs the integration of understanding both others and oneself. I learned that to understand the voices and silences of others, we must also remember to reflect upon our own thoughts and feelings. I also learned that we must take care to remember not to only listen and care for others but also to listen and care for ourselves. My long-term goal as an educator and researcher is to continue my inquiry into our emotional and psychological lives and how this affects our relationships with others and ourselves. Perhaps, in the interim, I will achieve my personal goal, which is to learn to trust and accept myself as I do others. Thus, my pedagogical philosophy as a lifelong learner, educator, and researcher is that the "curriculum of life" must include the invaluable lesson of how to love unconditionally—not only others but ourselves as well, which includes accepting our silences instead of trying to avoid or stop them.

This book will assist educators of all ages by providing them with ideas to integrate the concept of silence into their classroom, and to address issues of self-growth, especially the spiritual and emotional aspects. In particular, I hope that this book will interest educators or "developmental interventionists" who are curious about exploring the needs of the "whole adolescent" in education. I wrote this book intending to appeal to a variety of educators and researchers, ranging from early adolescent educators and researchers to university professors specializing in socioemotional and spiritual/moral development. This book may also have an international appeal given that the topic of spirituality, emotionality, and education has become of interest to many educators across the globe.

I do not see this book as a definitive answer to any of the questions with which I have grappled. Rather, I hope that this book adds to the conversation in a much larger discourse about the inner and social worlds of adolescents and what adults can do to help them to trust themselves and to address the silences of adolescence. I hope that you enjoy my attempt to solve the puzzle of silence and schools. I hope that my words encourage you to reflect upon how silence affects you personally now and how it affected you during your adolescence. I also encourage you to reflect upon and to question how silence affects those adolescents whom you know in everyday life. If my conversation contributes some insight or if it creates new questions, it will have been well worth my efforts.

ACKNOWLEDGMENTS

Throughout the researching and writing of this book, I have had the invaluable support of numerous individuals. I owe a debt of gratitude to Brock University for providing a rich opportunity to learn from some of the finest scholars in education. I appreciated the timely response and constant support from my editor, Joseph DeVitis. I thank my editors Phyllis Korper and Chris Myers at Peter Lang for their time in responding to my questions, and to helping me with the production during the manuscript production process. I also thank the members of the production team at Peter Lang including Sophie Appel, Ace Blair, and Lisa Dillon for their guidance and patience.

I wish to thank all those involved with the schools in which I have conducted my research studies on adolescents' and children's thoughts and emotions over the years including the children, teachers, principals, school staff, and parents. Throughout the years, both at Dalhousie University and Brock University, I have had the pleasure to work with numerous graduate student research assistants on various research projects and I thank them all for their assistance and support. I thank Janet Astington and Wilfred Innerd for serving as my mentors, friends, and colleagues as I progressed through the stages of graduate school and for continuing to be a source of inspiration as I continue my research journey. I also thank my various committee members who helped guide my graduate work including Mary Louise Arnold, David Booth, Anne McKeough, Jack Miller, Susan Murphy, David Olson, and Shelagh Towson for their constant support and mentorship. I thank Chris Moore, my colleagues, and former students in the Psychology Department of Dalhousie University for their support during my postdoctoral fellowship. I thank my colleagues and friends involved with the *International Journal of Children's Spirituality*, especially Cathy Ota, Jane and Clive Erriker, Jack Priestly,

Mark Halstead, and Mark Chater for furthering my thoughts around adolescents' emotional and spiritual development. I thank Larry Nucci in the College of Education at the University of Illinois at Chicago for taking the time to read and comment on my book.

I thank Michael Manley-Casimir, Dean of the Faculty of Education, Brock University, Coral Mitchell, and John Novak from the Department of Graduate and Undergraduate Studies in Education, Brock University, and all of my colleagues and friends at Brock University for their warm support during the book preparation process. I have had the opportunity to discuss my ideas for this book in various classes that I have taught at Dalhousie University and Brock University, and I thank all of my past and present students for furthering my thoughts around the many ideas expressed in this book.

I thank the Faculty of Education, Brock University for their financial support of my communication with Peter Lang. Background research and reflection underpinning the ideas and data presented in this book was supported, in part, by funding from various grants and scholarships received from Brock University, the Ontario Institute of Educational Studies of the University of Toronto, Dalhousie University, and the Social Sciences and Humanities Research Council of Canada Postdoctoral Fellowship and Standard Research Grant #410–2003–0950.

Early versions of portions of this book are published in the *International Journal of Children's Spirituality*. Grateful acknowledgement is hereby made to copyright holders for permission to use the following copyrighted material:

International Journal of Children's Spirituality, Vol 3, No. 2, 1998, pp. 109–121, "Is silence really golden? The role of spiritual voice in folk pedagogy and folk psychology." Reprinted by permission of the publisher. All rights reserved.

Most importantly, I thank my parents and sister for their patience, tolerance, and humour while I devoted my time and energy to this project. Their love and emotional support has made this book possible.

INTRODUCTION

Schooling the Silences: A Psychocultural Exploration

The "holes" define the "shape."
(BRAHAM, 1995, p. 37)

This book aims to bridge the gap between theory and practice in the fields of human development and education regarding the notion of silence. Expanding on Belenky, Clinchy, Goldberger, & Tarule's (1986) notion of silence as "a position of not knowing in which the person feels voiceless, powerless, and mindless" (Goldberger, Tarule, Clinchy, & Belenky, 1996, p. 4), this book views the notion of "silence within the classroom" from the lens of both an educational researcher and a practitioner. I attempt to explore the meanings and functions of silence experienced by adolescents in the classroom: What does silence mean? What are the functions or what do we do with the silences? How do the functions differ if we create our silences or if others impose them on us? To answer some of these questions, this book provides empirical evidence as well as suggestions for both educational and clinical practice.

What does it mean when there is silence in the classroom? What are the experiences of adolescents when they are silent or exposed to silence in the classroom? What is happening in the hearts and minds of silent adolescents? To answer these questions, this book borrows from both psychoeducational research and holistic educational philosophies that explore the roots of classroom silence. I examine how individual differences and classroom culture—including gender, ethnicity, and language—affect our experiences of silence in school settings and suggest ways in which educators can redesign and rethink educational programs that acknowledge the notion of silence. To explore the landscape of classroom silences from the perspective of a researcher and educator, I outline multiple meanings of silence that adolescents may experience within the classroom.

It is hoped that this book's attempt to unravel the meanings of classroom silences will encourage educators and researchers to instill and foster the unspoken love of learning among the youth they work with.

Organization and Outline of the Book

By providing research findings and practical applications, this book can be inspirational in a theoretical and conceptual sense as well as practical for both research and teaching purposes.

This book is divided into four main chapters, each highlighting an important aspect of classroom silence. Chapter 1 critiques theoretical issues that surround concepts of silence and voice in adolescents. I also connect the literature on social cognition and spirituality to issues of silence. Chapter 2 explores some of the possible causes of classroom silences, their characteristics, and how they influence the school life of adolescents. In other words, why do some adolescents feel silenced by others or feel the need to silence themselves? Are the silences helpful or hurtful to the adolescents' personal and social lives? Chapter 3 describes some examples of when and where adolescents may experience silence in the classroom. To explore this question, the chapter outlines the extant literature on particular examples of current experiences of classroom silences. In particular, the chapter focuses on silences created by situations of exclusion, including status variables such as ethnicity/race, gender, and social class. I also explore the notion of silences experienced by adolescents with learning exceptionalities. Chapter 4 examines the practical implications of silence and the strategies and directions that educators and researchers might take in work aimed to support the development of healthy voices and hearts in adolescents.

Overall, this book aims to address the paucity of research on adolescents' concepts of silence within the classroom and how this may be linked to self-growth. Socioemotional and spiritual development are emphasized and provide current and relevant psychoeducational research that may lead to new questions and lines of inquiry.

· 1 ·

MEANINGS OF SILENCE: EXPLORING THE LANDSCAPE OF CLASSROOM SILENCE

What is left repressed, or what cannot be uttered, is often as significant to the whole shape of the life as what is said.
(BRAHAM, *1995, p. 37*)

Introduction

Given the complexity surrounding the concept of silence, this chapter aims to provide a road map to some of the meanings and definitions of silences within the context of adolescence and education. That is, to explore the question of what silences mean to adolescents, this chapter explores the multiple meanings and definitions of silence within the psychocultural context. More specifically, I review and connect the literature on silences to related areas of inquiry, including social cognitive development and spirituality in adolescence. I end this chapter with an educational model that may provide a conceptual framework to address the role of the spiritual voice in adolescence.

The Cultural Landscape of Adolescence: Shifting Silences

The main thread that weaves the pages of this text together involves the topic of silence, or what is not talked about is sometimes more important than conversation. This chapter begins with the assumption that we need to consider the culture as well as the adolescent within that culture. Drawing largely on psychocultural approaches to development and education (e.g., Bronfenbrenner, 1977; Bruner, 1996), the newly constituted discipline of cultural psychology or a psychocultural approach asserts that the person and the context cannot be considered as separate, distinct entities (Vygotsky, 1978; Wertsch, 1985). Similarly, Fiske, Kitayama, Markus, and Nisbett (1998) argue that "psychological processes are culturally contingent" (p. 915) and that researchers need to focus on how individuals construct cultures by incorporating cultural models, scripts, meanings, and practices into their cognitive, emotional, and social processes. Thus, this chapter applies the psychocultural approach to the concept of adolescence, schooling, and silence, and discusses the meanings, functions, and implications of silence for adolescents in the classroom. Particularly, I explore the questions: what is silence, how is it experienced within the classroom, and what do both adolescents and adults who work with adolescents do with it?

Many researchers and educators agree that adolescence (approximately 9–18 years) is one of the most pivotal times in an individual's overall development (e.g., McDevitt & Ormrod, 2004; Selman, 1980; Santrock, 1993). Regarding identity development and social interactions, according to the classical developmentalist G. Stanley Hall (1904), adolescence is the age when youths shift their energy from themselves to their social relationships and experience the "storm" and "stress" of life. Also, according to both Hall (1904) and Erikson (1968), the central task of adolescents includes the development of one's own identity within the social context. Thus, the adolescent's task is to develop a self-understanding within the social relationships.

Surprisingly, despite the significance of this crucial transitory time, the majority of past research has focused on adolescents' cognitive abilities (Harter, 1999). Why have researchers continued to neglect the spiritual and socioaffective aspects of adolescent development? Is there anything distinctive about their affective development and the place of spirituality in their lives? To answer such questions, this book considers how young adolescents make sense of themselves and the world around them. As Adams and Berzonsky (2003) suggest, as we enter a new millennium, researchers and educators who work with youth need to be open to new questions and new conceptions of adolescence because historic, scientific, and lay conceptions of adolescents have diverged.

In addition to the reasons previously mentioned, early adolescence is often considered to be of developmental interest due to the emergence during this period of reflective/abstract thought (e.g., Piaget, 1965; Chandler, 1987), an increase in gender-role expectations and behaviours, and the increase of self-conflict (e.g., Blos, 1979; Harter, 1999; Hill & Lynch, 1983). Furthermore, the lack of research at this developmental level on gendered social and self-understanding suggests that such an investigation would be fruitful. Early adolescence can also be viewed as a transitional phase, a discontinuous shift in the self-system. The characterization of the transition to adolescence as discontinuous is consistent with psychoanalytical, sociobiological, and cognitive-developmental models. Particularly during this time, conflict episodes may represent a rich microcosm through which novel self, peer, and parent relationships emerge and stabilize. A large amount of empirical and theoretical work supports the notion that early adolescence begins a period of shifting power dynamics that may give rise to competing goals and results in a higher density of conflict opportunities. As Baumrind (1991) suggests, adolescent maturity is thought to grow from "the balance between agency and communion, between separation and connectedness, and between conflict and harmony" (p. 120).

As adolescents struggle for balance, they may experience conflict, which in turn may lead to experiences of silences with themselves and others. That is, interpersonal conflict may lead to silenced conversations whereas intrapersonal conflict may manifest as a lack of private speech or inner dialogue. Thus, adolescents may begin to feel at conflict with themselves and with their own competing worlds of the public and private. Given that the adolescent needs to accomplish two main tasks, that of individuation and social connection, many researchers have noted the complexity and paradoxical qualities of this time that have implications for silence and voice.

Autonomy, Identity, and Silence

Notions of "silence" and "voice" illustrate the key role that language plays in psychosocial development (see Damasio, 1999, Donald, 2004, and Nelson 1996, for further discussion), and have often been associated with issues of autonomy, identity, and self-expression during adolescence (e.g., Harter, 1999). Zimmer-Gembeck and Collins (2003) suggest that autonomy is often widely used to refer to a complex set of psychosocial issues that are of particular importance during adolescence. Some view autonomy as a quality or trait of the individual, whereas others define autonomy as partially or fully dependent upon an adolescent's relationship with others or a response to others. Likewise, some definitions emphasize freedom from the constraints of childhood dependence on others.

In contrast, other definitions focus on the freedom to pursue goals, to make choices, and to regulate one's mental and social world. Overall, given that autonomy reflects multiple dimensions of emotions, action, and thought, achieving autonomy is viewed as one of the key normative psychosocial developmental issues of adolescence. Given that the three dimensions of autonomy (cognitive, emotional, and behavioural) are often viewed as interdependent (Zimmer-Gembeck & Collins, 2003), the term has been defined as a sense of individuation from parents and a time of relinquishing dependence on them.

Although all aspects of autonomy play a role in the experiences of silence in adolescence, emotional autonomy in particular may hold some special significance. Emotional autonomy is often defined as the ability of the adolescent to change conceptions of, and relations with, parents, including developing more mature conceptions of parents as adult people (Steinberg & Silverberg, 1986). In general, given that research is in its infancy regarding how the various dimensions of autonomy relate to the broader spectrum of adolescent psychosocial development, researchers need to continue to explore the role of autonomy and the thoughts and emotions linked to experiences of autonomy. For example, do those adolescents who feel much more autonomous also feel more free to express their voice, or are they immune to any social pressure to express one's thoughts when there is silence? In contrast, do adolescents who feel as though they are silenced by others or that they do not wish to be heard feel less autonomous and feel a greater dependence on others? Such questions may help researchers link issues of silence, voice, autonomy, and identity and therefore require further investigation.

Silence and Voice During Adolescence: Empirical Evidence

As soon as you trust yourself, you will know how to live.
JOHANN WOLFGANG VON GOETHE (*1749–1832*)

Regarding silence and voice with respect to adolescents' autonomous functioning, various researchers have explored the notion of voice and silence in adolescents over the past twenty years (e.g., Gilligan, 1982; Harter, 1999; Pipher, 1994; Rogers, 1993). In general, voice represents the ability to say what one is thinking, expressing an opinion. Although the various researchers interpret and use the metaphor somewhat differently, overall, voice represents one's ability to express one's identity and thoughts. Everyone possesses an "inner" and "outer" voice, in which the inner voice represents our genuine thoughts and feelings, and our outer voice is the voice we choose to communicate with others in terms of self-presentation.

According to Anne Rogers (1993), a significant learning occurs when we connect with emotion-laden experiences. Rogers argues that courage is integral to self-expression. That is, by "speak[ing] one's mind by telling all one's heart" (Rogers, 1993, p. 271), courage represents a connected mind, voice, and emotion. Rogers and her colleagues associated with the Harvard Project on Women's Psychology and Girls' Development found that their research indicated that some female adolescents might lose "trust in the authority of their own experience" (Rogers, 1993, p. 273). However, this loss of trust and voice may differ according to racial, class, and cultural backgrounds. For example, Rogers and her associates' research found that white, middle-class girls' loss of voice seemed to result from their efforts to conform to social expectations for female-appropriate behaviour and self-expression. Girls learn that it is unacceptable to discuss certain topics or to express certain emotions such as anger. To conform to these expectations, some girls decide to become "silent" and to stop saying what they really think and feel. The question that researchers continue to grapple with includes determining to what extent those girls who choose to go "silent" change their inner voices. Further, a related puzzling question concerns the extent to which girls' voices express their genuine thoughts and emotions, or their "true selves."

As others have noted (Fivush, 2004; Nelson, 1996), the use of language to represent our psychological worlds is a complex developmental process. Given this complexity, the underlying reasons why some adolescents choose to go silent (either publicly or privately) and the implications of such public or private silence are important for educators. For example, as a means of self-protection, silence can be used to avoid the threats to relationships that could result from the voicing of unacceptable thoughts and emotions. Ultimately, this public silence may affect girls' internal voices as well, developing into what Rogers describes as "psychological resistance—the disconnection of one's own experience from consciousness" (1993, p. 289).

Harter (1999) has claimed that autonomous functioning may be contingent upon the context and may vary according to the adolescent's perceptions of received support within each context (e.g., school, home, etc.). Harter's notion of "level of voice" (ranging from complete silence to authentic or speaking your heart and mind) suggests that an adolescent's level of voice is systematically higher in some context than others (e.g., school context, home, peers—either male or female). For example, in one study, Harter found that adolescents' voices were the highest with close friends and the lowest with classmates of the opposite gender, teachers, and parents. Issues of autonomy, voice, and silence will be addressed in more detail in Chapter 2.

As Blos (1979) noted, the ability to act independently of others and an interest in connecting with others are thought to be associated with psychological and physical well-being during adolescence. However, an unusually high level of independence paired with a negative orientation to others has the potential to be psychologically, physically, and socially damaging. The majority of evidence shows that the autonomy support provided by others and the adolescent ability to function relatively autonomously have positive influences on various aspects of adolescent functioning. The majority of adolescent researchers would agree that a balance between independent, self-confident action and positive social relationships fosters optimal psychological adjustment and development.

Why Are the Silences of Adolescents Special?

Over the past decade, psychoeducational research has come to envision adolescents as interpretive psychologists who depend upon a mentalistic construal of reality to make sense of their social world (see Bruner, 1996). This psychocultural approach to education provides a new framework in which to investigate the phenomenon of adolescents' social understanding or social cognition, including studies that explore "theories of mind" (e.g., Astington, 1993), various aspects of the "self" (e.g., Harter, 1999), and how these areas of social thought are connected to social behaviour and experiences of silence and voice. Although a growing body of evidence suggests that a positive link exists between social-cognitive thought and social action (e.g., Spatz & Wright Cassidy, 1999), few studies have examined such a link in children beyond the early school-age years (Watson et al., 1999). Given these past findings with younger children, it can be expected that such links may also exist between social-cognitive thought and behaviour among adolescents involving the role of language.

Despite the fact that the school is a complex social institution that provides a data-rich environment in which to explore how preadolescents make sense out of their social world, little is known about the role that social-cognitive processes play in self-development and social relations within the school context (Eccles & Roeser, 2003). Schools provide the main context within which adolescents develop particular aspects of their voice and self-identity. Given that schools are formal organizations and have their own characteristics (values, activities, rituals, norms), the school as a culture may influence all aspects of adolescent development. Viewed as a "culture," schools have the power to create an atmosphere that can either promote or impede self-expression.

A psychocultural approach to social understanding focuses on adolescents' abilities to recognize themselves and other people as psychological beings. It can draw on various social-cognitive and epistemological theories and research (e.g., Gilligan, 1982; Selman, 1980) and may shed some light on the wealth of findings from psychosocial studies that show a significant drop in self-worth, a loss in voice, and an increase in reflection and self-conscious emotions around the age of eleven (Buss, 1980; Harter,1999). Similarly, there is substantial evidence of declines in academic motivation, and attachment to school and academic achievement across the early adolescence years (approximately 11–14 years of age) (e.g., Eccles & Roeser, 2003; Simmons & Blyth,

1987). Such developments can have a direct influence on adolescents' inner worlds and how they choose to express themselves. In other words, schools have an important impact on how adolescents choose to voice their thoughts and cope with classroom silences.

Given the complexities surrounding the adolescent experience (both personal and social), the adolescent personal fable has often been discussed in negative terms because of its potentially dangerous consequences. That is, given that adolescents often believe that problems afflicting others will not happen to them (e.g., Elkind, 1967), they may disregard some natural limitations, sometimes even the permanence of death. Such beliefs of infallibility may lead to the engagement of risk-taking behaviours (e.g., driving while inebriated, extreme risk sports). The personal fable, however, may also have protective value against suicidal and depressive behaviour. For example, Cole (1989) found that adolescents who endorsed optimistic views of the future and life-affirming values were less likely to resort to suicidal thoughts or behaviour. Cole speculated that adolescents with a strong sense of their own invulnerability, and hence who neither see themselves as possible targets for silencing nor feel the need to silence their own voices, will likely see themselves as capable of coping and handling life's problems. Thus, in line with other researchers, Cole supports the idea that aspects of the adolescent personal fable may act as a buffer against suicidal thoughts and behaviour.

In contrast, sometimes impulsivity, fueled by the sense of invincibility and coupled with a failure to recognize personal limitations, may lead adolescents who feel alienated from their family and peers to develop self-harmful thoughts and perhaps attempt self-harmful behaviours such as suicide. The report on adolescent suicide formulated by the Group for the Advancement of Psychiatry (1996) suggests that the changes that characterize adolescence leave some young people at risk. A heightened sense of self-consciousness, fluctuating levels of self-esteem, and a degree of impulsivity may set the stage: The developmental characteristics may place particular adolescents at a heightened risk for inappropriate response to stress under the best circumstances. Even a relatively minor perceived loss, rejection, or disappointment in oneself can trigger self-destructive urges and thoughts, which can lead to self-silencing and self-alienation.

Adolescence is also a special time when many youth establish a degree of autonomy from their families and take significant steps in personal identity formation. At the same time, peer relationships become increasingly important during the adolescent years. Families and peers may have positive and negative consequence concerning issues of voice and silence. Although trusting and authentic relationships can provide an opportunity for adolescents to express their voices, such positive experiences are not always the case. For instance, when adolescents do not feel comfortable to voice their own opinions, they may distance themselves from their friends and families. Also, given North America's relatively age-stratified society, adolescents and their peers are apt to undertake these transitions simultaneously, producing a social milieu that may not be a positive source of support (Robbins, 1998). Thus, adolescents may feel silenced by their families or peers, which in turn may lead to greater self-silencing, and consequent depression, inner conflict, or similar emotional distress.

The Shifting Landscape of Adolescence: Sociocultural Perspectives on Gender, Sexuality, and Literacies

Recently, the academic discourse of adolescence has become increasingly complex and multivoiced (Finders, 1997; Santrock, 1993). The assumptions that underlie the developmental period known as adolescence directly shape teaching practices, curricular decisions, and social roles within the classroom. However, such discourse can construct "terministic screens" that tend to homogenize students, and may render many of their behaviours invisible to school personnel and researchers. As Burke (1990) explains, terministic screens work like multicoloured photographic lenses to filter attention towards and away from a version of reality: "Even if any given terminology is a reflection of reality, by its very nature as a terminology it must be a selection of reality; and to this extent it must function also as a deflection of reality" (p. 1035). Selection, therefore, implies deflection.

Britton (1970) refers to language as a representation, as "a verbally organized world schema" (p. 28), a map used for guidance from one experience to the next. Literacy, then, can provide a window onto the complex processes at work as individuals move from one context to another. Literacy and the mesh of lives, classrooms, and relationships in which they are embedded serve as a window onto the processes in operation as adolescents begin to negotiate adult gender roles that change across social settings.

Social interactions are performances that are enacted for particular audiences (Goffman, 1959). In other words, social roles shift depending on who is present and what the established expectations are of those present. Social roles, including those of gender should be defined as a performative act that represents multiple and shifting selves. This sociocultural approach to self and language suggests that the "self" is a permeable, fluid, dynamic, and developing process that is culturally created (Vygotsky, 1978). That is, individuals' self-views, emotions, and motivations take shape and form within a framework provided by cultural values, ideals, structures, and practices (Kitayama, Markus, & Matsumoto, 1995; Markus & Kitayama, 1994; Neisser, 1988; Wang, 2004). Thus, as Bruner claims (1990), "self is dialogue contingent" (p. 101).

Also, given the interest in the co-creation of the self in adolescence and how the cultural stories and self stories are interwoven, researchers have begun to investigate how cultural stereotypic gender-role expectations influence adolescents' self-perceptions within the school context (e.g., Harter et al., 1997). Various researchers have suggested that gendered stereotypic beliefs held by adolescents may also help explain gender differences in academic self-belief (Bosacki, Innerd, & Towson, 1997) and peer relations (Crick et al., 2001). However, given the complexity of adolescents' social world, research on why girls and boys may view confidence and competence in multiple contexts through a different lens remains sparse. Furthermore, the lack of attention on sociocultural issues in epistemological theories combined with recent research on adolescent girls' stereotypic gender-role expectations and negative self-concept advocates the need for further exploration of sociocultural influences including race, social class, ethnicity, and gender on issues of voice and silence (e.g., Goldberger, Tarule, Clinchy, & Belenky, 1996; Hill & Lynch, 1983).

Silence and Social Relations in Adolescents

Children's and adolescents' abilities to communicate effectively with others depends partly upon knowledge and skills that have little or nothing to do with language per se. Social conventions that govern appropriate verbal interaction are called sociolinguistic behaviours. For instance, children learn that they may have to greet others and to end a conversation with some form of a sign-off. Such behaviours fall within the broader domain of pragmatics, which includes not only rules of conversational etiquette—taking turns in conversations, saying good-bye when leaving, and so on—but also strategies for initiating conversations, changing the subject, telling stories, and arguing persuasively. Children continue to refine their pragmatic skills and sociolinguistic conventions throughout the preschool years and elementary grades; however, this development is affected by cultural differences as different cultures often learn different conventions, particularly in the area of social etiquette.

Regarding the feminist approaches to viewing silence, drawing on the earlier works of Perry (1970) and Gilligan's (1982) works on personal epistemologies, Belenky and colleagues (1986, 1996) framed the concept of silence within their theoretical framework of epistemological development among women. Goldberger and her colleagues view silence as a position in which an individual feels as if he or she does not know something, as if he or she is missing out on an important piece of knowledge. This sense of loss or incompleteness may lead the person to feel powerless, mindless, and voiceless. Expanding on this one-sided view of silence, scholars have explored how culture affects personal experiences of silence, and have investigated the conditions within which adolescents become silent. For example, is silence a choice or command? What are the functions and meanings of silence in one's culture?

To describe this distinction between being silenced by others and choosing to be silent among others, or self-silencing, Goldberger and her colleagues suggested that structural silence (or societal rules that dictate when individuals should speak or be silent) may lead to particular individuals feeling "silenced." That is, such structural silence may drive some people to a defensive stance of silence and passivity that stem from feelings of fear and threat. In contrast to this structural silence in which an individual has either little or no control, Goldberger and colleagues refer to *strategic* silence. Situational and cultural factors can dictate individual strategic silence in which the individual deliberately chooses to be silent and is still able to engage in conversations as an active contributing knower.

Regarding the role silence and conversation play in the subtleties of social interaction, researchers remain challenged by the questions of how well children understand the mental states and emotions of others, how this ability influences their experiences of silence, and how these experiences connect in a way that influences their sense of self-worth and social behaviour. Understanding how adolescents co-construct their knowledge of others and what they do with this knowledge within social situations is similar to feminists' interests in how the sociocultural construction of knowledge is affected by sociopolitical structures. Given that feminist analysis often offers "a sharper articulation of the different strands—intellectual, imaginative, and affective— involved in human ways of thinking" (Lloyd, 1998, p. 172), I draw on the feminist lens to help unpack Nelson, Henseler, and Plesa's (2000) notion of psychological pragmatics.

Psychological pragmatics refers to a dynamic knowledge system comprised of self-views, emotions, and cognitions that undergoes constant creation and re-creation through social interaction (Nelson et al., 2000). This approach to psychological understanding is grounded in experiential knowledge gained in socioculturalinguistic contexts and is consistent with the principles of feminist epistemologies. This dialogical system allows us to understand the mental states of ourselves and others within a framework of action provided by cultural values, ideals, structures, and practices. Building on psychocultural theories of self-systems and social behaviour (e.g., Bussey & Bandura, 1999), researchers have started to explore the complex links between psychological pragmatics and self-worth within the school culture. Thus, researchers have started to explore the claim that the sense of self may play an intervening role in the co-creation of our ability to be psychologically pragmatic (mental state understanding enacted through social interactions). Given the lack of research on the gendered links between social thought, peer culture (e.g., values, linguistic, and behavioural norms), and school behaviour (e.g., Bosacki & Astington, 1999; Underwood, Galen, & Paquette, 2001), future research is needed.

As many scholars have suggested (e.g., Bruner, 1996), quite often, the focus of language educational programs is on the verbal components and promotes verbal and social skills that encompass verbal ability. In contrast, few language programs focus on fostering the nonverbal skills, including the art of listening and observation (e.g., Haynes, 2002). In addition, few educational programs focus on the pragmatic or sociolinguistic skills involved in social and emotional learning. Various holistic educators have mentioned this gap in both the developmental and educational literature, particularly regarding the lack of focus on the promotion of "intrapersonal skills," which entail periods of silent contemplation and reflection. Children and adolescents need the opportunity to "listen to themselves," including their thoughts, feelings, and physical sensations (Cohen, 1999).

As Piaget noted, "There is no cognitive mechanism without affective elements" (Piaget, 1981, p. 3); emotions play a critical role in learning and particularly in language development (Denham, 1998; Denham et al., 2002; Saarni, 1999). The connections among emotional development and language are complex and have strong implications for the educational context, particularly the elementary and secondary school classroom. As many researchers on emotions note, sometimes the expression of emotion is contingent upon a particular label or emotion word. Thus, building on the previously mentioned Goldberger's (1996) notion of structural and strategic silence, both types of silences may have different emotional implications. Regarding the case of structural silence, an adolescent may feel "silenced," either due a lack of knowledge of the emotion word or by the "other" who does not allow the child to speak. Such a type of silence may be linked to social situations and interpersonal interactions. Regarding the experience of strategic silence, an adolescent may choose not to express a particular emotion or articulate a particular emotion label. This experience of strategic silence may be more personal in nature, and although the motivation to self-silence may be influenced by the interactions of others, the decision to remain silent remains at a more private level (Jack, 1991, 1999).

Given the importance of emotions in adolescents' lives, decisions regarding verbal expression are often value- and affect-laden. To name or label an emotion is to make a statement of value. Emotion understanding or knowledge refers to the ability to identify the expression on a peer's face or comprehend the emotions elicited by common social situations (Denham, 1998; Denham et al.,

2003). As an integral part of emotional competence, I have chosen to use Saarni's definition of emotion understanding as the ability to discern one's own and others' emotional states and to use the vocabulary of emotion effectively (Saarni, 1999).

In the past 15 years, there has been a surge of interest in the development of emotion understanding among children and adolescents (Saarni, 1999). Transcultural research shows that across the world, most children begin talking about emotions around two to three years of age (Denham, 1998). Recent research has shown that beginning in the preschool years, emotional lives become quite complex (see Denham et al., 2002). For example, research has shown that between the ages of two and four, children learn to label emotions accurately and begin to understand that certain situations are linked to certain emotions (see Denham, 1998; Harris, 1989). They show substantial ability to use emotion-descriptive adjectives, understand these terms in conversations with adults, and begin to employ emotion language to meet their own emotional needs. However, despite the increasing interest in children's and adolescents' emotional development, much remains to be learned about the complex processes involved.

Cognitive-developmental research has shown that across most cultures, children begin to first talk about the simple or basic emotions (e.g., happy, sad) (Denham, 1998). Accordingly, such emotions have been claimed to be innate and exist transculturally. Interestingly, the more complex emotions (social and moral), also sometimes referred to as secondary emotions, involve more complex reasoning and cognitive development. Emotions such as pride and embarrassment require the child to reflect upon her or his self-concept and to imagine the value judgment of others.

Despite the importance of emotions to language and social development, the complex or self-conscious emotions have remained somewhat neglected in the study of adolescents' emotion understanding. The majority of emotion research on children and adolescents has focused almost exclusively on the "simple" or primary and basic emotions (i.e., emotions linked to underlying physiology), such as happy and sad. In contrast, complex or secondary "self-conscious" emotions such as pride and embarrassment that involve the ability to self-evaluate against internalized standards of behaviour have received considerably less attention (Saarni, 1999). Thus, although a strong theoretical link exists among complex emotions, sense of self, and social relations, little is known about how such a nexus develops and differs in children and adolescents (Lewis et al., 1989).

As noted earlier, although strategic silence suggests a sense of personal agency in that it represents a speaker's decision to either refrain or withdraw from a conversation, the speaker's decision may be independent of any outside forces or, alternatively, the individual may feel pressured to comply with the silence and may therefore feel "silenced." Thus, the process of "silencing" is complex, and the decision to remain silent in a public forum may also have either positive or negative affect attached. For example, regarding academic learning, an adolescent who is called upon in class and chooses to remain silent may lead to a number of possible scenarios. One scenario could be that the silence either frustrates the teacher or challenges the teacher to encourage a response. A second scenario could involve the adolescent's peers, who then treat the silent adolescent differently. Thus, the decision to remain silent in the classroom has implications for both the teacher and the peers in that the reactions solicited from the audience (teacher and peer) may create a mainly negative emotional reaction such as increased self-consciousness and possible anxiety.

In contrast, adolescents asked to engage in structured class silence or "quiet time" such as silent reading may experience positive emotions. That is, this task provides the opportunity for adolescents to remain silent and to listen to themselves (exercise their imaginative and creative abilities by listening to both mental and physical messages from within). Both strategic and structural silence, as defined by an absence of verbal expression, provide an opportunity for an individual to listen to her or his thoughts, emotions, and physical sensations, which, in turn, may have either positive or negative influences on an adolescent's sense of self-worth and personal competence.

Similar to academic experiences, within the school context, social situations also entail experiences of silence, and such experiences may either ameliorate or exacerbate the adolescent's sense of social competence and confidence (Kessler, 2000). Given that a psychocultural approach to personal experiences of silence is founded on an interest in identifying what resources (experiential, cognitive, affective, linguistic, etc.) are most useful to the adolescent in a social world, we need to explore what the adolescent needs to know and feel to participate effectively in a variety of social contexts. Once these resources are acquired, how do adolescents apply these tools to social situations? Moreover, how does an adolescent's psychological and self-knowledge emerge out of experience in different pragmatic circumstances? The psychocultural approach assumes that the abstract knowledge construct is built out of experiential, pragmatic knowledge acquired in an interpreted, social world. This developmental view of psychological understanding agrees with various scholars' thinking on the connections between thought, language, and behaviour within the social world (e.g., Bruner, 1996; Dunn, 1988; Vygotsky, 1978).

One situation commonly found among adolescents includes the case of social withdrawal and shyness (Rubin, Burgess, & Coplan, 2002). Within this framework, silence is often connected with negative social experiences and emotions, and silence may carry different psychological meanings that represent different motivations underlying the silence. These experiences of silence may be especially pronounced during social group situations, where verbal expression is often equated with confidence, popularity, and social status. Such situations occur frequently during childhood and adolescence, when an adolescent who holds psychological power over another adolescent in the social hierarchy chooses to harass or psychologically damage the adolescent with lower social status by choosing not to speak to the adolescent. That is, a popular adolescent may choose not to speak to another peer or not to respond to the adolescent's request. This "silent treatment" is often considered a form of psychological or emotional harassment if the adolescent receiving the silence is hurt emotionally, as the silence may be interpreted as a sign of rejection.

Alternatively, adolescents who find it stressful to join social groups or who are painfully shy may choose to remain silent in a group situation to avoid the negative feelings that may arise from possible rejection (Rubin et al., 2002). That is, adolescents may wish to say something to another peer, but the thought of rejection, social evaluation, and/or ridicule may prevent them from taking the risk to express their thoughts. If adolescents feel inhibited in a sense that they wish to contribute but cannot due to fear, some adolescents often decide either to remain silent or to withdraw from the social situation. In contrast to adolescents who choose to remain silent, those adolescents who are verbally and socially competent may experience feelings of control and powerfulness, as they may be aware of their ability to influence another adolescent's behaviour. Other adolescents may also choose to remain silent in that they are socially disinterested. They may lack the motivation to approach others while at the same time not necessarily have the motivation to avoid others. That is, when such individuals are approached by others, they will not remain reticent and retreat and may not experience wariness and anxiety (Rubin et al., 2002).

Social silence may also be experienced as ostracism or "being silenced" by others. This phenomenon of "feeling invisible," of being excluded from the social interactions of those around you, is discussed in more detail later on in the book, and is discussed in relation to forms of psychological and emotional harassment or bullying. The seemingly simple act of silencing someone else or performing the "silent treatment" has significant ramifications for all aspects of development, particularly during adolescence, when the peer group plays a large role in psychosocial, spiritual, and emotional health (Lightfoot, 1997). As many researchers on adolescents and the phenomenon of peer pressure have noted, engagement in some risk-taking behaviours may sometimes be due to the need to belong and to avoid ostracism and rejection (Williams, 2001).

Related literature on school bullying, peer harassment, and aggression has noted that the covert, indirect bullying acts such as social exclusion and the spreading of rumors may have greater emotional and psychological implications, including lowered sense of self-worth, compared to more direct and physical types of bullying such as punching and shoving (Crick et al., 2001; Marini, Dane, Bosacki, & YLC-CURA, 2002; Goodwin, 2002). As William James (1890) noted over one century ago, "A man's Social Self is the recognition which he gets from his mates. . . . If no one turned around when we entered, answered when we spoke, or minded what we did, but if every person we met 'cut us dead,' and acted as if we were nonexisting things, a kind of rage and impotent desire would ere long well up in us, from which the cruelest bodily tortures would be a relief; for these would make us feel that, however bad be our plight, we had not sunk to such a depth as to be unworthy of attention at all" (pp. 293–294). Chapter 2 extends the discussion around the experience of being socially silenced by others through ostracism, when I describe some of the social situational factors within the classroom involved with silencing.

In general, for some adolescents, silence may be viewed as a source of inspiration and as a psychological and emotional venue for quiet reflection or intense intellectual engagement. However, for others, silence may be accompanied by loneliness and emotional pain. The latter vision of silence may thus bring wariness in social company, victimization, and fear of rejection. In short, both the antecedents and consequences of the behavioural expression of silence remain contingent upon the individual and the context.

Early developmental theories and supportive data suggest that peer interaction influences the development of social cognition, and ultimately, the expression of competence social behaviour. Social interaction (with either peers or adults) also influences children's understanding of the cultural and subcultural rules and norms that guide social behaviours. This understanding of normative performance levels enables the child to evaluate her or his own competency against the perceived standards of the peer group. Related to the social group and being silenced or to the silencer, sometimes when silence is combined with solitude, this may relate to spiritual awareness or a sense of meta-awareness in which the individual becomes aware of "being aware." They are, as Buber (1970) stated, "manifestations of relation," or moments of complete engagement with what-is-there.

If social interaction does play a crucial role in the development of social competencies and the understanding of the self in relation to others, a question for researchers concerns the developmental consequences for those adolescents who, for whatever reason, refrain from engaging in social interaction and avoid the company of others. This question drives much of the current research on social withdrawal and the accompanying experiences of silence. For example, recent research suggests that the knowledge on the developmental consequences of social silence is constrained by cultural norms. Some studies suggest that in Western societies, shyness/social withdrawal may be less acceptable for boys than for girls (Sadker & Sadker, 1994). Furthermore, compared to Western countries, shyness and social silence are more prevalent and carry more societal value in Eastern countries such as China (Chen, Rubin, & Li, 1995). Clearly, future research is required to elucidate these provocative findings.

Spirituality, Silence, and Language

Although the word *silence* is ubiquitous and often found throughout many educational and psychological literatures, many researchers claim that silence may serve as a prerequisite to reflection and an integral part of the creative process (reflection and practice) (e.g., Goldberger et al., 1996; Kessler, 2000). This book focuses on silence as a form of communication and an integral part of the sociolinguistic repertoire that is learned and followed by children and adolescents. The "art of conversation" entails a sociolinguistic repertoire of practice that allows adolescents to learn and practice sociolinguistic behaviours that are guided by social and cultural conventions that govern appropriate verbal interaction. The art of conversation thus entails both the act of speaking *and* listening.

As Berryman (2001) suggests, silence may communicate as a call but involves no sound. Silence can signal as well as sound calls. Given the ambiguity of the language used to refer to silence, in various languages, there is a cluster of words that refer to communication without sound. In English, they are "stillness," "silence" and "quiet." All three must be considered in the interpretation of silence because no single one contains all that is meant by the whole. One of my tasks in this book is to depict the complexity of silence within the classroom of the adolescent. I will also return the notion of "quiet" later on in the book when I describe the use of the label "quiet student" in the classroom and the emotional and psychological factors involved in that use of a label to describe a human being.

Silence is one of three calls used by human beings to signal aspects of their spirituality (Berryman, 2001). The two remaining calls are the two basic emotions of sadness and happiness expressed by the acts of crying and laughing. The roles of emotion and language play in the experiences of silence will be discussed later on in the book. To further explore the concept of "silence," stillness refers to both movement and sound. For example, when the river is still and not moving, it remains silent. Movement and sound are related, as movement can be viewed in the medium of light (waves or quanta) as it stimulates our eyes as well as in the medium of air as sound waves stimulate our ears. The distinction between silence and quiet is on the basis of motivation. For example, the motivation to be quiet usually stems from inside of us, whereas silence may be imposed on us from the outside. Classroom silence, for example, can be imposed to force an outward calm, while at the same time increase inward agitation and anxiety.

A recent example of the connections between silence and spirituality or religiosity is the group of Carmelite nuns who live in a monastery outside of Montreal, Quebec, who have taken a vow of silence. Recently, however, the surviving 19 nuns have agreed to break their vow of silence for the benefits of science. A research team led by Dr. Mario Beauregard, a neuroscientist with the psychology department of the University of Montreal, is interested in exploring the "neurobiology of faith and belief" by exploring the brains of the nuns when they are experiencing a spiritual moment or one of "religious rapture," as one nun as stated (Steeves, 2003). The researchers will use functional MRI (Magnetic Resonance Imaging) techniques to examine the pattern of blood flow within the nuns' brains as they are asked to re-create times of spiritual bliss or "religious rapture." As Beauregard states, he would like to have a clear, biological picture of an experience that mystifies even those who have lived it. This human ability to create and understand mental states continues to remain an unsolvable puzzle for researchers across a wide array of academic disciplines from neurobiology to philosophy and education.

Although the term *spirituality* refuses to be defined or captured by one definition (e.g., Flanagan, 2002), I will address spirituality here in the sense of having the ability to be aware and accepting of your inner world at the present moment, or holding a meta-awareness about your state of being. Spiritual voice, discussed later on in the book, refers to the ability to express one's authentic or genuine thoughts and feelings, or the notion of expressing one's thoughts and feelings with all of your heart. What follows below is a brief overview of how spirituality may play a role in one's ability to be silent.

Spirituality: A Brief Overview

Given the connection between silence and spiritual experiences, researchers are interested in exploring the following questions: What does it mean when there is spirituality in the classroom or psychologist's office and how is it connected to silence? What are the experiences of children and youth when they claim to be spiritual or have had a spiritual experience? What happens in the hearts and minds of children and youth when they experience the spiritual? This section of the chapter borrows from both psychoeducational and cognitive science research and holistic educational philosophies that explore the roots of spirituality to examine how individual differences in spirituality are influenced by sociocultural factors such as the media, school, religious beliefs, gender, ethnicity, and language among children and youth.

To explore the landscape of spirituality and silence in youth, I outline multiple meanings of spirituality and related terms such as religiosity, morality, and moral or social emotions from the perspectives of both researchers and practitioners. Theoretical and practical implications are discussed to bridge theory and practice in the fields of human development and education to help unravel the meanings of spiritual development and spirituality and to encourage educators and researchers to consider how silence and spirituality may play a role in the educational experiences of the adolescent.

Conflicts exist between two self-views or visions of persons entrenched within two different worldviews. One view depicts humans as possessing a spiritual component or an incorporeal mind or "soul" (Flanagan, 2002), similar to the worldviews or ways of knowing (e.g., Goldberger et al., 1996; Bruner, 1996). In contrast, the second view states that a soul does not exist and that we are finite, social animals (logico-scientific or paradigmatic view). This humanistic versus scientific image reflects the centuries-old debate of body vs. mind, animal vs. human, which in turn guides philosophies underlying academic disciplines such as psychology and education (Flanagan, 2002). The question of "what makes us a good person?" continues to puzzle both educators and psychologists alike. Although I do not claim to provide any answers to this question, I hope to create additional questions that may inspire further inquiry and dialogue surrounding the role silence plays in psychology and education, especially in the mind and soul of adolescents.

Spirituality, Religiosity, and Faith Development

Given the complexities of psychology, education, and spirituality, basic definitions involving psychology and spirituality need to be outlined. Webster's (1989) dictionary defines religion as "a man's expression of his acknowledgment of the divine; a system of beliefs and practices relating to the sacred and uniting its adherents in a community such as Christianity; something which has a powerful hold on a person's way of thinking, interests, etc." (p. 841). Spirituality is defined as "attachment to all that concerns the life of the soul," (p. 958), with soul defined as "the immortal part of man, as distinguished from his body; the moral and emotional nature of man, as distinguished from his mind; the vital principle which moves and animates all life" (p. 948). Finally, psychology is defined as "the scientific study of human or animal behaviour; the mental and behavioural characteristics of a person or group; the mental characteristics associated with a particular kind of behaviour," derived from the Greek word "psyche," meaning soul plus logos or discourse (p. 806). Education is defined as "instruction or training in such a way as to develop the mental, oral and physical powers of an individual" (p. 298). Examination of these conventional definitions reflects the many complex connections among the concepts and suggests that each term could not exist in isolation; each term is reciprocally dependent upon the other.

I do not here attempt to define the term spirituality (see Hardy, 1966); I agree, however, agree with Mair in that spirituality is a "growing word" that "is bound to mean more than we say and is likely to change, grow and shrink in various ways, as our journey continues" (Mair, 1999, cited in Mallick & Watts, 2001, p. 71). To sharpen my own theoretical stance, I also draw on Kelly's (1969) work for compass bearings. Kelly claimed that we are in search of a strategic advantage in a long-term quest for understanding. This is the sense in which I have chosen to conceptualize spirituality: peoples' attempts to make meaning of circumstances, not simply through an appreciation of the immediate, observable conditions but through reflective, sensitive means. It is a willingness to question and to look continuously for meaning and purpose in life, an appreciation for depth of life, a personal belief system. Given the need for reflection and self-examination throughout the teen years, silence therefore plays a crucial role during adolescence.

The majority of research suggests that spirituality deals with connections and relations to ourselves, others, and the world around us. Spirituality refers to both a sense of interiority or an inner reality and a sense of being connected beyond one's own self, connected to something "greater" (Watson, 2000). Moreover, in line with other holistic thinkers such as Palmer (1999), I do not define spiritual in terms of any faith tradition, but I tend to think of the word "spiritual" in terms of a human quest for connectedness with something of more mystery and wonder than ourselves. As Palmer (1999) suggests, this life-long quest for connectedness, aims to explore the puzzle and intrigue around human life.

Conceptions of Mind and Models of Spirituality: Historical and Theoretical Issues

According to Flanagan's (2002) approach (humanist or perennialist vs. constructivist or scientific), our minds reflect the broader worldviews that underlay the psychological approaches that guide developmental research and approaches to spirituality in children and adolescents. Given the emphasis of education and psychology on the mind, many cognitive psychologists, educators, and philosophers have summarized the main problem in both education and psychology (e.g., Bruner, 1996; Gardner, Csikszentmihalyi, & Damon, 2001; Flanagan, 2002; Andresen, 2001).

Consistent with Flanagan, many educators and researchers agree that there is a disconnect between the two main approaches to human nature and inquiry in general. Perennial philosophy claims that what is right and good conforms to divine knowledge of the right and the good, followed by moral truths. Thus, perennial philosophy claims that there is an objective moral truth, a right way to think and behave, a rationally communicated pathway to attain goodness. In contrast, the scientific image does not require the secular moral philosophy that discusses the emotional approach to ethics (Flanagan, 2002), or as Noddings (2003) and others refer to as "the ethics of caring." A scientific or positivist view of the mind claims that the physical sciences set the standards for objectivity and rational belief and thus frame ethical judgments in terms of rationality and objectivity.

In the late nineteenth century, Edwin Starbuck, a pupil of the first professor of psychology (William James), begin researching the so-called scientific study of religious experiences (Andresen, 2001). Starbuck was the first person to construct a questionnaire that inquired into peoples' beliefs and encouraged James to write on religion and neurology. Similar to Starbuck, James approached individual experience (including religious experience) according to the systematic norms of the "objective" or physical sciences.

In his 1890 address of religious experience, James began the humanist or individualistic movement towards human experience and offered a cognitive approach to religious experience (Andresen, 2001). He considered the relation between mental states and experience of the divine. James' work created the foundation for the constructivist and cognitive science approach to the mind, which inspired Piaget's (1963) work on understanding children's concepts of God as a parent who fulfills cognitive needs. Piaget emphasized children's cognitive representations and understanding of their parents and the origins of the world. Theory of mind research is also grounded in this view.

A few decades following James (1890), Freud (1918) launched his approach to religious experience, and although it included the mind, he focused his psychoanalytic theory on neuroses and claimed that both magic and religion are projections of neurotic wish-fulfillment and psychological delusions. In contrast to James, Freud believed that God represents a surrogate parent needed to diffuse anxiety. In contrast to Piaget, who claimed that cognitive accounts deal with people's cognitive limitations and their implications for biological and psychological development, Freud initiated relational accounts and explored personality traits and dispositions attributed to divine beings. Although Freud claimed the investigation of religious experience to be one dimension in an overall science of mind, his work has inspired researchers interested in the psychoanalytic dimensions of religion and spirituality including religious belief and how it connects to parental attachment (e.g., Kirkpatrick, 1997).

In addition to the cognitive and relational approach to spirituality, the attempt to understand the origins of the mind also leads to theorists who work on evolutionary adaptation, especially as it relates to language. Extending his earlier work on language and the mind, Pinker (1994) claims an adaptationist perspective on belief in which religion and spirituality are seen as a by-product. Closely related biological or sociobiological models of the human experience, also guided by the scientific or positivist approach, also claim that biological accounts of spiritual and religious experiences exist (e.g., Hinde, 1997). Such accounts encourage theorists and researchers to consider how biology, culture, and cognition are interrelated, particularly regarding questions about the extent to which silence affects the ways of thinking and feeling.

Contemporary Psychological Perspectives on Spirituality and Silence:
Cognitive Psychology, Faith, and Self-Development

Consistent with past researchers outlined above, current thinking of developmentalists, including sociocognitive research and emotional development, reflect the two opposing worldviews, the cognitive (scientific) and the relational or cultural (humanist). However, to address the complex issues surrounding psychology and education, a psychocultural approach is required that represents dynamic and interconnected theories that reflect multiple perspectives and worldviews (e.g., Bruner, 1996; Steiner, 1976). Such a psychocultural approach can help educators and researchers to explore the connections between the experiences of spirituality and silence in the classroom.

To answer the question of how schooling, teachers, and learning have become separated or disengaged from spiritual awareness, some educators have begun to explore how spirituality, cognition, and silence are connected within the school system (Myers, 2000; Goldstein, 1997). Contemporary concepts of spirituality include connections to cognition and language, and can be applied to all ages across the lifespan. For example, Myers (1997) discusses the notion of a spirituality of caring as a shared construct of those within a given community who support, nurture, guide, teach, and learn in caring, hopeful ways. The four conditions include 1) a provision of hospitable space; 2) the acceptance, embracing, and providing of experience; 3) the presence of authentic, caring adults; and 4) an affirmation of the process of learning—of being able to spiritedly transcend present conditions.

How, then, can researchers apply this construct of a spirituality of caring to explore the question of what happens to a child's sense of the genuine and spiritual between young childhood and adolescence? Furthermore, does exposure to silence exasperate or ameliorate such spiritual development? From a psychological perspective, early adolescence (9 or 10 to 12 or 13 years of age) is recognized as a pivotal time in all aspects of development, including cognitive reflexivity (e.g., Piaget, 1963), self-concept formation (e.g., Harter, 1999) and interpersonal relations (e.g., Rosenberg, 1989; Selman, 1980). Despite recognition of this complex and multifaceted developmental milestone, a holistic approach to exploring the links between self and social understanding and the development of spirituality remains to be taken. Thus, research needs to explore children's and adolescents' perspectives of complex concepts such as a sense of self and of spirituality.

Consistent with a broader view of spirituality, Hay and Nye's (1998) definition includes a heightened stage of consciousness as awareness sensing, mystery sensing, and values sensing. To help explain spirituality within a cognitive framework, Hay and Nye provide a core construct of relational consciousness that suggests that children are able to distinguish between the self and other before conceptualizing what it is to be spiritual. Developed from Hay and Nye's research interviews with 6-year-old and 10-year-old children on their conceptions of spirituality, the term *relational consciousness* reflected two main aspects: 1) heightened level of perceptiveness or consciousness, and 2) conversations in a context of how the children related to things, other people, her/himself, and God.

Relational consciousness presupposes the expression of spirituality as an interactive phenomenon; it suggests that language provides access to spiritual processes of thought and experience. This relational consciousness encompasses child-God consciousness, child-people consciousness, child-world consciousness, and child-self consciousness. Relational consciousness supports Vygotsky's (1978) theory of thought and language, which claims that thought or belief systems emerge in the connection between socially derived linguistic influences and internal experiences. Thus, belief systems involving faith, self, and so forth are socially interpreted and might be conceptualized as inclusive of preverbal sensory experiences located in the child's social ecology. Such theories have implications for notions of silence: What happens to internal or private language experiences when adolescents either choose to withdraw or are prevented from participating in social interactions?

Such a sociocontexualized basis for language acquisition and representational thought accommodates the unique perceptions and experiences of the individual adolescent. Cognitively, the adolescent's relational experiences precede the development of spiritual narrative, and then mediate a recursive process of interaction between narrative and experiences of persons, objects, or the divine. Regarding the notion of silence, although youth may be cognitively competent to engage in higher-order reasoning and thinking about spirituality, this does not guarantee that the youth will express her or his thoughts and feelings. For example, a youth may perceive herself to be very spiritual although this spirituality may remain unarticulated and private. As with adults, children and adolescents might choose not to share their thoughts and feelings regarding spirituality with anyone but themselves.

Trust, Faith, and Moral Language

As Hay (2001) suggests, spirituality defined as relational consciousness is the natural antecedent of both religion and morality. Spirituality provides the underpinning of ethics and supports Levinas' writing as ethics as a first philosophy (Hay, 2001). Levinas (1989) emphasizes personal responsibility and empathy; the ethical impulse precedes all social construction, dialogue, and mental functioning. Similar to the developmentalist Jerome Kagan's (e.g., 1984) notion that the moral or self-conscious emotions such as shame, guilt, and pride precede moral cognitions involving issues such as fairness, justice, and so on, Levinas states that the role of understanding and experiencing one's own and others' emotions plays a crucial role in ethical thinking and moral reasoning. Regarding silence, researchers need to explore the implications of a limited or nonexistent moral vocabulary for faith development as well as what happens when an adolescent may possess a sophisticated repertoire of moral language, but chooses silence over conversation. Researchers and educators who work with adolescents need to explore the underlying reasons for these actions, and the implications such decisions have for the learning experience within the classroom.

Although influenced by Erikson (1968), the principal psychological tradition in which faith development theory stands is the constructive developmental work of Baldwin, Dewey, Piaget, Kohlberg, and their intellectual descendants (Fowler, 1981). The constructive developmental approach focuses on the operations of knowing, valuing, and committing that underlie the dynamic pattern of interpretation and orientation that is faith. This psychological tradition is heir to Kant's 1781 designation of the a priori categories of mind that provide the means to order and make coherent sense of the data provided by our senses. It is also heir to Hegel's 1807 work on the evolution of consciousness and the stages of reflective selfhood. In contrast to the strict focus on the logico-mathematical model of intelligence, faith development theory has tried to take account of the constructive involvement in faith of intuition, emotion, and imagination (Oser & Scarlett, 1991).

To operationalize faith as the activity of meaning making, various developments have attempted to conceptualize faith as a construct that has both developmental and structural levels (e.g., Fowler, 1981; Oser & Scarlett, 1991). Fowler views faith as a "person's or group's way of moving into the force field of life" (1981, p. 4). Fowler's definition of faith is a shared construct built in an interactive, triadic way in that self interacts with self, with others, and with the "shared centres of value and power" in a dynamic relational fashion. These shared centres of value and power are those ultimate concerns in which self and others invest trust and loyalty (e.g., God, money, fame, etc.). Faith, then, could be seen as the relation of self and others and an ultimate concern for something like the educational and nurturing process connected with the institutions and persons committed to youth. The concept of faith in this sense is a shared construct of language and meaning, both personal and communal.

As children grow, they expect the world to meet their needs appropriately; as they develop such a sense of basic trust, they can hope. Erikson (1968) describes such hope as "The ontogenetic basis of faith . . . nourished by the adult faith which pervades patterns of care" (p. 118). Children's understanding of faith develops over time through concrete experiences with those who hold, support, communicate, and stand with them. Thus, as children grow and become adolescents, they co-construct their meaning of the world through language. That is, through conversations with their peers, teachers, and family members, adolescents begin to integrate the shared centres of value and power into their developing identity.

Regarding faith development, Fowler (1981) claims that as children approach adolescence, they begin to move away from prescribed beliefs to a more reflective approach that emphasizes social relations, and is at ease with mystery and uncertainty. In Fowler's theory of faith development, he posits five stages that reflect how individuals become more aware of their own belief system as one of many possible worldviews, contemplate the deeper significance of religious symbols and rituals, and open themselves up to other religious perspectives as sources of inspiration. During the intuitive-projective development stage (three to seven years of age), children's fantasy and imitation allow them to be influenced by stories, models, and behaviours that demonstrate the faith of adults. During this intuitive-projective state, children also develop an awareness of right and wrong actions.

During the mythic-literal stage (7–11 years), children begin to internalize the stories, beliefs, and observances of their religious and cultural community, which they may take literally. For example, they may hold concrete images of God living on top of the world watching over everyone. Adolescents have a coherent set of deeply felt beliefs and values, which provides a basis for identity and self-development. Although once they reach the synthetic-conventional stage (after the mythic-literal stage), they may not yet examine the personal ideology systematically or critically. Oser and Scarlett (1991) elaborated on Fowler's (1981) faith development theory to incorporate a richer picture of human faith development.

According to Berger and Luckmann (1967), the systems of meaning that people construct and maintain increasingly centre on their individual psychological needs, given the individualism of modern society. Berger claims that peoples' religions "no longer refer to the cosmos or to history, but to individual psychology." Consistent with this claim, recent cross-cultural research on North American children, adolescents, and adults reflects a tendency for North America's moral self-language and cultural stories to reflect values of autonomy and self-survival in contrast to respect for others, interdependence (e.g., Hoffman, 1984).

Spirituality and the Moral Self

Given that spirituality assumes that the person is able to distinguish between the self and other, William James' representation of the first developmental-oriented model of the self claimed that the "me" represented those qualities of self that were material (body, possessions), social (relations, roles), and spiritual (consciousness, thoughts). The "me" was termed "self-as-object," containing principles of a physical self, an active self, and a social self. The "I" was not included in this categorical framework, and was represented in terms of the self's subjective nature. The "I," interpreted as awareness of agency over life events, was termed "self-as-subject" and contained principles of continuity, distinctness, and agency.

Given the past literature that suggests adolescents have a first language of individualism by reflecting the goal of maximizing their own interests, the goal of an expressive individualist is to express her or his inner identity to the fullest, free of social constraints or conventions. Bellah et al. (1985) hold that "second languages" draw upon older biblical traditions that define the person less as an individual and more as a member of religious, social, and political communities. The biblical tradition emphasizes building a society that is conducive to an ethical and spiritual life. Again, what are the implications (cognitively and emotionally) if adolescents either have the language skills or choose to remain silent? For example, if an adolescent chooses to remain silent or to opt out of moral discourse, will she or he have a less developed moral sense of self?

According to Shweder (1990), three types of ethics involve different conceptions of the self. Moral discourses within the ethic of autonomy define the person as an autonomous individual who is free to make choices, within limits. Moral discourse within the ethic of community describes the person in terms of her or his membership in groups, such as family, the community, or the nation. Moral discourse within the ethic of divinity envisions the person as a spiritual entity. A person's behaviours are to conform to the guidelines ordered by a given spiritual or natural order.

Shweder's (1990) concepts of the moral self build on both Marcia's (1980) constructs of identity formation and Erikson's (1968) description of adolescence as a time in development that involves an identity crisis (or diffusion) surrounding choice of occupation, sexual orientation, and decisions about religious or political commitments. Marcia (1980) interviewed adolescents to explore how they sought information that would lead to a personal choice and to what extent they had a commitment to particular issues. According to Marcia, adolescents responded to interviews regarding self, religion, politics, and so forth in four categories: identity diffusion (little or no commitment), foreclosure (made a commitment according to parents), moratorium (searching or struggling for identity—cannot make a commitment), and identity achievement (crisis has been resolved and a commitment has been reached). Given the strong emphasis on language, researchers need to explore nonverbal measures and tasks to investigate moral discourse. What implications does this sense of moral self have for adolescents' experiences with language and silence within the educational system?

Conceptions of Mind and Models of Teaching and Learning: Role of the Spiritual Voice

Given Dewey's (1897) belief that education should draw on psychological insight to help us understand children's competencies, this section outlines the models of teaching, learning, and mind introduced earlier. It is my hope that such an advance in understanding young adolescents' minds and their spiritual voices will lead to an improved pedagogy (see Bosacki, 1998, for a more detailed discussion of the models). Given the link between spirituality or inner meaning, emotion, and "voice" (the articulation of one's subjective experience), I have chosen to use "spiritual voice" to represent the complex web between the three concepts.

Similar to Gilligan's (1993) use of voice, spiritual has been added to emphasize the link to the spiritual or most inner part of the self, the part that one must access in order to acquire a genuine sense of understanding, one that requires both emotional and intellectual knowledge (Miller, 1997). Furthermore, although spiritual voice may suggest links to religion and a sense of a higher power, due to limited space, the complex philosophical and educational issues of religious implications remain to be addressed further. For a detailed discussion of religion and children and schooling, see Coles, 1990.

To address the issue of spiritual voice that may constrain learning in the classroom and self-development, Belenky et al.'s (1986) five epistemological perspectives or "women's ways of knowing" are integrated into Olson and Bruner's (1996) four models of mind, teaching, and learning. At issue is the

TABLE 1. Ways of Knowing and Models of Mind

Ways of Knowing	Models of Mind
1. Silence	1. Adolescent as Doer
2. Received Knowing	2. Adolescent as Knower
3. Subjective Knowing	3a. Adolescent as Thinker (Subjectivist Epistemologist)
4. Procedural Knowing	3b. Adolescent as Thinker (Objectivist Epistemologist)
5. Constructed Knowing	4. Adolescent as Knowledgeable Expert

Notes. Comparison between Belenky et al.'s (1986) Epistemological Stances or Ways of Knowing and Olson & Bruner's (1996) Models of Learners' Minds. Adapted from Bosacki, S. (1998). Is silence really golden? The role of spiritual voice in folk pedagogy and folk psychology. *International Journal of Children's Spirituality*, 3, 109–121, p. 112.

dialogical relation that exists between folk psychology (assumptions we hold regarding mind and knowledge) and folk pedagogy (a set of commonsense ideas about teaching and learning) and its contingency on both culture and context. Thus, the possibility that conceptions of self and mind may be the product of pedagogy as well as the reverse has strong educational implications and can therefore act as a lens for understanding students' approaches to learning and for devising teaching strategies (Strauss & Shilony, 1994). Borrowing from other researchers interested in a psychocultural approach to education (e.g., Belenky et al., 1986; Nelson et al., 2000; Olson & Bruner, 1996; Tomasello, 1999; Tomasello, Kruger, & Ratner, 1993), four models of learner's minds are outlined below, each with varying degrees of appropriateness to different educational goals. To intertwine feminist psychoeducational theory with cognitive psychology, Olson and Bruner's four dominant models of learner's minds (adolescent as doer, knower, thinker, and knowledgeable expert respectively) are used as a framework to examine Belenky et al.'s five different epistemological perspectives: silence, received knowing, subjective knowing, procedural knowing, and constructed knowing (see Table 1).

Adolescent as Doer (The Silent Servant)

Within this model, the learner is conceived as a "doer" who acquires the ability to do and know through imitation. Procedural knowledge (or "knowing how") is acquired through concrete experience, not words. The teacher is viewed as a craftsperson who demonstrates the behaviour that is to be learned. On the imitative view, competence only comes through practice, where the focus of the teaching/learning would be on demonstrated skills and ability.

According to Belenky et al. (1986), in such contexts, learners see themselves as "deaf and dumb" with little ability to think. They survive by obedience to powerful and/or punitive authority alone. They have little awareness of the power of language for sharing thoughts, insights, and feelings. Hence, learners experience themselves as mindless and voiceless and subject to external authority.

Although some theorists claim this model of demonstration and apprenticeship to be a part of "traditional" education (Olson & Bruner, 1996), it may still play a part in some modern folk pedagogies of teachers and learners. Given that students' spiritual voices reflect their belief that they have something to say and that they have a right to be fully heard (Stanton, 1995), this self-belief may thus enable them to express their thoughts within the classroom.

However, given the reciprocal link between teaching and learning, a student's ability to articulate her or his spiritual voice may be influenced by teacher expectations (e.g., Strauss & Shilony, 1994). For example, a teacher may assume that a learner lacks a particular talent or skill and may influence that learner's self-view of being incompetent; thus, the learner may remain silent. Alternatively, if a student believes that she or he will not be able to accurately imitate the teacher (due to a fear of failure), that learner may appear to be incompetent and the teacher will assume that the child has not learned the particular skill.

In this scenario, it is the teacher's task to first develop a trusting and caring relationship with the student. Within such a relationship, the teacher's role is to encourage learners to first become aware that they possess a spiritual voice and that it is safe for them to develop and express it within the classroom. Consequently, this discovery of one's ability to articulate her or his spiritual and mental life may lead to a sense of confidence that will enable the learner to question the teacher. Eventually, the aim is not only to foster the learner's ability to perform skillfully but also to foster a sense of security and confidence within the learner. Such emotional and spiritual security may supply further encouragement for the child to learn various concepts taught in the classroom (Coles, 1997).

Adolescent as Knower (The Silent Listener)

Within this model, the learner is conceived as a "knower" who acquires the ability to know through listening. Propositional knowledge (or "knowing that") is acquired by either listening to the teacher or reading text. This didactic view of teaching envisions the teacher as an "authoritarian expositor" waiting to fill the child's mind with facts. On the didactic view, competence is assessed by whether or not the learners can reproduce what the teacher told them (either through speech or writing), where the focus of the teaching/learning would be on telling the learners what to learn.

According to Belenky et al. (1986), from this teaching/learning perspective, the learners see themselves as merely receiving or reproducing knowledge from the all-knowing external authorities but not capable of creating knowledge on their own. An important aspect of competence is the ability to be a good listener, to remember and reproduce knowledge (Donaldson, 1992); thus, the learner may seek out strategies for remembering received knowledge. Due to the great emphasis on listening, there is no encouragement to develop one's voice by speaking up in the classroom and expressing one's opinion. Hence, the lack of emphasis on the use of one's voice in the classroom may eventually lead learners to believe that they do not have a voice, that their thoughts and opinions are not worthy or valid.

Although this model of didactic instruction remains the most widely used line of folk pedagogy in practice today and despite the fact that there are certain contexts where it may be useful to view knowledge as given and "objective" (Bruner, 1996), learners do not believe that they can create knowledge on their own within such a model. From this view, the learner is looked upon from the outside or the third-person, objective perspective that deals with only intellectual knowledge. The teacher is not interested in the child's mental and spiritual experiences, but is only concerned with the transmission of intellectual knowledge. Obviously, this model's conception of the learner as a passive listener and "parrot" has implications for the learner's self-view. For instance, if learners view themselves as mere intellectual knowledge-receivers rather than spiritual knowledge-creators, how will they develop the ability to use their imagination or to take the emotional risk of creation? Furthermore, how can adolescents learn and practice self-regulatory processes such as self-motivation and self-relaxation if they are unaware that they themselves have the power to control their learning?

Also, the notion of taking knowledge as given may prevent learners from the ability to read beyond the given text (e.g., what the textbook and teacher says is true). In such a scenario, where the learner is afraid to truly learn or create, it is the teacher's task to attempt to see things from the learner's perspective, and to seek out and listen to the student's spiritual voice (Kessler, 2000). This ability to understand the other person's mind entails a dialogical relationship between the teacher and the learner that will be further elaborated on in the fourth model. Within such a relationship, the teacher's role is to encourage the learner not to be afraid to question "objective" or intellectual knowledge, and to develop the ability to create knowledge of one's own.

More importantly, the teacher needs to encourage the learner how not to be afraid of failure. Such a fear may preclude the learner from expressing her or his voice and from creating new knowledge. Hence, unlike silent imitators who remain unaware that they can control how they think and feel, silent listeners may be aware of their mental life, but for some reason (fear of self/ teacher?) they cannot or will not articulate their experience.

Adolescent as Thinker or Epistemologist

In general, this model emphasizes a folk pedagogy of mutuality or intersubjectivity. This model views learners as thinkers or epistemologists who construct a model of the world to aid them in construing what they experience. Such a model presumes that all human minds are capable of feeling, holding beliefs and ideas, which through dialogue and interaction can be moved towards a shared frame of reference. The teacher is viewed as a collaborator, a colleague who assists learners as they attempt to interpret information and create meaning.

Although the following set of assumptions of mind and learning are grouped under the heading of Olson and Bruner's (1996) "Child as Thinker," this also describes Belenky et al.'s two epistemological positions of subjective and procedural knowing (where procedural knowing is divided into separate and connected). Thus, the category "adolescent as thinker" describes two different views of the adolescent, including adolescent as a 1) subjectivist epistemologist (a combination of subjective and connected knowing) and 2) an objectivist epistemologist.

Adolescent as Poet or Subjective Epistemologist

Within this model, the learner is conceived as a "thinker" who acquires the ability to know through listening to one's inner sources (both spiritual and emotional). Accordingly, truth and knowledge are conceived of as personal, private, and subjectively known or intuited where the learners believe that their own opinions are unique and valued. Moreover, although learners are capable of exploring different points of views and seeing things from multiple perspectives, they are not overly concerned about the correspondence between their own truth and external reality. Similar to a poet who is concerned with meaning, interpretation, and insight, knowledge is acquired by listening to one's own inner voice for the truth; thus, the subjective thinker is a "connected knower of the self" and speaks from her or his feelings and experiences or from the heart, listens, and needs others to listen without judging.

Given that "there is no cognitive mechanism without affective elements" (Piaget, 1981, p. 3), although emotion and spirituality play a crucial role in all of the models, they may receive special or at least an equal status to that of cognition in the subjectivist position. A subjectivist thinker relies on intuition and thus may give equal credence to both thought and emotion. For example, in my own research (Bosacki, 1997), through interviews on inter- and intra-personal understanding with preadolescent girls and boys, I learned that the role of spiritual voice within the school context may be powerful in the development of social understanding. In response to some of my questions concerning a socially ambiguous situation (see Appendixes and Bosacki, 1998 for further details), many of the 11- and 12-year-olds that I interviewed often defined the verb "wondering" as "an in-between feeling." Although learning may occur independently of self-acceptance and self-understanding, to truly be able to create knowledge, one must feel the discovery of realization, that "a-ha" feeling. As one 11-year-old girl stated, "I feel as if I know it."

This epistemological position poses interesting implications for models of teaching/learning. From Belenky et al.'s (1986) perspective, the learners see themselves as receiving and creating knowledge from the all-knowing self as opposed to the all-knowing external authorities. To illustrate, in my interviews with preadolescents, to assess their social or interpersonal understanding, after children were asked questions that concerned predicting how characters in a social story would think, feel, and act, they were asked to justify their answers by being asked, "How do you know that?" In one instance, an 11-year-old boy responded to my question, did he know that, he retorted, "I don't know, I just know what I think." Thus, although the boy was unable to articulate why he answered the way he did, he felt that he was right. For him, his source of knowledge was himself, not the teacher or text.

However, what pedagogical model is appropriate for when children do not feel the need to adjust their theories of subjective knowledge to fit the theories of objective knowledge? The key to competence is the ability to be a good listener to both oneself (subjective voice) and to the other (objective voice) (Stanton, 1995). The question regarding what kind of teaching strategies will foster such a competence in "disciplined subjectivity" (Wineburg, 1991) must thus incorporate a sense of balance and connection, which will be further discussed in the model where the learner is viewed as an expert critic or connoisseur.

Adolescent as Scientist or Objectivist Epistemologist

This epistemological perspective views the learner as a "thinker" who acquires the ability to know through learning and applying objective procedures such as logic and analysis. In contrast to the subjective thinker, the objectivist epistemologist focuses on third-person, objective analysis and aims to see the world as it "really is." Accordingly, truth and knowledge are conceived of as different frameworks of information formed by multiple perspectives. Similar to a scientist who is concerned with finding as opposed to creating knowledge, the objectivist epistemologist or "separate knower" (Belenky et al., 1986) focuses on definition, explanation, and rationality. Unlike the subjectivist thinker who believes one's spiritual voice speaks the truth, the learner-as-scientist's voice aims for cultural definitions of accuracy and precision and modulates her or his voice to fit the conventional standards of logic or discipline.

In contrast to the subjectivist epistemological position, the objectivist or separate way of knowing (Belenky et al., 1986) remains the dominant model of both folk psychology and folk pedagogy. It is this objectivist and logical view that is valued in both our modern society and our schools. However, before educators assume that such a stance may be more sophisticated or developed than the subjective one, they must consider the possibility that some learners deliberately choose to take the objectivist stance. For instance, some learners may take an objectivist or strictly intellectual position to avoid the perhaps emotionally painful task of self-analysis.

Furthermore, instead of making the assumption that the objectivist position is the correct one, educators need to question why some learners choose to develop their voice outside of cultural constraints whereas others attempt to please authoritarian figures by complying with cultural conventions of knowledge. In other words, to answer the question of when the cultural/objective model becomes the self/subjective model, instead of focusing on learners' answers, educators need not only listen to but also question why some learners choose to ask (or not to ask) particular questions. Moreover, given the debate between learning and understanding (e.g., Gardner, 1985, 1991), is it true that understanding only occurs when one "feels" as if one knows? Thus, can the separate knower experience true understanding if only intellectual knowledge is acquired? It is this ability to understand that brings us to the last perspective.

Adolescent as Expert Critic (The Courageous and Caring Connoisseur)

This perspective reflects the highest levels of both Olson and Bruner's (1996) models of mind and pedagogy and Belenky et al.'s epistemological positions. The learner is a knowledge constructor or creator who is capable of not only making the distinction between first-person/subjective or spiritual knowledge and third-person/objective or intellectual knowledge but can also integrate both knowledge types successfully. That is, the learner realizes that knowledge has a history and she or he is capable of contributing to the cultural archive through the application of knowledge to practice. Through the connection of both spiritual and intellectual knowledge, the learner can play the role of both poet and scientist. Thus, the learner is adept at critiquing arguments as well as empathic listening and spiritual understanding, or what Sternberg (2003) refers to as the expert or wise learner. This wise adolescent is capable of integrating interpersonal (other people's), intrapersonal (one's own), and extrapersonal understanding (more than personal, such as institutional) and applying this knowledge to practice towards the attainment of a common good. This learner is a courageous connoisseur, a connected learner (Belenky et al., 1986), one who is not afraid to "speak one's mind with all one's heart" (Rogers, 1993).

The pedagogical model is one that emphasizes teaching for wisdom in the sense that adolescents are encouraged to seek truth through dialogue and collaboration, where the teacher is viewed as a consultant or "midwife" who aims for self-transformation by hoping to change herself or himself in addition to encouraging change in the learner. The classroom thus becomes a metaphor for a construction site, where the "connected teacher" (Belenky et al., 1986) both participates and observes the classroom (Stanton, 1995). Finally, as Sternberg (2003) suggests, as educators of youth, we need to teach a new generation of wise learners who are capable of using their expertise to attain the common good on behalf of their communities.

However, as some writers have already mentioned (Barresi & Moore, 1995; Debold, Tolman, & Brown, 1996), within this view of the learner as knowledgeable, the task may be more complex than merely distinguishing between opinion and fact. Subjective and objective knowledge exists for both the self and other. Thus, as expert critics, learners must learn to become wise in that they need to learn to distinguish between subjective and objective knowledge about the self, other, and community and apply this knowledge towards a common good. This poses a difficulty for both teachers and learners: How can learners develop a sense of "healthy skepticism" about the gap between opinion and fact when they cannot access first-person or subjective information about the other?

Moreover, what are the consequences of a schooling and cultural system that values third-person/objective information about the self rather than first-person/subjective information? For instance, how can we explain when adolescents justify self-beliefs or acquire forms of self-knowledge that appear to contradict facts that are objectively true (e.g., a gifted adolescent who receives top grades believes that she or he is an academic failure)? Finally, why do some school systems promote the silence of the subjective voice, and how can educators promote the ability to integrate the subjective and objective voice among adolescents?

In sum, a choice of pedagogy inevitably communicates a conception of the learning process and the learner; real schooling is never confined to one model of the learner or one model of teaching. While there are common elements among the models, such as the role of spiritual voice and teacher-learner relationship (i.e., there must be a sense of trust, a lack of fear in order for true competence and confidence to develop in the learner), teaching is both inquiry and practice, both research and application, where various models and methods are tried and evaluated. Models of pedagogy involve processes that are required to advance knowledge and understanding in the learner and to assist children in evaluating their beliefs and theories reflectively, collaboratively, and archivally (Olson & Bruner, 1996).

Moreover, the order in which the models of different types of adolescents were presented were not necessarily representative of an advanced sophistication but suggest the increasingly internal view of thinking, learning, and knowing. Similar to other psychological theoretical models, the framework presented here is dependent upon the context within which it occurs. For example, in the case of a novel learning situation where learners may doubt their own spiritual voice, the learners' decision to remain silent does not necessarily place the learner in the silent listener category. Finally, regarding the application of this model to status variables such as gender, social class, race, and ethnicity, given that all adolescents possess a mind and heart, the present framework can be adapted to fit the needs of adolescents according to their respective gender, social class, and family cultural heritage. In sum, the aim of such a theoretical framework is not to label, but to serve as a source of inspiration for future investigations of links between epistemology and educational practice.

Educational Implications

It is essential that the fields of education and social sciences (psychology, anthropology, sociology, etc.) continue to work collaboratively towards a psychocultural educational approach. Such an approach would advance conversation/dialogue (interpersonal, intrapersonal, and extrapersonal) through pedagogical practices that encourage engagement and question through mutuality, reciprocity, and care rather than detachment and distance.

In the same vein, as Postman (1995) highlights, to achieve the contradictory educational aims of today's school system (encouraging compliance and capacity to critique), educators need to provide a means to integrate the inner, first-person, subjective voice (voice of spirit?) with the outer, third-person/objective voice (voice of reason?). In other words, educators of today are faced with the problem of "aiding and abetting" (Bruner, 1996) children to comply but at the same time to teach them to be critics of the cultural conventions that guide their compliance!

In the end, as Olson and Bruner (1996) remind us, pedagogy is never innocent, never without consequences. School curricula and classroom climates will always reflect implicit cultural conventions and intentions often concerned with issues of social class, ethnicity, and gender. Consistent with many contemporary constructivist educators and developmentalists (e.g., Donaldson, 1992; Sternberg, 2003), I believe that our educational aim is not worship but discourse/interpretation through critical reflections and wise discussions that lead to self-transformation or personal growth in the attainment for a common good (Donaldson, 1992).

In my view, it is crucial that educators become cognizant of the often-made assumption that equates competence with confidence. Adolescents need to be encouraged to see themselves as both confident and competent knowers who all share the potential to become wise learners. They need to perceive themselves as courageous creators of knowledge so they can not only solve but also find problems and purposes. Most important, children should not be afraid to express their ideas and feelings, even if they are not "right." Following Dewey's (1938) notion that children learn by doing, children also learn by failing and thus educators need to create schools that provide the environment for both documenting error and for revealing the true state of affairs.

To promote the creation of a connected classroom that encourages adolescents to become wise, courageous, reflective, and creative, teachers must foster the development and use of the spiritual voice. Perhaps the most effective way to promote this spiritual voice is for teachers themselves to act as role models for the students. That is, by sharing their own spiritual and emotional experiences with their students, teachers can validate the importance of expressing one's spiritual voice within the classroom.

As I will outline in further detail in Chapter 4, given the link between arts and language-based, holistic teaching activities and spiritual/emotional development (e.g., Donaldson, 1992; Coles, 1990), teachers can also implement a variety of teaching activities to foster the spiritual voice. For instance, the use of activities that promote both critical reflection and self-expression such as bibliotherapy, journal writing, psychodrama, and meditation have the potential to foster the connection between intellectual and spiritual/emotional knowledge (see Miller, 1993, and Olson, 1997, for further examples). Also, activities that are ambiguous and open-ended may also have the potential to encourage children to take risks and be creative by expressing their spiritual voice. Thus, such activities may encourage children to seek patterns of self-discovery by learning to listen to and integrate their inner voices with their experiences of schooling, and will be discussed in more detail related to classroom context.

Through the recognition and validation of their spiritual voices, adolescents may then learn to integrate self-inquiry with the various lines of curriculum inquiry taught in the classroom. Such a connection may encourage adolescents to become engaged with the present, to encourage manifestations of relation, be it a book, communicating with another person, daydreaming, or similar activity. The possibilities are endless, and the learning to develop an enhanced awareness of everyday life may also lead to a greater sense of comfort, calmness, and peacefulness with oneself and one's surroundings. Finally, given today's chaotic world of constant noise and business, such a calmness may be of particular value given that the majority of adults living in modern

Western worlds are required to function as competent multitaskers, engaged in a variety of tasks simultaneously, without fully appreciating or engaging fully in any one task.

Summary

Given that education is a moral and spiritual enterprise (Coles, 1990), our task as those who work with adolescents is to continue to fuel the sense of possibility by continuing not only to study how the mind is created and used but also to apply such theoretical knowledge to the practical educational context of the classroom. Thus, I revert to the theme with which this chapter began: the time is long overdue for us as educators to explore the issue of silence among adolescents in the classroom through the reexamination and redefinition of the current frames of education, culture, and mind as we aim to create an interdisciplinary research area that attempts to integrate all three. Our ultimate goal as humanistic, constructivist educators is not to produce unfeeling, direction-following experts but to encourage adolescents to develop a heart and mind of their own, which in turn will assist in the growth of the love for learning and the need to constantly search for meaning. Eventually, such a vision of "schooling" will include wise adolescents who have developed enough courage to begin to wonder why silence is considered to be golden, and thus feel safe enough to question verbally society's value of silencing the subjective. Silence should not be feared within a caring and connected classroom. Given that this chapter outlined the meanings of silence, in the next two chapters, I discuss what may cause some adolescents to be silent. I describe some of the characteristics and consequences of this silence and explore the question of when and why some adolescents feel silenced in the classroom.

·2·

SETTING THE STAGE:
CAUSES AND CHARACTERISTICS
OF CLASSROOM SILENCE

Speech is silver, silence is gold.
(SCHWEICHART, *1996, p. 306*)

Introduction

To understand silence experiences within the classroom, and to know what to do with them, we first need to explore the roots of silence. What causes silence among adolescents in the classroom, and what are some of the underlying factors involved in the creating of personal and social silences? This chapter consists of two distinct sections. The first section sets the stage of silence by describing some of the social-cognitive roots or some possible causes of silence, distinguishing between general social cognitive research and the more specialized discipline referred to as "theory of mind." I then describe how recent research on the various components of theory of mind within adolescence may help us to further understand the connection between how adolescents know and feel and what they say or do not say. The second section draws on relevant developmental sociocognitive literature and explores the characteristics and tentative consequences of classroom silence in adolescence. More specifically, I explore how silences may either help or hinder an adolescent's social cognitive development. The chapter ends with an overview of some methodological and ethical cautions when studying silence among adolescents within a school context.

Roots of Silence

To explore the connections between adolescents' mental and social worlds, over the past decade, sociocognitive research has increasingly come to envision young people as interpretative psychologists (Astington & Olson, 1995; Bennett, 1993; Erwin, 1993). That is, such research views the adolescent as an intersubjective theorist (Bruner, 1996), as one who depends on a mentalistic construal of reality to make sense of the social world. Based on the collective works of various social-constructivists (e.g., Berger & Luckmann, 1967; Bruner, 1990; Case et al., 1996; Gergen & Walhrus, 2001; Vygotsky, 1978) and symbolic-interactionists (e.g., Baldwin, 1902, 1913; Cooley, 1912; Mead, 1934), such an approach proposes that children and adolescents come to understand or make meaning from their experiences guided by the tenets of relativism, constructivism, narrative, and self agency.

The Vygotskian notion that cognitive growth stems from social interaction and dialogue is congruent with holistic or humanistic and psychocultural approaches to development, which focus on connections between thought and language (Bruner, 1996). This approach draws on various theories that assume adolescents create and then rely on both emotional and cognitive structures to make sense of the world (e.g., Piaget, 1981). Such an integrative approach may assist researchers to answer the increasingly common question of how and why adolescents come to make meaning from their social experiences and eventually become "socioemotionally literate" or socially intelligent in varying degrees (e.g., Goleman, 1995; Levinson, 1995). Thus, the larger question considers whether a conceptual framework can provide a unifying theory that emphasizes the interactions among thought, emotion, and action, and what implications this has for notions of silence and voice among adolescents. That is, to what extent does social and self-knowledge affect how adolescents communicate and act with their families, teachers, and friends?

Social Cognitive Research: Theory of Mind

In search of a theory that can help explain the connections between mental state understanding and social communiation, social scientists have recently begun to investigate the sociocognitive abilities that help adolescents to understand and navigate through their social world. The main goal of such research is to find a theory that will assist in their exploration of how children and adolescents acquire the knowledge that others are thinking and feeling beings. Accordingly, over the past decade, many researchers have approached the area of social cognition from what is referred to as a "theory-of-mind" (ToM) perspective. This unique way of viewing social understanding has also been referred to as folk psychology, commonsense psychology, or belief-desire reasoning (see Astington, 1993).

A ToM perspective on psychological development is unique in that it is founded on the premise that all humans are folk or commonsense psychologists. That is, humans understand social information by means of ascribing mental states to others and thinking that overt behaviour is governed by these states. This ability to "read" others' minds and to predict how people will act in social situations focuses on the understanding of mental states such as beliefs, desires, and intentions (Moore, 1996). More specifically, to understand social behaviour, children must first understand mental representation. That is, they must understand that there is a difference between thoughts in the mind and things in the world (Astington, 1993). By inferring mental states from people's actions, children learn to understand that minds are active and contain mental states that can bring about events in the world. Thus, the same world can be experienced in different ways by different people. Each person may have a distinctive belief about reality.

This relatively new approach to social cognition claims that a largely implicit conceptual framework containing intentional elements allows children to understand, explain, and predict their own and other people's behaviour and mental states (Wellman, 1990). In line with this view is the widely held assumption that this mentalizing ability allows children to make sense of social behaviour by ascribing desires and intentions to others' actions for the specific purpose of regulating their interactions with others (Astington, 1993). Moreover, it is believed that the ability to recognize, represent and understand others' thoughts and emotions in early childhood provides the sociocognitive foundation for the later development of social and emotional competency (Dunn, 1988).

Interestingly, although the interest in the development of folk psychology has been paralleled by an interest in the sociocognitive processes of the adolescent (e.g., Alsaker, 1995; Brooks-Gunn, 1989; Harter, 1999; Matthews & Keating, 1995), the two research areas have failed to connect. Perhaps one of the greatest impediments that has prevented researchers from adapting a ToM approach to adolescent development has been the lack of conceptual agreement among ToM theorists. Examples of some of the ongoing conceptual debates include the argument of how exactly a "theory of mind" develops beyond preschool, and exactly what are the processes that develop (Flavell & Miller, 1998). Although ToM research could enrich investigations of adolescent social cognition, particularly in the areas of self-concept (Wellman, 1990), perspective-taking (both affective and cognitive) (Chandler, 1987), and person perception (Yuill, 1993), the two research areas (theory of mind and developmental adolescent psychological research) have continued to work mainly independent of one another, without building on each other's findings.

ToM understanding, or the ability to "read" others' mental states in the context of social action, can also be referred to as psychological understanding (Bruner, 1996); this ability to read others' mental states enables children to understand multiple perspectives and to communicate with others (Nelson, Henseler, & Plesa, 2000). Recent research in children's theory of mind shows that by age five, children begin to understand that people have desires that lead them to actions, and these actions are based on beliefs. Beyond the age of five, however, little is known about the links between psychological understanding and social experience. Given that children who possess high levels of psychological understanding are more likely to "think about their own and others' thinking" during the school day, such an ability has important educational implications. For example, recent research shows that this ability to make a meaningful story out of people's thoughts and actions plays a role in self-regulated learning and language competence such as storytelling. Moreover, research has shown that the ability to "read others" or to make sense of the signs and symbols evident in human communication has an influence on children's self-conceptions and their social interactions. The next section examines how we can use some of this research on adolescent minds to help us to understand why some adolescents choose silence over speech.

Adolescent Theories of Mind: A Case for Complexity

Despite the claim that adolescence is a pivotal time in many areas of sociocognitive development, including cognitive reflexivity (e.g., Piaget, 1981), self-concept formation (e.g., Damon & Hart, 1988; Erikson, 1968; Harter, 1999), and interpersonal relations (e.g., Rosenberg, 1989; Selman, 1980), a psychocultural approach to exploring the links between such sociocognitive areas remains to be taken. Such an inquiry may promote a better understanding of the two main tasks of adolescence, which are 1) the intrapersonal task of constructing a coherent psychosocial identity (Damon & Hart, 1988; Erikson, 1968; Rosenberg, 1989), and 2) the interpersonal task of understanding multiple and contradictory intentions of others, allowing judgments to be made in an uncertain world (Chandler, 1987). Thus, drawing on various social-cognitive (Selman, 1980) and epistemological theories and research (Gilligan, 1982; Perry, 1970), a folk psychological approach to social cognition may help to illustrate the linkages among the understanding of mental states in others, self-concept, and social relations. Research on how adolescents make sense of themselves and others may help us to understand their social-communicative patterns and how they interact with others.

Past research studies have focused mainly on the aspect of children's theory-of-mind development, which involves their recognition of false belief

(Wimmer & Perner, 1983). Around four years of age, children understand that people act on their representation of the world, even in situations where it misrepresents the real situation. At this age, children can represent and reason from people's first-order beliefs (a single mental state): X believes p. From as young as age five or six, children are able to represent and reason from second-order beliefs (two or more mental states): X believes that Y believes that p (Sullivan et al., 1994). The development of this second-order understanding has received little attention in the literature. This is surprising, given that much of our social interaction depends on what people believe about other people's beliefs (Astington, 1993).

The importance of second-order reasoning has been shown to be related to children's ability to understand speech acts such as lies and jokes (Leekam, 1993) and in their ability to understand self-representational display rules (Banerjee & Yuill, 1999). Although research on ToM and social and self-competence remains in its infancy, there are some research findings that suggest that such higher-order reasoning is also fundamental to children's understanding of complex emotions, their self-concept, and social interactions. For example, in some of my own work (e.g., Bosacki & Astington, 1999; Bosacki, 2000, 2003), among sixth-grade early adolescent girls and boys, I found that more sophisticated ToM ability was positively related to social competence for boys only. That is, the better boys were at reading social situations, the more likely they were to be rated as socially competent by their teachers and peers. Interestingly, this relation was not influenced by how boys felt or thought about themselves. For example, a boy who was an effective social interpreter was also rated as an effective or competent social communicator by his peers and teachers regardless of how he felt or thought about himself. Thus, boys who had a negative sense of self-worth or low self-esteem could still have been capable of understanding and interacting effectively with others.

In contrast, for girls, the link between ToM and social competence was moderated by self-perceptions. In other words, girls who scored relatively high on the ToM measure (i.e., possess a sophisticated ToM understanding) and also reported a relatively negative sense of self, received relatively low social competence ratings from their teachers and peers. For example, regardless of whether or not a girl could read or understand social situations, if she held a negative view of herself or felt badly about herself, she was also rated as less socially competent by her teacher and peers. Thus, how girls felt about themselves influenced the connection between their ToM ability, or their ability to "read other" in social situations, and how their teachers and peers viewed them socially.

Both social cognitive (e.g., Bennett, 1993; Chandler, 1987; Harter, 1999; Selman, 1980) and theory-of-mind theorists (e.g., Wellman, 1990) agree that the ability to understand self and others within the context of social relations develops in complexity throughout one's lifetime, and may be associated with sociocultural factors such as gender or language (e.g., Astington, 1993; Lillard, 1997). However, how this growth comes about and what it consists of remains debatable (e.g., Bennett, 1993; Brooks-Gunn, 1989; Harter, 1999). Recently, various authors have emphasized that in order to acquire a better understanding of the concept of a general, overarching theory of mind, one must map out or chart what the adult or mature theory of mind consists of (Flavell & Miller, 1998). Although a few attempts to examine ToM understanding have been expanded to the early adolescent years (e.g., Chandler, 1987; Feldman, 1992; Mansfield & Clinchy, 1997; Nelson, Henseler, & Plesa, 2000), the majority of literature on adolescent social cognition remains largely within the field of social or social-cognitive psychology, and explores mainly Euro-North American samples. Thus, ToM researchers need to further explore the role of silence and voice within a theory-of-mind framework (Dunn, 1988; Levinson, 1995; Mansfield & Clinchy, 1997). Thus by focusing on the understanding of the perspective of both oneself and others, exploring adolescent sociocognitive development may help to illustrate how adolescents' behaviours and communicative tendencies are shaped and made meaningful by their internal repertoire of actions, feelings, and thoughts.

An overview of the literature reveals that the majority of social-cognitive research in adolescents includes studies on attribution and perspective or role-taking (both of self and other) (e.g., Selman, 1980, 1989; Damon & Hart, 1988), person perception (e.g., Yuill, 1993), and empathetic sensitivity (e.g., Ferguson, Stegge, & Damhuis, 1991). Similarly, the realm of social-cognitive research has failed to integrate the mainly cognitive studies of higher-order mental processes among adolescents (e.g., Boyes & Chandler, 1992; Miller, Kessel, & Flavell, 1970).

For example, studies have shown that the emergence of relativist thought, or the process of becoming a reflective knower (Chandler, 1987), co-occurs with the ability to understand the meaning of promising (Astington, 1988), social commitment (Mant & Perner, 1988), sarcasm and irony (Happé, 1994; Keenan, 1995), self-conscious emotions such as shame and guilt (Tangney, 1991), and metacognitive and meta-linguistic verbs (verbs that represent mental states) (Astington & Olson, 1995). Moreover, despite the increasing interest in the development of a constructivist theory of mind beyond middle childhood (Astington, 1996; Gopnik, 1993; Lalonde & Chandler, 1997; Mansfield & Clinchy, 1997), at the time of this writing, there have been no studies that have attempted to conceptualize or systematically study the workings of the adolescent mind as a culture-specific, dynamic, multifaceted, conceptual network of cognitive and affective components that may serve as a template for self- and other-understanding.

Furthermore, as researchers continue to define social understanding in adolescence within the framework of ToM research, perhaps such explorations will help to illuminate the wealth of findings from psychosocial studies that show a significant drop in self-worth and use of voice (e.g.; Gilligan, 1993; Harter, 1999) and an increase in self-consciousness and experiences of silence (Buss, 1980; Simmons, Rosenberg, & Rosenberg, 1973) around the age of 11. Although Chandler (1987) attributes the development of relativistic thought as the main cause of generic self-doubt (implying a decrease in self-worth), more research is needed on early adolescent thought and social-emotional development to investigate both the drawbacks and benefits of developing an advanced ability to understand the minds or interior lives of others (Belenky et al., 1986). Moreover, despite the recent popularity of cultural psychology (Bruner, 1996), a large gap still exists in the ToM literature concerning sociocultural issues such as gender, social class, and ethnicity (Astington, 1996; Lillard, 1997). A psychocultural approach to self and social understanding may contribute to recent findings that have shown an increase in adolescent stereotypic gender-role expectations and behaviours (e.g., Hill & Lynch, 1983) and in the development of a negative self-concept among preadolescent girls (Brown & Gilligan, 1992). Thus, such a lack of communication between disciplines advocates the need for social cognition to be explored within the cultural context, particularly psychological pragmatics (Behrens, 2004; Mansfield & Clinchy, 1997; Wang, 2004). Such research may help us to uncover some of the pieces of the puzzle surrounding the question of why and how adolescents experience silence within the educational context.

The need for an integrative, multifaceted view of an advanced theory of mind is supported by the assertion that the age of adolescence (10–13) is the second period of individuation (Blos, 1979), when the fusion of interpersonal and intrapersonal understanding allows the preadolescent to form a sense of identity (Erikson, 1968). The majority of literature on preadolescent social cognition has assumed that both self and person perceptions develop in parallel; that is, self and other concepts arise simultaneously from social interactions, both develop in the same fashion, and both share the same features (e.g., Baldwin, 1902). Alternatively, in agreement with other social-cognitive theorists (Damon & Hart, 1988), a ToM perspective may provide an avenue for investigation of the dynamic relations between these two processes.

Until recently, little effort has been dedicated to the identification and explanation of factors associated with individual differences in the acquisition of a mentalistic understanding of one's own and other minds. Drawing on various theories of social-cognitive processes, particularly that of attribution theory (e.g., Werner, 1948), conceptual role-taking (Chandler, 1987; Piaget, 1981; Selman, 1980), empathy (e.g., Harris, 1989), and person perception (e.g., Livesley & Bromley, 1973), ToM research provides a framework from which to investigate how the understanding of self and other relates to social interaction. Given the philosophical foundations of folk psychology and Chandler's (1987) conceptual formulation of social understanding in preadolescence, researchers have yet to describe how this understanding influences self-concept and social relations in preadolescence. Such a framework will provide the opportunity to study the influences of a developing ToM on preadolescents' construals of other people, the self, and the reasons behind social behaviour.

Similarly, the notion of ToM as an ability to co-construct or narrate one's social reality may also provide a framework in which to investigate the consequences of the process of becoming "perspectival"—that is, becoming a constructivist epistemologist may have an effect on one's social and emotional development (Boyes & Chandler, 1992; Chandler, 1987). For example, although cognitive developmentalists have suggested that as children enter preadolescence they move from a dichotomous, true/false view of knowledge and mind to a more constructivist or "degrees of certainty" view (Kitchener & King, 1981), such a notion has failed to include aspects of emotional and social development such as self-understanding or social relations. It is therefore important to investigate traditionally researched areas of preadolescent social understanding from the new perspective offered by ToM theorists, including issues of voice and silence.

Chandler (1987) has proposed that a collaborative approach towards understanding the adolescent's mind may help to illustrate the social-cognitive and emotional processes that occur during preadolescence, when a shift from a realistic to a constructivistic epistemology occurs (e.g., Chandler, 1987; Erwin, 1993; Lalonde & Chandler, 1997). More specifically, Chandler suggests that the investigation of conceptual role-taking, empathetic sensitivity, and person perception may provide a clearer picture of how adolescents make sense of others' social behaviours. That is, the examination of these three constructs may help to explain the social-cognitive processes underlying how adolescents communicate with themselves and others. For example, to what extent does the capacity to understand emotions in others affect adolescents' experiences of silence within the school setting? Accordingly, the following section provides a brief overview of research findings in each of the three social-cognitive constructs. The section focuses on how the exploration of various components of ToM can further the discourse on the adolescent experience concerning voice and silence.

Conceptual role-taking. As already noted by various ToM and social-cognitive researchers (Astington, 1993; Bennett, 1993; Flavell & Miller, 1998; Harris, 1989; Perner, 1991), research on children's understanding of mind is reminiscent of the notion of social role-taking or perspective-taking in the 1960s and 1970s (e.g., Flavell, et al., 1968; Miller, Kessel, & Flavell, 1970). However, the majority of studies performed during the sixties and seventies involved preschool and early grade-school children. Although an attempt was made by cognitive developmentalists such as Michael Chandler, John Flavell, Robert Selman, Lawrence Kohlberg, and Jane Loevinger to investigate perspective-taking and ego development in older children, the majority of the studies involved older adolescents and did not specifically focus on the social-cultural factors (see Kroger, 1996).

The most detailed account of the differentiation of self from other has been provided by Selman (1980). Selman created a model of interpersonal understanding that explains the way in which children become capable of coordinating their own point of view with those of other people and thus develop appropriate role-playing skills. According to Selman's five-stage theory, children gradually progress from an egocentric stage to becoming able to appreciate that others do have points of view and that these may be different from their own. Selman's model contends that preadolescents (i.e., 10- to 13-year-olds) are capable of understanding multiple perspectives simultaneously. Known as the third-person or mutual perspectives stage, the preadolescent is able to abstract the self from an interactive situation and view the perspectives of each person involved in the interaction. Their own viewpoint can be reflected upon from that of other persons. Furthermore, Selman's (1980) model has also been criticized for an overemphasis on the structure of various stages too closely tied to Piagetian stages of cognitive development (see Schaffer, 1996).

Theory-of-mind research also re-addresses children's and adolescents' problems with egocentrism (Chandler, 1987; Elkind, 1967; Piaget & Inhelder, 1956). Adolescents' failure to differentiate between their own thoughts and the thoughts of others is referred to as the imaginary audience syndrome, whereas overdifferentiation between their own and the thoughts of others is known as the personal fable. From a ToM perspective, adolescents who suffer from egocentrism are not able to understand what someone else would think or feel. They are unable to imagine being in the same situation. That is, since they cannot take the roles or perspectives of another person, they are unable to put themselves in "another person's shoes." Research has shown that interpersonal understanding is a better predictor of adolescent egocentrism, whereas formal operations did not predict any forms of adolescent egocentrism (Jahnke & Blanchard-Fields, 1993). These results suggest that the links among self and other reasoning and processing capacities are complex and suggest the need for further investigation.

Regarding experiences of silence, how can the exploration of social cognition of adolescents help researchers to understand those adolescents who have a tragic or negative personal fable, or a fable that has been negated, erased? For example, what happens when an adolescent claims to have no self-story, or no audience, or both? How can social cognition researchers help to uncover the adolescent's possible experience of feelings of marginalization and invisibility? Also, why have these questions remained unexplored?

Empathetic sensitivity. Given that young children's emotional understanding is considered to provide the foundation for the later development of empathy (ability to recognize emotions in others) and prosocial behaviour (Eisenberg & Mussen, 1989), research on social cognition in adolescence explores how communicative competence may influence adolescents' ability to interpret and understand both the thoughts and feelings of self and other. According to Hoffman (1984) and Davis (1980), empathy contains both affective and cognitive components and is related to one's ability to interact with others in role relationships. Although a growing number of developmentalists are showing an interest in the role that understanding emotions or empathetic sensitivity plays in the understanding of minds (e.g., Astington, 1993; Baron-Cohen, 1995; Chandler, 1987; Dunn, 1995; Hobson, 1991), research that explores the connections between emotional/cognitive factors and social communicative ability in adolescents remains sparse.

Research has shown that the majority of adolescents are able to understand and mention multiple internal states and relate them to each other in a coherent fashion (Harris, 1989; Bruchkowsky, 1992). Studies have also shown that once children reach preadolescence, they develop the ability to understand that a person can have conflicting emotions and/or hide emotions from others (e.g., Harris, 1989; Harter & Buddin, 1987). Related research on the more complex or self-conscious emotions such as shame and guilt show that, until preadolescence, the majority of children are not capable of understanding these complex emotions, or the fact that one can have conflicting emotions (e.g., Griffin, 1995; Tangney 1991). Regarding silence experiences, to what extent do adolescents' abilities to understand emotions in others and themselves influence their feeling of being silenced or their sociocommunicative patterns with others?

Furthermore, the importance of empathy in one's social understanding has been supported by research from two independent, although related, areas. ToM research on preschoolers, which has shown that in addition to cognitive understanding, emotional understanding plays an independently significant role in social interactions (Astington & Jenkins, 1995; Bartsch & Wellman, 1995; Dunn, 1995; Lalonde & Chandler, 1995). Similarly, social-cognitive studies of empathy in preadolescence have generally found that empathetic responding is positively related to popularity or peer acceptance (e.g., Erwin,

1993) and to peer competence (e.g., Ford, 1982; Zahn-Waxler & Robinson, 1995). Thus, to achieve a fuller understanding of an adolescent's theory of mind, the two research areas need to connect. I will elaborate on the role emotions play in adolescents' identity development and social experiences later on in the book, particularly concerning the experiences of silence.

Person perception. Although research on person perception stems from diverse theoretical and methodological perspectives (Shantz, 1983), the basic assumption is that social interactions are strongly influenced by one's conceptualization of others. That is, how one perceives others is affected by one's social experience (and vice versa) (e.g., Mead, 1934). In general, research has shown that children's understanding of the behaviour and personality of others progresses along a developmental continuum that reflects cognitive processes towards higher-order, more complex abstractions (Schaffer, 1996). This continuum reflects a shift from viewing others in terms of concrete, observable characteristics (e.g., "She is pretty") to an increased understanding of others in terms of abstract, psychological characteristics (e.g., "He is more shy than his brother"). During early adolescence, research has shown that there is an increase in the use of psychological comparisons and categories reflecting consistent traits, interests and abilities, and beliefs (Barenboim, 1981; Livesley & Bromley, 1973).

Although studies of person perception and related studies of gender stereotyping have occurred independently of ToM research, the ability to attribute or ascribe gender-role stereotypes relates to the general rubric of trait attribution and thus suggests indirect implications for ToM research (Edwards & Potter, 1995; Flavell & Miller, 1998; Yuill, 1993). This ascription of gender-role stereotypes can be viewed as a heuristic device that enables girls and boys to understand their own and others' intentions and beliefs (Erwin, 1993). Consequently, the representations of these social roles may help shape evaluative perceptions about the self and other that, in turn, could be used to guide social interactions (Levinson, 1995).

For instance, the notion that the self-concept plays a role in the understanding of social-role ascription is supported by a study with preschoolers that found both emotional self-evaluation and cognitive development may influence the acquisition of gender-role concepts (Kuhn, Nash, & Brucken, 1978). With regard to adolescence, Harter, Waters, Whitesell, & Kastelic (1997) recently studied the links between self-concept, levels of "voice," and gender-role orientation. Results from Harter et al.'s study showed that levels of voice, or the ability to express one's opinions, were highly correlated with self-worth. Furthermore, girls who endorsed a traditionally "feminine" gender-role orientation reported lower levels of self-worth. Taken together, results suggest that the ability to represent and understand others as psychological beings is related to self-perceptions and feelings, which in turn may affect social relations and one's experiences of silence among cultural contexts.

The explanatory or predictive use of trait terms and gender roles shares some of the concepts that are associated with ToM research by illustrating how people create implicit personality theories in order to predict or explain others' behaviour. Although person perception and trait attribution research continues to grow, the area continues to be neglected by ToM researchers (Yuill, 1993). In general, research gleaned from social-cognitive psychology has shown that preadolescent girls and boys interpret each other's behaviours based on gender-role stereotypic attributes such as greater sociality and emotionality to girls (Powlishta, 1995) and greater instrumentality and autonomy to boys (Honess, 1981; Urberg, 1982). Such findings provide support for various feminist epistemological theories (e.g., Chodorow, 1978; Gilligan, 1982) that claim females' conceptions of self and others are more psychologically oriented or rooted in a sense of connection and relatedness to others whereas males define themselves and others in terms of behaviours or accomplishments. Thus, social-cognitive research could help to further the discourse on gendered experiences of silence by exploring gender-role ascription and development of specific processes that enable preadolescents to create gender-typed implicit personality theories.

Self-Conception and Self-Understanding

In addition to the aforementioned higher-order social-cognitive processes, an inquiry into an adolescent's mental world must consider the role of the self-concept in the development and application of these processes (Wellman, 1990). As asserted by Shantz (1983), the developmental processes involved in understanding oneself and in understanding others appear to be intricately interwoven and support the view that both self and other perception derive from social experience (Berger & Luckmann, 1967; Mead, 1934).

Similar to ToM research, the study of the self has had to deal with the problem of internal theoretical conflict since the field's conception (Baldwin, 1902; Cooley, 1912; James, 1890; Mead, 1934), perhaps causing its continued popularity within various social science disciplines, especially in psychology (e.g., Bruner, 1990; Kegan, 1994) and philosophy (e.g., Bakhtin, 1981; Morrison, 1994; Nagel, 1986). Conceptually, the "theory" theory of the self shares the greatest affinity to ToM research given that it emphasizes the individual's construction of the self and deals with one's feelings and beliefs directed towards oneself (Damon & Hart, 1988; Harter, 1999). In addition, self-concept research has recently moved from the monolithic conception of self (e.g., Coopersmith,

1967) to a cultural-specific one that is both multidimensional (Harter, 1999; Neisser, 1988) and hierarchical in nature (Marsh & Shavelson, 1985). This notion of the dialogical or "omnibus" self suggests that the self is a cultural-specific, dynamic, multilayered entity that reconceptualizes itself as a combination of cognitive abilities and emotional and social experiences (Bruner & Kalmar, 1997; Cedarblom, 1989; Markus & Wurf, 1987; Wang, 2004).

From a developmental perspective, the self-concept becomes increasingly differentiated with age and gradually shifts from the physical and active self in early childhood to the psychological and social self in early adolescence (see Damon & Hart, 1988; Harter, 1999). During early adolescence, the concept of the self increases in complexity and abstractness; the self is now conceptualized primarily in mental—rather than physical—terms. Many researchers have noticed the similarities in children's understanding of self and other, that they both progress along a developmental continuum from concrete, physical, and situation-specific views of the self to abstract, psychological, and trait-like self-definition (Schaffer, 1996). Accordingly, although an interactionist or psychocultural approach to self-concept research is in its infancy (Bruner, 1996), a growing number of social-cognitive researchers have begun to investigate how children and adolescents come to understand the complex experience of their own individuality and how this differs from their understanding of others (e.g., Damon & Hart, 1988; Hart & Fegley, 1995; Selman, 1980). For instance, studies that have investigated the concepts of self and other have found some developmental differences between the two concepts, suggesting that it may be possible to have a greater understanding of oneself than other, or vice versa (Damon & Hart, 1988; Hatcher et al., 1990).

An ongoing debate among self-concept researchers involves the question of how to integrate the cognitive and affective aspects of the structure of self. While the majority of past researchers (e.g., Coopersmith, 1967; Rosenberg, 1989) have defined one's cognitive representation of self in mainly affective terms, claiming that self-esteem assesses how negatively or positively one feels about one's selfhood, more recent research has begun to focus on the more cognitive and cultural aspects of the self by investigating the justifications of these self-evaluations. As Damon and Hart claim, asking "how much" understanding a person has does not approach the crucial question of how the self is understood (1988, p. 14). Subsequently, researchers have begun to incorporate both qualitative (e.g., interview) and quantitative (e.g., self-report questionnaire) methods to obtain a clearer picture of the conceptual system of self-conception and its cognitive underpinning of self-understanding, which encompasses the thoughts, attitudes, and beliefs about oneself that distinguish self from others (Damon & Hart, 1988). Moreover, with cultural-specific, multidimensional self-concept research in its infancy, many researchers are advocating further research in this area, especially questioning whether or not the structure of the self-concept is equivalent across gender (Marsh & Shavelson, 1996; Harter et al., 1997; Wang, 2004).

Within the research domain of ToM, the concept of the self has been increasingly mentioned, particularly regarding the issue of whether or not mental states are equally ascribed to both the self and other (e.g., Barresi & Moore, 1995; Gopnik, 1993; Gopnik & Astington, 1988; Moore, 1996). Unfortunately, there exists a large gap between the research fields of ToM and social cognition, with the latter offering a wealth of literature on the relation between self-concept and social development in preadolescence whereas the former continues to focus on infants and preschool children. Thus, by approaching self-concept development from a ToM perspective, the complex relations between theory of mind and theory of self may become a little clearer. A fuller, more complex model of social understanding, then, may shed some light on the various research questions concerning self-concept during preadolescence. For example, a more complete model of social and self-understanding could help to explain findings of recent studies that have shown experiences of silence (Gilligan, 1982), self-consciousness (Rubin & Asendorpf, 1993), social anxiety (Rosenberg, 1989), and loneliness (Parkhurst & Asher, 1992) increase in tandem with social-cognitive development.

In addition, this social-cognitive model could also be used to test the various theories of ToM development by comparing self and other interpretations. For instance, theory-theorists would expect self- and other-understanding to develop in tandem (e.g., Barresi & Moore, 1995; Gopnik, 1993), whereas the simulation theorist would expect self-understanding to develop before other-understanding (e.g., Harris, 1989). Alternatively, given that a sense of self is derived from social interactions (e.g., Cooley, 1912; Mead, 1934), a social-constructivist ToM theorist would perhaps predict that other-understanding (interpersonal) would develop before self-understanding (intrapersonal). Also, regarding Sternberg's (2003) notion of extrapersonal understanding, to what extent can social-cognitive theories help to explain broader conceptualizations of a sense of self within the larger cultural context?

The investigation of self-development within the framework of ToM also provides an opportunity to explore the roles that language, voice, and silence play in self-conception. Although the notion that language influences the individuation process is not new (e.g., Bakhtin, 1981; Vygotsky, 1978), Bakhtin's claim that the "selfing process" takes place in the context of relationship, such as the ongoing dialogue between self and others, has gained popularity within psycholinguistic and feminist epistemological circles. In particular, recent literature has focused on the changing social nature of the selfing process as expressed in "voice," or the articulation of one's subjective experience (e.g.,

Harter et al., 1997). Furthermore, many researchers claim that the development of this voice and/or self becomes differentiated according to gender during early adolescence (e.g., Brown & Gilligan, 1992; Debold, Tolman, & Brown, 1996). The fact that the self is developed within, and by complex social interaction and experience of language, suggests that self-conception entails one's ability to speak (and listen) to oneself and to others. Similarly, to what extent can such research help to explain the "silencing process" in the context of peers and the school setting?

The majority of current ToM research on self and other have found significant correlations between the understanding of mental states in self and other (e.g., Pratt & Bryant, 1990; Wimmer & Hartl, 1991). Such findings support the theory-theory hypothesis that claims children use the same conceptual system to reason about their own and other people's second-order mental states. Alternatively, there are a few social cognitive (Damon & Hart, 1988; Hatcher et al., 1990), cross-cultural (Ochs & Schieffelin, 1984), and ToM preschool studies that provide support for the Meadian/Vygotskian claim that one needs to understand the concept of "other" in order to understand the self. Due to these conflicting findings, a collaborative effort between educators and social-cognitive and linguistic researchers is needed to investigate the role silence plays in adolescent self- and other-understanding. Using methods gleaned from 1) the more general research area of social cognition and 2) the more focused research area of children's understanding of mental states, a psychocultural approach to adolescent social cognition may become an exciting avenue for future research on adolescents' experience of silence within the psychological and educational context.

Adolescents' Theory of Mind and Self-Concept

Despite the theoretical connection between ToM understanding and the self-concept (Wellman, 1990), few studies have investigated this link directly, particularly with respect to cultural context (Banerjee & Yuill, 1999; Johnson, 1997). Furthermore, in relation to ToM, no studies have looked at various self-representations such as verbal and graphical, or other aspects of the self-system such as self-evaluation or self-agency (Bruner, 1996). With regard to mental-state understanding, findings have shown relatively sophisticated cognitive abilities such as the ability to understand recursive mental states in others (e.g., "She thinks that he thinks . . .") may be linked to feelings of negative self-worth (Farber, 1989; Veith, 1980). For instance, Veith (1980) found that preadolescents' ability to understand recursive mental states in others was related to a relatively negative view of the self. Similarly, feelings of low self-worth and depressed mood have been found to be linked to sophisticated mental-state reasoning capacities, particularly among highly academically competent preadolescent girls (e.g., Gjerde, 1995; Kerr, 1994).

In contrast to past research that suggests a positive link may exist between psychological understanding and self-concept (Selman, 1980), some investigators claim that the later correlates of ToM and feelings of self-worth may not be uniformly positive (Dunn, 2000; Hughes & Dunn, 1998). There is some evidence to suggest that high levels of children's psychological understanding result in greater sensitivity to teacher criticism and lower self-esteem (Dunn, 1995; Cutting & Dunn, 1999; Veith, 1980). In addition, studies have shown that children and adults with high levels of psychological understanding may experience diminished self-concept and emotional problems, given the time spent on self-reflection and imagining what others think of them (Hatcher & Hatcher, 1997). Also, given the finding that children who scored high on second-order ToM tasks were able to better understand self-presentation rules (Banerjee & Yuill, 1999), perhaps children who are adept at reading social cues are adept at pretending to be who they think people want them to be.

Such self-presentation skills may suggest the ability to edit and/or perhaps silence particular aspects of the self and personal voice. Thus, investigations of links between psychological understanding and self will illuminate the complex connections between understanding oneself and others. Taken together with other studies on adolescents that have shown links between cognitive abilities and self-concept (Bhatnager & Rastogi, 1986; Bosacki, 2000), these results support Farber's (1989) contention that high psychological mindedness may have deleterious consequences such as a negative self-concept. Overall, such findings suggest that social and emotional correlates of interpersonal understanding or "psychological mindedness" need to be further examined in adolescents, particularly in how such sophisticated mental capacities may enable adolescents to become highly proficient "editors" or "silencers" concerning particular aspects of the self (Park & Park, 1997).

Language, Sociocommunication, and Emotions

As mentioned by past theorists and researchers (e.g., Blos, 1979; Coopersmith, 1967; Harter, 1999), early adolescence is considered the stage of re-individuation, when the child reorganizes and differentiates the self-concept. Given that the sense of self is derived from social experience (e.g., Berger and Luckmann, 1967), preadolescents' social experiences with their peers play a significant role in the development of their self-concept (Rosenberg, 1989; Selman, 1980; Sullivan, 1953). Accordingly, a psychocultural approach to social and self-understanding in adolescence may assist in the investigation of the links between cognitive representations of self and other and their links to social communication. That is, how adolescents think and feel about, and make sense of social situations and themselves, may influence how they interact with others. Thus, by focusing on the cognitive and emotional elements of social understanding, both ToM and social-cognitive theorists have suggested that higher-order mental states are necessary for effective social interaction (e.g., Flavell & Miller, 1998; Happé, 1994; Perner, 1991; Selman, 1980).

According to folk psychology, social interaction is actually an interaction of minds that consists of mental states expressed through speech acts or acts of silence. That is, social interaction does not proceed directly via the interaction of these mental states but proceeds indirectly by way of language (Astington, 1993). This notion is expressed in various speech act theorists' claims that communication relies on both speaker and hearer taking account of each other's knowledge and intentions (Austin, 1962; Grice, 1968; Searle, 1969) and the corresponding definition of communicative competence as intention attribution (Levinson, 1995; Sperber & Wilson, 1986). Thus, experiences of silence can occur whether or not the speaker and listener acknowledge or understand each other. Both the speaker and the listener may create the meaning of the "silence acts" and the interpretation may be influenced by additional nonverbal communication (e.g., body language, posture, tone of voice, etc.).

In relation to cognitive development during adolescence, as previously noted, by the age of 11, children are capable of abstract, recursive thought (Piaget, 1963). Case et al. (1996) have shown that by age 11, children's increased processing abilities (i.e., central conceptual structures) allow them to integrate multiple perspectives and relate them to each other in a coherent fashion (Case et al., 1996). Within the context of narrative thought, studies on narrative complexity and cognitive competence have shown that the structural complexity of children's narratives increases with age and that this increase may be attributed to information processing capacity (McKeough, 1992).

Research on children's narrative shows that 10- to 11-year-olds are capable of understanding and creating interpretive narratives (e.g., Fox, 1991; McKeough, Templeton, & Marini, 1995). For example, in a study to explore the developing awareness of mind in children's narrative writing, Fox (1991) found that the majority of 11-year-olds were capable of spontaneously writing stories that focused on Bruner's (1986) landscape of consciousness as opposed to the landscape of action. That is, most of the 11-year-olds' narratives involved a self-reflective protagonist or several characters capable of thinking and feeling. Such narrative tasks, then, may be a useful vehicle to investigate children's cognitive ability to simultaneously represent and reflect upon the relation between two events. Given that such a cognitive capacity may underlie social-emotional reasoning skills (Bruner, 1986; Case et al., 1996), a growing number of researchers have suggested that narrative tasks may provide some insight into how adolescents make sense of themselves and others (e.g., Astington, 1993; Hatcher et al., 1990; Tager-Flusberg, Sullivan, Barker, Harris, & Boshart, 1997).

With regard to mental states, language, and social interaction, various researchers have agreed that the understanding of mental states in others is reflected by the use of both metacognitive (e.g., believe, think, know) and metalinguistic verbs (e.g., assert, say, concede) (representing mental states and speech acts respectively) (e.g., Astington & Pelletier, 1996; Slomkowski & Dunn, 1996). The use of such mental-state verbs has implications for higher-order interpersonal relations in that it represents one's own stance or position towards another person's mental states (Laing, 1961; Leech, 1980). For example, if John states "Leslie claims that she is hungry," this statement implies that Leslie believes it is true that she is hungry, but the speaker (John) may not share Leslie's belief. Thus, the expression of mental states in speech acts facilitates interpersonal communication and provides the basis for the ability to "read each other."

The importance of speech acts for social communication also has implications for those individuals who choose to remain silent; silence is ambiguous in that the receiver of silence (or "silencee") can interpret the received silence in many ways. For example, if one is the recipient of another's silence, the silencee may believe that either the silence represents a lack of the speaker's willingness to share one's mental state with the other, or that the silence refers to the speaker's lack of mental state (i.e., speech = mental state, lack of speech = lack of mental state).

Although adolescents' ability to relate to their peers may partly be influenced by their ability to understand mental states in others as expressed through their speech acts, peer relations are often excluded from studies that investigate psycholinguistic and pragmatic issues. For example, although links between communicative ability and theory of mind have been studied with preadolescents in terms of speech acts, such as the understanding of irony and promising (Astington, 1988; Happé, 1993; Keenan, 1995), within this age group, related areas of social cognition (including social competence) have yet to be approached from a ToM perspective. Furthermore, few studies investigate the role of silence in speech acts and how sociocultural factors may affect the situation. To address this gap in research, studies on adolescents' understanding of mental states and their acquisition of mental-state verbs may assist in the investigation of how adolescents come to understand intentional relations in the peer milieux, including the understanding of silence, feelings, intentions, and beliefs of others (de Villiers, 1995; Astington & Pelletier, 1996).

Language also plays a role in how adolescents make sense of emotions in others. A related area of higher-order mentalizing is emotion understanding, particularly regarding complex and ambiguous emotions. In contrast to the simple or basic emotions (e.g., happy, sad), to understand complex emotions (e.g., pride, embarrassment), children must hold in mind two separate pieces of information: other people's and societal norms (Saarni, 1999). That is, children must imagine what others think of their behaviour and self-evaluate against internalized behavioural standards. Although complex emotion understanding hinges on cognitive abilities such as second-order reasoning and self-evaluation, no studies have investigated the links between the three concepts. Despite the growing interest in the links between ToM and emotion understanding, these studies have focused on preschoolers, first-order ToM understanding, and basic emotions such as happy and sad (Cutting & Dunn, 1999; Hughes & Dunn, 1998; Hughes, Deater-Deckard, & Cutting, 1999). Research on the links between second-order, or higher-level ToM, and the understanding of complex emotions has just begun (Carpendale & Shelton, 1999), and future researchers will need to explore this relation longitudinally, and include sociocultural factors.

A substantial part of children's emotion understanding is mediated through language processes—in particular, in cultural settings such as parent-child conversations in the home or in peer conversations during free play (Kitayama, Markus, & Matsumoto, 1995). A psychocultural approach to emotion development assumes that the development of language and emotion concepts are interdependent and have their origins in social interactions with more skilled partners (Rogoff, 1990; Vygotsky, 1978). Many researchers have asserted that emotion words or labels play a large role in the development of the child's conceptualization of emotion (e.g., Saarni, 1999). Thus, according to Kopp (1989), emotion language "provides children with an especially powerful tool for understanding emotions" (p. 349). Several recent studies have highlighted the importance of language abilities in children's understanding of emotions and have suggested that the links are complex, especially when investigating emotion understanding across different genders and countries (Cutting & Dunn, 1999; Jenkins & Astington, 1996; Harris, 1989).

Despite the potential to shed light on adolescents' developing emotional world, few studies have investigated children's and adolescents' understanding of complex emotions from a psychocultural perspective (e.g., for exceptions, see Bybee, 1998; Capps et al., 1992; Harris, 1989). Given Maccoby's (1998) conceptualization of gender as a culture, a psychocultural approach to the study of self-conscious emotions could help to unpack the links among language, gender-role socialization, and emotion understanding. Extant literature has focused on emotional expression among older children and adults, with results in general suggesting that girls or women exhibit a higher level of self-conscious emotion understanding and experience than boys or men (see Bybee, 1998, Markus & Kitayama, 1994).

Given that many of our interpersonal interactions involve comprehending and responding to emotion, or discussing emotion-laden situations and issues, strong emotion is not a rarity. Oatley and Duncan (1994) conducted a diary study of emotional experiences among adults. On average, their research participants recorded one episode of emotion each day that was described as strong enough to consume thoughts to be accompanied by a perceptible bodily response, and to simulate some urge to action. The importance and salience of emotional experiences, as a feature both of subjective consciousness and of the interpersonal relationships, contrasts with the comparative rarity of emotion words in conversation. Even though emotion, even strong emotion, occurs frequently, and we give priority to reading others and managing our own emotion, emotion language is a very small proportion of natural speech. People do not usually use emotional labels with much frequency in regular conversation.

Although we talk about emotion all the time, surprisingly, in natural conversation, reference to emotion is often made in oblique terms, and not often with specific labels for emotion. Emotional labels, by virtue of their rarity, are a powerful statement of value, and it would seem, are seldom applied in a value-neutral way. The act of labeling emotion is an act of evaluating the content of experience or behavior on several dimensions: its authenticity, rationality, legitimacy, and hedonic tone. Naming an emotion conveys something about controllability and intensity. Few researchers have undertaken the task of collecting information about emotion talk in everyday conversation, as it could take hours of tape recording to yield a handful of emotional labels. Anderson and Leaper (1998) investigated conversations about people and emotion and found that undergraduate women and men talked about the same kinds of emotions and referred to specific emotions equally frequently. Given the low frequency of emotion words, such silences around emotion terms remains to be explored. For example, researchers need to explore why some adolescents choose to talk about particular emotions over others and how does this preference differ across gender, ethnicity, social class, and so forth.

Shields (2002) discusses how the completeness of conventional accounts of emotional socialization are now being questioned by social-constructivists or psychocultural views of development. In general, consistent with a psychocultural approach to development, social-constructivists claim that developmental progress is defined in terms of the child's approximation and variation on culturally agreed-upon norms of conduct. Developmental progress is defined in terms of a fixed, mature state. Regarding emotional socialization, family and peer groups cultivate a "nice girl" orientation in girls (quiet and compliant) that deletes anger from the normal emotional script and, in contrast, encourages the expression (and understanding) of happiness, shame, fear, and warmth or friendliness. Boys, however, are encouraged to express (and understand) emotions that reflect a sense of entitlement, anger, contempt, pride, and so on, while other emotional expressions are dampened.

Emotions also figure prominently in social experiences of silence, although this is seldom explicitly acknowledged. As many researchers have noted, emotions are significant because they help to regulate social behaviour that is also governed, in part, by the cultural context. Commonly observed behaviours, whether it is young adolescent girls acting appropriately quietly and kindly or adolescent boys acting loud and boisterous towards teachers, are not a result of a blind adherence to powerful norms or of a principled holding fast to a system of values and beliefs. As D'Andrade (1984) and others suggest, normative behaviour typically feels "good" or "right."

Markus and Kitayama (1994) suggest that the connection between good feelings and normative behaviour is intertwined with the developing sense of self. That is, Markus and Kitayama suggest that a cultural group's ways of feeling are shaped by the group's habitual and normative social behaviour. In turn, these ways of feeling influence the nature of this social behaviour. Thus, how adolescents experience silence implies affective reactions and also shows the variation in social behaviour, which provides a window on the interdependence between emotion and culture. For example, some adolescents have learned that "good girls" are quiet and "bad girls" are loud; such a lesson may influence their social behaviour and emotional states.

Thus, the nature of the lock and key arrangement between the social order and emotional responses has been of pervasive interest to many social scientists and educators interested in how the self provides a meeting point and a framework for the relation between the individual and the social world. Each person is embedded within a variety of sociocultural contexts or cultures (e.g., country or region of origin, ethnicity, religion, gender, family, birth cohort, profession, etc.). Each of these cultural contexts makes some claim on the person or plays a role in that person's mental schema or script that involves a set of beliefs and practices that (i.e., a cultural schema or framework) about how to be a "good" person. A sense of the "good" is an integral part of one's sense of the self, and one's sense of self shapes what is "good" (e.g., of value, concern, appropriate, etc.) and what is not (Oyserman & Markus, 1993). The self, then, is an organized locus of the various, sometimes competing and contradicting, understandings of how to be a person. This self-concept functions as an individualized orienting, mediating, interpretive framework giving shape to what people notice and think about, how people make meaning from information, to what they are motivated to do, and to how they feel and their ways of feeling.

According to Neisser (1988), a psychocultural approach to development suggests that the self is the entire person considered from particular points of view, and contingent upon different contexts; it is the ways in which the person is made meaningful or given significance. Thus, the concept of the self as the particularized locus of various sociocultural influences suggests that adolescents maintain some kind of agency in their socialization (self-socialization). As Maccoby (1998) claims, this notion of self-socialization helps to explain why two adolescents in similar sociocultural contexts (e.g., two 14-year-old adolescent girls in a ninth-grade classroom) are unlikely to experience silence and emotion exactly the same way in a given set of circumstances.

For example, if an adolescent girl chooses to break her silence and "talk back" to the teacher, her sense of self will determine the nature of "good" feelings and of the social behaviour that will promote and foster these good feelings. This means that emotional experiences are mediated by one's self-concept. It is the self-concept that acts as a selective filter or a personalized translator of the social context; what is as experienced as happy or joyful (or sad or angering) depends upon the mediating self. Being moral (i.e., proper, right, or appropriate) according to one's group, feeling good, and being a person are all intimately connected. This moral space may provide a compass for adolescents who are searching for answers to questions about what is good/bad, what is worth doing and what is not, what has meaning and importance for you, and what is secondary.

Psychological Understanding, Self, and Social Relations in Adolescence

To understand the silences of adolescence, we must also understand the voices and actions of adolescents. Accordingly, to help us understand some aspects of the adolescent mind, heart, and voice within the context of the school classroom, the following sections briefly outline research on links among psychological understanding, self-concept, and social relations. Such research agendas, then, may provide a rich database for the exploration of what silences mean to adolescents within the school setting.

To study the role of peer relations in self and social cognitions, a large amount of research has been conducted on the link between self-concept and social behaviour. In brief, the majority of studies show that positive feelings of self-worth are related to positive social experiences and prosocial behaviour (e.g., Boivin & Hymel, 1997; Patterson, Kupersmidt, & Griesler, 1990; Schaffer, 1996). More specifically, such studies have shown a positive relation between self-concept and social competence (e.g., Harter, 1999), self-concept and peer acceptance (e.g., Jones & Gerig, 1994), and self-concept and attachment (e.g., Jacobsen, Edelstein, & Hofmann, 1995). Although peer relations play a large role in the adolescent's social-cognitive and affective development (e.g., Abrams, 1989; Sullivan, 1953; Wentzel & Asher, 1995), teachers also continue to affect the adolescent's inner world. To support this view, Pekrun (1990) found that the influence of family, peers, and teachers had a cumulative effect on 10- to 13-year-olds' general and academic self-concept, with teacher support correlating the highest. In addition to teachers and peers, sociocultural factors such as family structure (i.e., birth order, number of siblings) (e.g., Peterson & Leigh, 1990; Sulloway, 1996), cultural background (e.g., Phinney, 1990; Ward, 2004), and media exposure (e.g., Wilgosh, 1994; Ward, 2004) have also been suggested to influence social-cognitive thought and behaviour.

Research findings on the link between social-cognitive abilities and social relations in preadolescents have been contradictory and inconclusive. Social-cognitive processes such as conceptual role-taking, empathetic sensitivity, and person perception have all been found to be related to both teacher and peer ratings of positive social behaviour ratings and peer acceptance (e.g., Ford, 1982; Pellegrini, 1985). In contrast, some studies have failed to find a relation between various social-cognitive abilities and sociometric status. In particular, studies have shown that aspects of social reasoning such as referential communication and means-ends problem solving were not related to peer popularity among sixth-grade students (Matthews & Keating, 1995; Rubin, 1972). As Dodge and Feldman (1990) suggest, the lack of consistent findings concerning social-cognitive skills and peer ratings highlights the need for further study.

Despite the fact that a large amount of research exists on adolescent social cognition, few studies investigate the connections among psychological understanding, self-concept, and social relations. As previous researchers have noted, this paucity of research could be due to the fact that the links between social thought, self-cognitions, and social behaviour become increasingly complex as children reach early adolescence (Dodge & Feldman, 1990).

Although social interactions and the understanding of complex emotions require second-order reasoning, these three areas have been studied separately. Despite the increasing number of studies on ToM and social behaviour in children, the majority focuses on preschoolers (e.g., Astington & Jenkins, 1995), with a few on older children (Bosacki & Astington, 1999; Watson et al., 1999). In general, results suggest that a sophisticated ToM is linked to greater social competence. However, the picture becomes more complex once self-concept, gender, and language are considered. A potentially rich context within which to investigate such connections is children's play behaviour during school recess. Play has been linked to language development and many areas of sociocognition, including ToM and self-concept (Hughes, 1999). In particular, past studies have shown that particular types of play in early childhood (e.g., pretend, cooperative) may be more linked to psychological understanding than others (e.g., Brown et al., 1996). Future research needs to extend the exploration of play behaviour and psychological understanding into adolescence.

In contrast to prosocial play behaviours, aggression may be linked to psychological understanding such as relational aggression (when one tries to damage the self-esteem or feelings of others) (e.g., Crick & Dodge, 1994; Underwood, 2002). In contrast to physical or overt aggression, little is known about adolescents who exhibit behaviours of relational or psychological aggression such as telling lies about one's peers. Similarly, research on behavioural disorders has focused mainly on physically aggressive children and adolescents as compared to those labelled as withdrawn or socially inhibited (Tremblay, 2000). In general, evidence suggests that physically aggressive children may have lower levels of psychological understanding than nonaggressive children (e.g., Hughes et al., 1998). Given the link between low self-worth and social inhibition (Rubin & Asendorpf, 1993), surprisingly few studies have examined sociocognitive abilities in socially withdrawn adolescents (see Harris et al., 1997, for exceptions). More research is needed to explore (a) psychological understanding and psychological aggression in adolescents and (b) the mental world and social experience of socially inhibited adolescents. To pursue this line of inquiry, I am currently working on a longitudinal research project with middle school children that builds on my past and current research on ToM and social behaviour by investigating social cognition, self-concept, and language within the naturalistic context of the school classroom and playground (Bosacki, 2004).

Given the previously mentioned link between social understanding and communicative competencies, adolescents' classroom experiences may be determined in part by their ability to understand mental states in others. Although the link between adolescents' mental state understanding and school experiences remains to be studied from a psychocultural perspective, past studies on preschoolers and young school-aged children have shown positive links between the understanding of false beliefs and 1) positive teacher ratings of social-emotional skills (Lalonde & Chandler, 1995), 2) skilled aspects of pretend play (Astington & Jenkins, 1995), and 3) peer ratings of likeability or popularity (Dockett, 1997). In addition to false-belief understanding, studies have also shown a positive relation between positive peer relations and emotional understanding/affective perspective-taking (Donelan-McCall & Dunn, 1996; Werner & Cassidy, 1997).

However, within the realm of ToM research, the links among adolescents' understanding of mental states, self-concept, and their social relations and silence remain relatively undiscovered. The few studies that have investigated links among social cognition, self-concept, and social relations in adolescents have not worked within a psychocultural framework. That is, such studies have not incorporated the principles of folk psychology or belief-desire reasoning into their research design or into the interpretation of their findings (e.g., Bosacki, 1998; Rubin, LeMare, & Lollis, 1990; Schultz & Selman, 1989). Thus, ToM research on adolescents needs to draw on the recent relevant studies on younger children that have examined mental-state understanding and social relations.

For example, past studies investigated the connections between school-aged children's personal and emotional school experiences and their mental-state understanding. Most recently, researchers have started to examine the personal school experience of young school-aged children and how this relates to their understanding of thoughts and emotions in others (Astington & Pelletier, 1996; Donelan-McCall & Dunn, 1996). In particular, Donelan-McCall and Dunn's study of six-year-olds' school experiences found positive links between emotional understanding and positive peer relations. Thus, such findings promote the need for further investigations of social understanding and social relations in adolescents within a school setting.

Furthermore, studies that have investigated the complex web of adolescent social cognition and social behaviour rarely examine how the self-concept and the notion of voice may influence the relation between social reasoning and social behaviour. The majority of research that investigates the various connections among three or more social-cognitive variables often assumes that the construct of the self-concept and voice acts as mediating variable. As Baron and Kenny (1986) note, research needs to investigate the possibility that various aspects of the self-concept may act as either a mediator or a moderator. To illustrate, Boivin and Hymel (1997) recently studied peer experiences and self-perceptions in preadolescents. Although Boivin and Hymel found that negative peer status and peer victimization mediated the relation between social behaviour and self-perceptions, they did not test to see if these mediating variables also acted as a moderator. By using only a mediational model, Boivin and Hymel assumed that social behaviour causes social preference or popularity. Alternatively, popularity could have acted as a moderator, either compensating or inhibiting the influence of social behaviour on self-perceptions. As Baron and Kenny (1986) suggest, as opposed to using the terms *mediator* and *moderator* interchangeably, when studying the complex interrelations among three or more social-psychological variables, both mediational and moderation models need to be tested.

Within the context of the present text, the influences of self-concept and voice may have either a mediating or moderating effect on the relation between social understanding and social relations. However, despite Baron and Kenny's (1986) claim, a recent study on preadolescents tested for the mediating and moderating effects of self-esteem, attributional style, and ethnicity between the relation of shyness and academic performance (Haines & Bartels, 1997). Results showed that self-esteem and a negative attributional style mediated the relation between shyness and academic performance. Future research needs to explore the mediating and moderating roles of adolescent voice on their social-cognitive abilities and their classroom experiences of silence.

Given the lack of empirical evidence for established links between self-concept and mental-state reasoning, and findings from past studies that show self-concept may have a negative influence on social behaviour, irrespective of social-cognitive ability (Schultz & Selman, 1989), it could be suggested that self-concept and voice may have an inhibitory influence on the relation between interpersonal understanding and social relations. That is, irrespective of one's ability to understand mental states in others, if one holds a negative view of the self, one would be perceived by peers and teachers as less socially competent.

Psychological Understanding and Schooling

The classroom setting is a powerful social context in which the psychological world of adolescents remains under construction. As various writers have noted, children often evaluate their own performances and sense of selves based on the feedback received from the school environment (e.g., Bruner, 1996; Harter et al., 1997). That is, an adolescent's sense of self and voice is determined in part by peer and teacher interactions within the classroom (Harter, 1999). Accordingly, peer relations help shape an individual's personality to the extent that an adolescent who avoids peer interactions or withdraws from the social milieu may be at risk of developing problems in the social-cognitive and social-behavioural domains (Sullivan, 1953).

Although mental-state understanding would seem to be foundational to a child's educational experiences, few researchers have studied the influence of psychological understanding or ToM on school success beyond the age of five or six (Astington & Pelletier, 1996; Bosacki et al., 1997). Regarding academic competence, associations have been found between ToM and the production of stories and general language ability (Astington & Jenkins, 1995; McKeough, 1992). ToM has also been claimed to facilitate children's ability to self-monitor their cognitive process and engage in reflexive thinking (Astington & Pelletier, 1996). Taken together, these claims suggest that psychological understanding is linked to higher-order, metacognitive thought. Thus, based on past findings with children, adolescents who possess high levels of psychological understanding may be more likely to "think about their own and others' thinking" during the school day.

In contrast, results from research on ToM and school social experience have produced contradictory evidence. Some studies have shown that sophisticated ToM and emotion understandings have a positive influence on school experience (Brown et al., 1996), whereas others have found that such understandings do not guarantee an easier or more positive life at school (Cutting & Dunn, 1999). For example, Dunn (1995) found that kindergarteners' ToM understanding was related to negative initial perceptions of school and sensitivity to teacher judgment and criticism. Perhaps the ability to read the other provides opportunities for children to be privileged to both positive and negative feedback. Access to such knowledge, particularly negative evaluation, may lead some adolescents to feel silenced; thus, future research needs to explore how psychological understanding and self-concept play a role in classroom silence experiences beyond childhood into adolescence.

Sociocognitive Psychology and Silence: Does Silence Help or Hurt the Adolescent?

This next section outlines the ways in which silence may affect the adolescent's developing sense of self. How does the silence experience differ if the silence is chosen by the adolescent or if the silence is imposed on the adolescent by others? Drawing on past relevant literature, I outline both the positive and negative influences of silence on various aspects of adolescent development, particularly the social, emotional, and cognitive areas. In others words, this section explores ways in which silences can either help and/or hurt the adolescent's confidence and competence, in both personal and social contexts.

Helpful Silence: Intrapersonal and Interpersonal

Silence experiences may be helpful to the adolescent in many ways, including the opportunities for developing a stronger self-connection and an increased sense of spiritual and self-awareness. Viewed as an absence of dialogue, silence may provide opportunities for adolescents to develop their listening skills by means of encouraging adolescents to listen to their inner voices and to develop a stronger sense of who they are as individuals. Opportunities of silence may promote the development of reflective thought and higher-order cognitive processes including contemplation and creativity.

Adolescents who experience silence may also experience strengthened relationships with others in the sense that they have learned more self-knowledge about themselves, which will add to the relationship with another person. As Jack (1991) suggests, if silence indicates a withdrawal from the authoritative voices of others, and the critical gaze and judgments of oneself, then that silence may hold the possibility of healing and helping. Such a withdrawal can offer a psychologically safe place of creative waiting and transformation (Hall, 1980). Silence may provide the adolescent with the opportunity to do "inner work" and to reclaim parts of the self that have been set aside or ignored within relationships with the self and others. The healing possibilities arise out of a dialogue of inner questioning and awareness to the real or authentic self. Thus, in this way, silence can provide valuable learning opportunities for the adolescent to gain self-knowledge and may create possibilities for movement and change, both intrapersonally and in relation to others.

Spirituality, silence, and mental health in adolescence. Regarding the connections between silence and spiritual awareness, although a cognitive locus for spiritual awareness has been suggested by an increasing number of educators and developmentalists (e.g., Levine, 1999; Harris, 2000; Hay, 2001), Goldman (1964) was the first to explore children's religious notions. The main point of Goldman's studies was that children's religious notions are not just fragmented or abridged versions of adult representations. Goldman was interested in the finding that children's concepts of religion diverged systematically from adults and particularly from the cultural input provided by religious education. Consistent with Piaget's predictions, the child's concept of God is overwhelmingly anthropomorphic to the "formal operational" stage (after age 11). For seven-year-olds, prayer works because of some physical conduit that allows God literally to hear people just as they hear each other. According to Goldman, children must wait until they are young adolescents to take biblical stories as symbolic and not as literal accounts of physical events. In the same way, it is at that stage that they grasp complex aspects of Christian morality and the idea that God is good (as compared with evil).

In general, these studies on cognitive understandings of the metaphysical and supernatural reflect a convergence of language acquisition with religious and spiritual thought. Unfortunately, little research exists on the roles that language, voice, and silence play in the connections among faith development, self-cognitions, and feelings. This lack of serious interest in detailed studies of children's and adolescents' religious concepts is surprising as most psychologists focus on the externals of religion such as explicit claims to belief and religiosity scales. Watts and Williams (1988) suggest that religious knowledge is the knowledge of God; that religious knowing involves coming to know a separate religious work and coming to know the religious dimensions of the everyday world.

Given that our modern North American culture values the compartmentalization of human development, this focus on individualism may promote a sense of disconnection between oneself and one's community. For educators and developmentalists, the question concerns when this disconnection occurs and why it often manifests as silence. How can we study these experiences of disconnect and silence and subsequently intervene to create programs that foster a spiritual dimension? How can we, as educators and researchers concerned with the spiritual growth of children, prevent such attitudes from developing in the first place? In what ways does conventional schooling encourage adolescents to be silent about their "hunches" and to hide or silence their inner life? How can we as educators truly believe that this will foster a sense of well-being and fulfillment later on in life?

To answer the question of how schooling, teachers, and books have become separated or disengaged from spiritual awareness, a fruitful area of study includes a focus on adolescents—an exploration of the spiritual experiences among adolescents and the role silence plays in these experiences. Although some writers discuss spirituality in terms of younger children, few researchers adapt these concepts to adolescents. For example, Myers (1997) discusses the notion of a spirituality of caring as a shared construct of those within a given community who support, nurture, guide, teach, and learn in caring, hopeful ways. The four conditions include 1) a provision of hospitable space; 2) the acceptance, embracing, and providing of experience; 3) the presence of authentic, caring adults; and 4) an affirmation of the process of learning, of being able to spiritedly transcend present conditions. Although Myers discusses such a concept of caring within the context of preschoolers, such conditions could be valuable as they may influence silences among adolescents. To what extent do the conditions of a spirituality of caring play a role in the experiences of silence in the classroom?

How can researchers apply this construct of a spirituality of caring to explore the question of what happens to an adolescent's sense of self and voice within a school setting? From a psychological perspective, early adolescence (9 or 10 to 12 or 13 years of age) is recognised as a pivotal time in all aspects of development, including cognitive reflexivity (e.g., Piaget, 1963), self-concept formation (e.g. Harter, 1999), and interpersonal relations (e.g., Rosenberg, 1989; Selman, 1980). Despite recognition of this complex and multifaceted developmental milestone, a holistic approach to exploring the links between self and social understanding and the development of spirituality remains to be taken. Thus, research needs to explore children's and adolescents' perspectives of complex concepts such as sense of self and spirituality.

Although I have not yet assessed adolescents' perceptions of spirituality and silence directly, given that spirituality and self are inextricably intertwined, my past and ongoing research involves listening to middle school children's and adolescents' voices on aspects of the self, including their thoughts and emotions, which sometimes refer to spiritual or religious experiences. For example, some of my own research may also help to shed some light on how silences play a role in the connections between concepts of self and spirituality in adolescence. To better understand how Canadian preadolescents perceive their belief systems regarding themselves and self-knowledge, I interviewed 239 preadolescent girls and boys (127 girls, 112 boys; 9–12 years old) on various issues including their perceived sense of self-worth. Borrowing from the work of Damon and Hart (1988), I asked students during their individual interviews to explore the subjective concepts of the self, including issues of continuity, distinctiveness, and agency (Bosacki, 2003).

In particular, to assess the notion of continuity (or to determine how we remain consistent over time), students were asked the following questions: If you can change from year to year, how do you know it's still you? What stays the same? If you had a different name, would you still know it's you? How would you know you're the same person? To assess children's conceptions of self-agency (or what/who determines the formation of self, the control of one's destiny), they were asked the following questions: How did you get to be the kind of person you are? How did you get to be the way you are? Finally, to assess children's conceptions of distinctiveness (or how they are unique individuals), they were asked: What makes you different from everybody in the world? How are you different from other kids in your class? What makes you special compared to the other children in your class?

Regarding the concepts of spirituality and an awareness of the faith in oneself and beyond, the self-agency questions were found to be particularly relevant. Responses also differed according to gender. The most frequent response for girls was a referent to their parents, such as "My mom has taught me to be who I am today." In contrast, the most common responses for boys included references to oneself, such as "I was born this way." Regarding the second most-common response, the order was reversed for both genders, that is, girls mentioned self-agency as the second-most reason how they got to be the kind of person they are, whereas boys mentioned parents. Both genders mentioned peers and other references equally. Regarding the other, few responses included references to a spiritual aspect of their lives (e.g., "I'm the way that I am because God made me like this.").

To explore Shweder's (1990) notion of moral discourse, the adolescents' responses to the question of "What makes you different" was coded according to the following categories: autonomy, community, and divinity. Findings revealed that most adolescents employed the language of autonomy, particularly the boys. That is, more boys provided justifications that reflected the ethic of autonomy, particularly as compared to the ethic of divinity. In contrast to boys, a larger percentage of girls provided justifications falling within the ethic of community. Overall, few responses included references to the divine and/or spiritual. The responses that did refer to the notions of divinity included references to God, the bible, and/or aspects of organized religion.

Regarding conceptions of religion, morality, and the application of these concepts to the classroom, a recent Canadian study explored children's and adolescents' reasoning about freedom of speech and religion. Helwig (e.g., 1997) found that by six years of age, children as well as older children and adults viewed freedom of speech and religion as universal moral rights that should be upheld in all countries. Younger children (6- to 8-year-olds) linked these rights mainly to issues of personal autonomy; however, older children (8- to 11-year-olds) and adolescents recognized broader societal, cultural, and democratic aspects to these rights. Older children saw freedom of religion as serving not only individual autonomy and personal expression but also as ensuring that group and cultural traditions are preserved and respected. Regarding the application of these concepts, older children (around 11 years of age) believed that it was acceptable for parents to prohibit their young children from practicing a religion different from their own (Helwig, 1997). They considered parents' rights to socialize their children as they wish. Overall, this study illustrates how researchers can apply findings on adolescents' reasoning ability to help further our understanding of the subtle and sensitive issues of the mental adolescent world, including issues of spirituality and silence.

As mentioned earlier in Chapter 1, another area of research that has begun to investigate spiritual development and silence in youth includes the theory-of-mind research (e.g., Coles, 1990; Gardner et al., 2001; Harris, 2000; Taylor & Carlson, 2001). Following the cognitive revolution of the 1970s and early 1980s (see Bruner, 1996, for a description), a research area that investigates mental-state understanding in children and adults emerged in the mid-1980s exploring children's understandings of false belief in both self and other. That is, this research explores the question of how children and adolescents come to understand that other people have thoughts, intentions, beliefs, desires, and emotions, as well as themselves (see Astington, 1993, for a brief history). Regarding cultures of classroom silence, how does this sociocognitive ability shape adolescents' experiences of silence within the context of spirituality and religiosity?

Overall, given the roles that silence and voice play in the complex relation between spirituality/religiosity and mental health, spirituality/religiosity has an empirically demonstrable influence on mental health. According to some researchers, spirituality and religiosity are broadly compatible with mental health coping and adjustment (Argyle, 2000; Hill & Pargament, 2003), critics notwithstanding (Ellis, 1980). Regarding educational contexts in particular, school psychologists and educators agree that spirituality and religiosity may act as a developmental asset, both in the lives of the individual youth and in their communities (Lantieri, 2001; Trulear, 2000; Youniss, McClellan, & Yates, 1999). Various factors that relate to religiosity in adolescents help to serve as building blocks of healthy development that assist youth to choose healthy paths and to make wise decisions. Such factors including religious involvement; service to others; and placing high value on caring, integrity, and honesty have found to have a significant positive influence on youth's lives in that such involvement provides a support network for some adolescents who do not feel comfortable in speaking or have to work on developing their true "voice." Furthermore, such opportunities for self-expression may also lead to greater connections with self and others, which in turn may deter adolescents from engaging in self-harming and unhealthy behaviours and choices ranging from drug abuse to depression and attempted suicide (Lantieri, 2001).

Regarding religious involvement, empirical findings show that religious involvement and commitment increase the qualities in youth that society values, such as school achievement, attendance, self-esteem (Ream & Savin-Williams, 2003). Religiousness (e.g., religious service attendance, participation in religious activities, and conceiving oneself as a religious person, etc.) may help to mitigate against undesirable behaviour, such as delinquency, juvenile court referrals, substance use, teen pregnancy, and sexual permissiveness (Corwyn & Benda, 2000; Litchfield, Thomas, & Li, 1997; McCree, Wingood, DiClemente, Davies, & Harrington, 2003; Miller, Davies, & Greenwald, 2000; Thomas & Carver, 1990). Some researchers suggest that religious adolescents internalize their religions' messages about care and concern for other people; compared to nonreligious youth, they are more engaged in their communities and care more about the welfare of themselves and others (e.g., Regnerus, 2003). For example, studies have found that religiosity is also connected to a strong work ethic, which promotes positive academic achievement and positive school behaviour (Lanteri, 2001; see Jeynes, 2002, for an overview). Although studies on religiosity/spirituality and mental health do not explicitly explore the connections between silence and mental health, given that many religious and spiritual activities (such as church services, individual praying, etc.) may involve opportunities for silence and reflection, such findings suggest that silence experiences within the context of some spiritual and religious events may help to strengthen adolescents' connections with themselves, their families, peers, teachers, and the larger community.

Positive psychology movement. Given the more contemporary, broader concepts of morality and spirituality, the notion of happiness and subjective well-being may also provide researchers with some answers to the inner, spiritual world of the adolescent. Related to concepts of affect and morality, within the discipline of developmental psychology, the research area called "positive psychology" may provide some insight into silences experienced by adolescents in the classroom. The theme of this new approach to adolescent development (the movement has yet to address issues of early or middle childhood) includes positive features of human nature and our worlds. Seligman and Csikszentmihalyi (2000) describe the movement as a response to psychology's history of focusing on pathology and health problems only.

In contrast to the relatively negative focus psychology has had on development, positive psychology aims to examine the positive features of human life that make our life meaningful, including the study of such topics as future-mindedness, hope, wisdom, creativity, spirituality, responsibility, and perseverance amongst others. Given that spirituality is listed in the mandate for this new research movement in psychology, the focus on both initiative (a characteristic that is associated with individualism and autonomy) and social connectedness could help to promote further research on the role that silence plays in adolescents' spiritual development, and may extend to research on leisure, play, and flow (e.g., Csikszentmihalyi, 1990).

Positive psychology may illuminate the connection between the experiences of silence and mental health in adolescents, and includes studies on the concept of flow and positive thinking. Csikszentmihalyi's (1990) research on flow, or what the humanist psychologist Maslow (1971) referred to as peak experiences, this branch of humanistic psychology may also provide an area for collaboration regarding cognition and religious experiences. This field area of research draws on findings from neuroscientists that suggest flow may be an altered state of consciousness, and this positive emotional state may have a neurological basis. This concept of flow has been studied in adolescents; past research has shown that adolescents who report experiences of flow are more likely to experience a greater sense of psychological well-being and successful academic achievement (e.g., Csikszentmihalyi, Rathunde, & Whalen, 1993).

Based upon the broad concept of mental health, the notion of happiness and subjective well-being may also provide researchers with some answers to the inner, spiritual world of adolescents. For example, Ben-Zur (2003) investigated the internal and social influences on subjective well-being in university students and middle adolescents (15 to 17 years of age). In general, the results found that mastery, optimism, and positive adolescent-parent relationships helped to contribute to the well-being of adolescents. Thus, the field of positive psychology and studies on well-being and health is an area for future research that may help to illustrate the complex links between adolescents' experiences of silence and mental health issues (Hill & Pargament, 2003; Seligman & Csikszentmihalyi, 2000). Regarding practical implications of positive psychology, the area of positive youth development (which I explain in more detail in Chapter 4) may also provide a way in which educators can promote the development of psychological well-being in adolescents.

Hurtful Silence: Intrapersonal and Interpersonal

As Buber (1970) suggests, dialogue not only refers to speech but also to a form of relation. Given that dialogue provides a way to develop connections with others, with the self, and with the world beyond, the absence of dialogue represents isolation and disconnection from the self and others. Thus, adolescents who either feel silenced by others or the need to silence themselves may experience some difficulties and negative emotions as they develop their sense of self and their relationships with others.

Self-silencing. Based on past literature that suggests some adolescents describe their "loss of self" with the silencing of their voices in intimate relationships (e.g., Harter, 1999), the absence of dialogue or silence may lead to the adolescent feeling isolated and excluded from social opportunities that may promote her/his self-development. According to Jack (1991), this type of self-silencing is particularly damaging to the self in the sense that it may hold despair and isolation. If adolescents do not feel that they can speak their true voice, then their silence indicates an absence of relation. The silence of this type has been found to be linked to depression and lowered sense of self-esteem (Harter, 1999; Jack, 1991). This experience of adolescents "losing their voices" is further described in Chapter 3 in terms of the influence sociocultural factors may have on this experience.

Self-alienation and social withdrawal may also help to reinforce adolescents' willingness to silence themselves. As Belenky and her colleagues have noted, "The continued injunction against articulating needs, feelings and experiences must constrain the development of hearts and minds, because it is through speaking and listening that we develop our capacities to talk and to think things through" (Belenky et al., 1986, p. 167). The notion that some adolescents soften or silence their voices may reflect the negative way they judge themselves or how they react to being looked at or judged by others and the culture. Such sensitivity to judgment (by both self and other) may influence their susceptibility to social withdrawal, lowered self-esteem, and possible depression (e.g. Belenky et al., 1986; Lamb, 2001; Pipher, 1994).

Although silence may provide opportunities for further self-exploration and reflective thought, for some adolescents, silence may create opportunities for negative self-talk, including judging and criticizing their own thoughts, and silencing their voices and opinions. This self-silencing may not only prevent adolescents from sharing their real thoughts and opinions but it may also prevent them from expressing emotion, particularly negative emotions such as anger. Silence may thus represent withdrawal from social interactions and stand as a statement about the condition of their inner worlds. That is, an adolescent may be so fearful of the judgments of others that it feels safer not to share one's thoughts and feelings. This fear of judgment and annihilation threatened what feels like the genuine or true sense of self. As a means of self-preservation, adolescents may learn to conceal their feeling and needs. Some adolescents may expect reprisal, condemnation, and loss if they reveal their true voices, so they may choose to veil themselves behind the safety of silence.

In contrast to promoting opportunities for creativity, adolescents who silence their voices in relation to others may also silence their creativity, which in turn may lead to feelings of worthlessness and self-hatred. Silence may stifle the adolescent's creativity in the sense that they will not be able to engage in spontaneous imaginative freedom. As Belenky and her colleagues discuss, "To learn to speak in a unique and authentic voice, women must 'jump outside' the frames and systems authorities provide and create their own frame" (1986, p. 134). Regarding adolescents, what happens if they do not feel secure or safe enough to explore or question these frames? What happens when some adolescents, due to long-term silencing (either by self or imposed by others), become unable to differentiate between the frames of others and the culture and their own personal cognitive schemas or frames? What happens when silence represents the loss of one's identity and purpose for living? Does long-term silencing lead to decreased self-awareness? In other words, does the expression "practice makes perfect" also apply to self-expression and self-awareness in the sense that the more adolescents engage in self-expression, the more they will become self-aware? Thus, as a preventative measure to self-concept and social problems, perhaps researchers need to explore why and when adolescents feel silenced, which may serve as a step in the prevention of mental health and social difficulties (such as depression, low self-esteem, and social anxiety) experienced by adolescents.

Silence and social relations. Regarding the power of silence within social relations, developmental psychologists have documented how some adolescents choose to use silence as a psychological weapon to shun or exclude individuals to preserve the group's cohesiveness and survival. For instance, the act of ostracism is pervasive in that it transcends time and cultural differences (see Williams, 2001, for an extensive discussion). The term's definition is derived from the Greek word "ostrakismos," a practice that originated in Athens circa 488–487 BC to remove those individuals with dictatorial ambitions from the democratic state (Zippelius, 1986). In particular, citizens would cast their vote to exile the individual in question by writing their preference on shards of pottery (*ostraca*).

The ubiquity of ostracism is also reflected in the many terms used to describe it, including "avoiding," "shunning," "exile," "the silent treatment," and "silencing." Although ostracism is complex and has multiple causes and consequences, three main characteristics gleaned from the relevant literature include ignoring, excluding, and rejecting, thereby creating a workable definition (Gruter & Masters, 1986). Individuals who deviate from others' expectations are often the targets of ostracism, and existing research shows that ostracism is an aversive interpersonal behaviour to the targets. Given that silence plays a role in the ambiguous definition of ostracism, it is often considered a nonbehaviour. For example, if adolescents realize that they are being intentionally excluded from a group, they may question themselves, "Is this really happening or is it my imagination?" Given that many adolescents experience increased self-consciousness and sensitivity, targeted adolescents may wonder why they are being excluded and how could they have provoked this treatment. For example, the private script of the sensitive adolescent may include statements like, "Why am I being left out?" "What don't they like about me?" "Am I a bad person and that's why they don't want to be in my company?"

Such ambiguity surrounding ostracism may lead some adolescents to develop extreme social anxiety, self-doubt, and lowered self-esteem. Developmental psychologists have documented the use of shunning and exclusion behaviours in children, used among other techniques as a form of peer rejection (e.g., Asher & Coie, 1990). For example, Barner-Barry (1986) describes a case where a preschool class systematically ostracised a bully (i.e., ignored him, excluded him from conversations and playing) without adult prompting, which led to apparent success. Such a case suggests that the use of ostracism as a means of controlling the behaviour of other is both adaptive and innate.

Regarding adolescence, research suggests that some teenage girls in particular favour ostracism as a strategy during conflicts or as a form of social aggression, described as "the manipulation of group acceptance through alienation, ostracism, or character defamation" (Cairns, Cairns, Neckerman, Ferguson, & Gariepy, 1989, p. 323). In contrast to girls, Cairns et al. (1989) found that adolescent boys preferred to resort to physical violence as a means of resolving conflict. As outlined by Underwood (2002), ostracism may be viewed as another form of social aggression, That is, in contrast to direct aggression, to ostracise someone, individuals direct aggression towards damaging another's self-esteem, social status, or both, and may take direct forms, such as negative facial expressions, body movements, verbal rejections, and/or social rumours. Ostracism may also be considered a form of relational aggression, which includes behaviours aimed at harming others through the purposeful manipulation and damage of their peer relationships and self-worth.

Consistent with social exclusion and peer groups, related research on sociometric and social competence, including peer popularity and social acceptance, have also examined the experiences of adolescents who have been silenced by their peers (e.g., Schuster, 1996). Schuster found that rejected children (those disliked by their peers) and neglected children (those not noticed by their peers) experienced victimization, for example. In particular, rejected adolescents were more likely to experience victimization, whereas neglected children were not. Both types of adolescents claimed to have felt victimized, although in different ways; rejected adolescents experienced more direct acts of rejection and social silencing. In Chapter 3, I review some research on the bullying and victimization experiences of adolescents with exceptional needs and I also discuss the role silence plays in the causes and consequences of bullying, including social and physical aggression, and victimization (physical and relational) in further detail.

Silence, social withdrawal, and shyness. Given the link between silence and solitude, as noted previously, some adolescents may find silence and solitude as a phenomenon that brings psychological safety and peacefulness; they may view silence and solitude as an inspiration and as a psychological venue for quiet reflection. In contrast, when adolescents experience victimization either by psychological bullying or harassment, peer ostracism, or other intrinsic reasons, such as low self-esteem, feelings of worthlessness, hopelessness, and depression, some adolescents may choose to withdraw from the social group. Solitude and silence may bring out adolescent wariness in social company, fear of rejection, victimization, and loneliness. To explore the negative correlates and consequences of silence and social withdrawal, in the past 20 years, a burgeoning literature has accumulated on the topic of social withdrawal or solitude as it brings with it loneliness and suffering (Rubin, Burgess, & Coplan, 2002).

Although past researchers and clinicians have used the terms *social withdrawal, isolation, shyness,* and *inhibition* interchangeably, social withdrawal refers to the consistent display of all forms of solitary behaviour when encountering familiar and/or unfamiliar peers (Rubin et al., 2002). That is, social withdrawal occurs when adolescents decide to consistently isolate themselves from the peer group over time. For some adolescents, this social silence and withdrawal may carry social and psychological costs. Overall, early developmental theories and data suggest that peer interaction influences the development of social cognition, and ultimately the expression of competent social behaviour. Peer interaction and dialogue also enable the adolescent to develop an understanding of the self in relation to others. Thus, as Rubin et al. (2002) and other researchers have noted (Williams, 2001), adolescents who refrain, for whatever reason, from engaging in social interaction and avoid the company of their peers may suffer some developmental cognitive and social-emotional consequences.

Past research reveals that the constellation of social withdrawal, social inadequacy, and peer rejection may be associated with internalizing problems such as low self-esteem, social anxiety, depression, and loneliness (e.g., Rubin & Burgess, 2001). Investigators have found that by middle childhood and early adolescence, socially withdrawn and silent children (i.e., children who are compared to others as less vocal in social situations) have negative self-perceptions and experience feelings of anxiety, loneliness, and depressed mood (Bosacki, Pelletier, & Astington, 1997; Rubin et al., 2002). Thus, given the negative psychological state of the relatively silent and withdrawn adolescent, researchers need to explore how peer relationships and dialogue with others can either exacerbate or ameliorate negative personal and social experiences.

For example, the most popular intervention for withdrawn children is social skills training and it has had moderate effects on increasing the social interactions of mildly to moderately withdrawn adolescents (Sheridan, Kratochwill, & Elliott, 1990). However, many intervention programs are hampered by various conceptual and methodological difficulties. One problem that is specifically related to social skills training for socially withdrawn, shy, and/or silent adolescents is that cognitively, the adolescents know what they should do in social situations, but they cannot move from thought to action. The action appears to be inhibited or prevented by adolescents experiencing strong negative emotions such as anxiety, fear, embarrassment, and/or shame (Silverstein & Perlick, 1995). Overall, the social and emotional development of socially withdrawn, shy, and silent adolescents may be challenged and perhaps impeded (Rubin et al., 2002). Thus, researchers need to be more active in exploring the reasons why some adolescents choose to withdraw socially and remain silent. Such research may help to develop ameliorative, if not preventive, interventions for these adolescents. However, given the complexities of classroom silence, such research may be hampered by methodological difficulties. To discuss such difficulties, the following section outlines some methodological issues that researchers may experience when attempting to unravel some of the complexities of the causes, correlates, and consequences of classroom silences.

Methodological Issues: Cautions Regarding the Study of Classroom Silence

As discussed in Chapter 1, the concept of classroom silence is complex, ambiguous, and cuts across different academic disciplines, including psychology, education, sociology, anthropology, psycholinguistics, and others. Given this complexity, I have argued throughout this book that a psychocultural approach may provide the researcher and educator with a lens complex enough to explore adolescents' experiences of silence within the school. In line with Fiske et al. (1998), I share their contention that "a premise underlying this work is that in order to participate in any social world, people must incorporate cultural models, meanings, and practices into their basis psychological processes" (p. 915–916). Given that the premises of cultural psychology imply commitment to contextualism as a general explanatory framework (that is, human behaviour, including adolescents' social behaviour, can only be understood in the context of its own unique historical moment, as Harkness [2002] suggests), a transcultural explanatory framework may help researchers and educators to make sense of silences in their classrooms across their students' various cognitive abilities, and various socioeconomic and ethnic/racial backgrounds.

Despite the importance of personally experienced silence to both psychology and education, research on the connections between silence experiences, religious/spiritual beliefs and psychological development (especially self-development) remain sparse. To date, the majority of the studies have focused primarily on cognitive development, but research on classroom silences entails observation of culturally structured practices and social interactions as they relate to school experiences. Regarding research methodology that resembles traditional fine-grained ethnographic observation and interviewing, a major challenge has been to establish a way to cross-validate the observations and testimonials of adolescents' experiences in particular contexts. In the extreme version of this approach, this is an impossibility since the person and the cultural context are one and the same. From this perspective, perhaps the only solution is for the research community to redefine its concept of science and research (Shweder 1991).

However, many developmentalists seek further evidence than what has been inferred from methods such as in-depth interviews and naturalistic observation. This challenge remains to be met, in part because it appears that some aspects of silence in particular contexts are very personal, sensitive, and "subjective." Further, regarding research ethics, to address the truthfulness of data, the exercise of individual perceptions in a social context is often distributed among the participants in a seamless fashion, and thus difficult to separate into individual thoughts (Super & Harkness, 1997).

Regarding research ethics, both Nesbitt's (1998) and Hay and Nye's (1998) research suggest that when examining sensitive issues such as silence and spirituality, respectful research must be one of the researcher's main priorities, and young people's verbal skills need to be valued. Particularly regarding interpretivist research approaches such as ethnographic research, implications of reflexivity in interpretation are also paramount. An empathetic and sensitive rapport, one that facilitates conversation about emotional and sensitive issues, is necessary to develop a reciprocal relationship between researchers and participants. As many interpretivist researchers suggest (both with the educational and psychological context) (e.g., Lather, 1986), to explore areas of great personal relevance and sensitivity such as spiritual and religious experiences, we need to conduct respectful research in that we actively respect what we do not know or understand, regarding our own views and the views of our participants. Thus, the need for researchers to maintain integrity through conducting ethical and respectful research remains paramount (Creswell, 2002; McGinn & Bosacki, 2004).

Regarding reflexivity and the issues surrounding the insider/outsider dilemmas of the researcher, interpretivist researchers such as ethnographers are responsible for addressing their subjectivity and personal biases in their own research. Researchers must also remain cautious in the sense that they will need to "bracket their own assumptions" or, as Peshkin (1988) claims, tame their own subjectivity, if they are to provide authentic interpretations of children's and youth's spiritual narratives and self-stories. As Nesbitt (2001) warns, ethnographic sensitivity entails an attentive listening not only during interviews but also when reviewing the tape recording and transcripts. Similarly, the notion of respectful research needs to be applied to those situations in which researchers ask participants to disclose personal and private information (Tilley, 1998). Such respect is necessary for exploring adolescent perceptions and experiences of silences that may connect to emotional and private experiences.

Finally, the benefits of both longitudinal study and research that explores cultural and gender difference would help to enrich the current research landscape on spiritual experiences in children and adolescents. Studies over time and cultures would help to illustrate the possible influences age, gender, and culture may have on adolescents' perceptions and experiences of silence.

Summary

In sum, researchers have only just begun to explore how adolescents make meaning of silence experienced in the school and how this relates to their sense of self and identity. Multidisciplinary studies could permit fruitful investigation into the links between cognitive and emotional development, and how this plays a role in adolescents' developing sense of self and understanding of others. Further, systematic research is also needed to explore the role of silence in the development of adolescents' spiritual awareness, and how spiritual and moral growth connect with and are influenced by other aspects of psychological understanding (i.e., self-knowledge).

·3·

CASES OF CLASSROOM SILENCE: SOCIOCULTURAL AND EDUCATIONAL ISSUES

There are hundreds of languages in the world but a smile speaks them all.
(SOURCE UNKNOWN)

*Personally, I am always very nervous when I begin to speak. Every time
I make a speech I feel I am submitting to judgment, not only about my ability
but my character and honor.*
(CICERO, *"In Defense of Cluentius XVIII," p. 51, cited in Everitt, 2003, p. 58*)

Introduction

The previous chapter described some of the psychological and social causes, correlates, and consequences of classroom silences experienced by adolescents. This chapter outlines specific cases of classroom silences, particularly regarding sociocultural and educational issues. Consistent with my psychocultural approach to classroom silences, this chapter first argues for the need for a psychocultural approach to studying classroom silences in adolescents and why we should focus on metacognition; the remainder of the chapter describes specific cases of classroom silences. In particular, I focus on status variables including ethnicity, gender, social class, and cognitive competence in the terms of learning exceptionalities. The final section describes specific classroom examples of when adolescents either feel silenced by others or feel the need to silence themselves, and focuses on sociocultural factors and implications for the classroom.

Metacognition and Silence in the Classroom:
The Need for a Psychocultural Approach

Despite the recent efforts of cultural psychology (e.g., Bruner, 1996), social science researchers continue to renew conversations regarding how researchers and educators conceptualize and use cultural differences, including race and ethnicity, from a cultural-historical perspective (Lee, 2003). Status variables including gender, ethnicity, and social class are often overlooked in both the developmental literature and religious/spiritual studies. The vast majority of research is conducted in North America and Western Europe and, as with all social behaviours and cognitions, researchers need to examine how cultural norms play a role in development. That is, researchers need to examine the means by which such norms are socialized, and the developmental prognoses for children, who, while displaying normative behaviour in one culture, do not conform to expected behavioural norms in their own country.

Tomasello (1999) claims, as did others before him (e.g., Mead, Vygotsky), that human culture depends upon the fundamental social-cognitive skill that involves the individual human being's ability and tendency to identify with other human beings. This capacity involving reflexive thinking reflects the ability to operate with symbols or signs. As I described in Chapter 2, social-cognitive skills such as mental-state understanding (e.g., false-belief understanding) are necessary for effective play and for any complex social game. For example, regarding the adolescent within the school setting, social interactions could be viewed as a game of social chess in that mental states are products of historical and cultural developments that work with a variety of preexisting human cognitive skills to help us understand the mental reasoning that motivates the actions of others. Such knowledge of others may help adolescents to navigate around the social game board of school life and beyond.

All human beings live in a world of cultural institutions such as language, government, science, religion, and so forth, which are all composed of cultural conventions. These kinds of social institutions and conventions are created and maintained by certain ways of interacting and thinking among groups of human beings. Social interaction and dialogue provides the basis for adolescents to develop not only social cognitive skills but moral reasoning skills as well. For example, through interactions and conversations with others, adolescents can learn to empathically engage with another human being, and to imagine what another person is thinking and feeling and use this knowledge to shape their actions. Issues of power come into play regarding moral issues; for adolescents to be able to put themselves in the place of the other, they are affected by how the "other makes the person feel." Thus, language alone will not enable the adolescent to develop a moral sense if she or he already feels intimated or fears the other in social interaction.

For example, many moral developmentalists (e.g. Damon, Piaget) believed that moral reasoning could not be "transmitted" from parent to child. They claimed that although children may learn social rules from adult injunctions such as "Don't fight," the ability to imagine others as moral agents with thoughts and feelings is developed more thoroughly through social discourse with peers who, compared to their parents, may hold more status in terms of knowledge and power.

For example, Kruger's (1992) study of moral reasoning skills, 7- and 11-year-olds were asked to independently engage in narrative tasks that involved deciding the distribution of particular rewards. Kruger found that those children who engaged in discourse with their peers as opposed to their parents reflected greater moral reasoning skills. The ability to morally engage with someone involves more than the understanding of explicit directives and verbalized principles; it is the process of engaging another mind and heart that is key (Tomasello, 1999). The verbal language is only one piece of the psychocultural landscape that characterizes human interaction. As Tomasello (1999) notes, linguistic discourse provides a rich source of information about other minds and hearts and reflects a mutual understanding between at least two minds and hearts.

To add to this already complex puzzle, sociomoral and social cognition are also influenced by cultural influences in that different cultures may use mental-state terms differently. In turn, such cultural differences may then affect adolescents' social cognitive abilities. For example, in Lillard's (1997) review of cross-cultural research, she concludes that across cultures, the main universal social cognitive skills may include the ability to understand mental states in others. In contrast, the more cognitively complex abilities such as psychological explanations are more likely to be influenced by others within the particular culture. Once children develop this universal cognitive competence, as they enter adolescence, they then begin to develop more sophisticated abilities such as reflexive thought within their particular culture (Lillard, 1997). Thus, the social and cultural experiences of the child will continue to shape and help grow their psychocultural developing ability as they develop into adolescents and adult. The process of engaging another mind and heart in discourse dialogically provides the foundation for psychocultural learning. To help develop this foundation, researchers need to explore the development multileveled, dynamic interdependency among socially appropriate behavior, the self, and emotion across different countries (Markus and Kitayama, 1994).

Across all cultures, formal schooling begins between the ages of five to seven and involves the ability to internalize explicit rules in the sense that children remember particular rules without being told (self-regulation), to engage in reflective discourse, and to talk about their own mental reasoning (metacognition). For example, they begin to understand and use embedded mental-state language, such as "She thinks that I think that I am angry." As Vygotsky (1978) suggests, the child begins to internalize the dialogue that first begins with the caregiver, then is learned and becomes part of the child's private speech or self-talk, which plays an important role in self-regulatory behaviours. Although the dialogue that is internalized may be different across countries, the underlying message is the same (control yourself) and it is this meaning that is interpreted by children through the internalization of parent-child conversations or intersubjective dialogues concerning regulating behavioural conduct.

Interestingly, although research suggests that self-regulation and private speech occur universally, very little research exists to discuss the accompanying emotions that adolescents may experience as they talk to themselves and regulate their own behaviour. Consistent with Bakhtin (1981) and Wertsch (1989) who suggest that perspectives can be represented by "voices" in the mind, the internalization of parental rules and regulating behaviours may be thought of as the internalization of their parents "voices." Therefore, given that such a voice also contains emotional tone, the internalization of an instructional directive has both a conceptual and a moral contingent. As Bruner (1996) suggests, when children begin to internalize parental orders, they also need to interpret the "deontic" aspect of the message, which implies some kind of emotional or moral aspect to the message. Given this emotional dimension of moral injunctions such as "you should behave in this way," few studies explore connections between personal speech, deontic reasoning, and emotional experiences and how such experiences may shape the experiences of adolescents in the classroom.

Within the framework of metacognition, little research exists on the links between social cognition, inner speech, and self-conscious emotions. As I discussed in Chapter 2, past research on self-conscious or complex emotions or those that require self-reflection (e.g., pride, embarrassment, shame, guilt) suggest that such emotions start to develop around the one-year mark, as evidenced by children acting shy and coy in front of other persons and mirrors (Lewis, 1995; Lewis, Sullivan, Stanger, & Weiss, 1989). Such self-conscious emotions continue to develop and emerge around the same time as self-regulatory behaviours among five- to seven-year-olds (e.g., Harter, 1999; Tangney, 1991), although very little transcultural research exists on the connections between self-regulatory behaviours, inner dialogue, and self-conscious or social emotions in middle childhood and adolescents. To help researchers and educators further understand the silence experiences of adolescents across cultures, such aspects of metacognition need further exploration.

Ethnicity and Race

The art of "being silent" often varies across cultures. Although mainstream Western culture focuses on expressive verbal ability as the main representation of cognitive competence, in some cultures, silence is considered to be sacred or highly valued. For example, initial greetings for Brazilians and Peruvians are often void of conversation and include long periods of silence. Arabs stop speaking as a way of signaling that they require privacy. Apaches and North American First Nations people often value silence (e.g., Trawick-Smith, 2003), where silence is considered an act of respect for another person yet is freely chosen, not adopted in response to powerlessness. As Nancy Goldberger (1996) described in her experience of speaking with North American First Nations people on the topic of silence, all the North American First Nation participants discussed the importance of silence and how it was culturally imposed. According to Goldberger, they reported that as children, they learned that they should not waste time in foolish talk. Many learned from their grandparents that silences have the advantage of being respectful by listening to the stories of others, as opposed to confrontation and physical strength. They learned that silence often meant politeness in that it was polite to be quiet and to let people have their "psychological space" and just wait.

An important sociocultural lesson involves learning when *not* to speak—knowing when to talk and when to listen. Such lessons are also basic to the production of culturally appropriate behaviour. As Markus and Kitayama (1994) suggest, the rules of speech tend to be more tightly regulated by personal relationships and social hierarchies. Similarly, the anthropological research findings by Basso (1970) revealed that with the Western Apache, there was a fierce reluctance to talk and that silence has culturally specific meanings. Basso found that an Apache individual may "give up words" for several reasons, including 1) the need to resist the influence or power of an unfamiliar person who may want something, 2) the need to teach something, 3) the desire to wait to see how someone has changed if they have been away for some time, 4) to prevent upsetting someone else who is emotional, 5) to be courteous with people who are sad, particularly during tribal ceremonies, and 6) to prevent revealing one's incompetence in ambiguous or uncertain situations. Finally, across all of Basso's research, he found no evidence to suggest that silence was dispositional. Silence was contingent upon the context of the situation and the relevant interpersonal relations.

Similarly, Schweichart (1996) observed that silence was highly valued in her native Filipino culture. More specifically, among Filipino people, those who talk too much may be seen as overestimating the power of their voice. Further, silence may be viewed as a sign of complex, reflective thought rather than a sign of weakness, fear, incompetence, or lack of voice. According to Schweichart (1996), silence often represents cognitive activity and thoughtful silence is a highly valued form of agency. Moreover, Schweichart (1996) contends that among Filipinos, silence attends wisdom.

Racial and ethnic silences in the classroom. Played out in the classroom, children and adolescents from mixed cultural backgrounds may be less likely to speak up in class; unfortunately, adults and peers may hold negative reactions to their silence (e.g., Menyuk & Menyuk, 1988). Such negative reactions may have a detrimental effect on a child's sense of self-worth, confidence, and social competence. For example, others may sometimes interpret silence as a representation of fear, an ambiguous message, or a source of information, and the perceptions and interpretations of social ambiguity may vary across individuals and cultures. For example, some people often interpret ambiguous messages as either positive or negative (see Dodge and Frame's [1982] work on children's interpretations of socially ambiguous situations). This may occur if some people feel uncomfortable in group situations when silence becomes awkward and may also represent issues of power and control (e.g., Kumar & Mitchell, 2003; Goldberger et al., 1997).

Given that the majority of Western communities believe that verbal expression represents general cognitive competence, students are expected to articulate their comments or questions. However, this focus on verbal expression with adults varies across cultures. For example, children raised in the Uip'ik Alaskan culture are expected to learn primarily by close, quiet observation of adults and they rarely ask questions or otherwise interrupt what adults are doing. Similarly, in Mexican American and Southeast Asian communities, as well as in some African American communities in the southeastern United States, children learn to engage in conversation with adults only when their participation has been directly solicited (Delgado-Gaitan, 1994; Lomawaima, 1995).

Eye contact and personal space are other components of nonverbal communication that vary across cultures. For example, for many people looking someone in the eye and direct speech are ways of indicating that they are trying to communicate or are listening intently. But in many African American, Puerto Rican, Mexican American, and Native American cultures, children who look adults in the eyes and who speak directly and assertively to adults are considered to be a showing signs of disrespect and may be judged as being rude and even rebellious (e.g., Bosacki, 1995; Grant & Gomez, 2001; Sangster, 2002). For example, in her interviews with adult North American First Nations women, Goldberger (1996) found that all of the adult women reported on feelings of inauthenticity during their early (Western) school years, including feelings of being stereotyped and invalidated. In her conversations with Goldberger, one woman, a graduate student in anthropology, claimed that she still found the issue of speaking a sensitive one because it affected how others saw her in her university. She claimed that speech versus silence was linked to identity and racism.

Despite the fact that the meaning of silence is culturally contingent, some researchers note that within the Western educational system, silence and interpersonal passivity have been interpreted as reflections of cultural dispositions or a nonverbal, nonanalytic learning style (Grant & Gomez, 1991). As researchers who write on issues of gender, race, and culture in classrooms warn (e.g., Razack, 1998; Sangster, 2002; Tatum, 2003), education that caters to conventional characteristics that promote speech over silence can perpetuate patterns of learned dependence in the classroom and extend to the perpetuation of cultural and racial stereotypes.

Drawing on psychocultural approaches to emotion understanding (e.g., Brody, 2001; Bruner, 1996; Harre, 1986; Shields, 2002), psychocultural theory and research claim that each person is embedded within a variety of sociocultural contexts or cultures (e.g., country or region of origin, ethnicity, gender, profession, etc.). Subsequently, each of these cultural contexts makes a claim on the person and is associated with a set of ideas and practices (i.e., a cultural framework or schema) about how to be a "good" person and how to interact with others (e.g., see Bruner, 1996; Maccoby, 1998). Such an approach envisions emotions as a language or script that acts as both a product and process co-created by experience within a culture. According to Lutz and White (1986), emotional cultures (group set of beliefs, vocabulary, and regulative norms pertaining to emotions) provide the adolescent with a source of reference that mediates social experience and organizes behaviour towards others (Saarni, 1999). Thus, the promotion of the belief that a transactional relation exists between the emotional culture and the adolescent's emotional competence or understanding may help educators to understand why some adolescents remain silent, particularly in multicultural classrooms (Saarni, 1999).

Regarding the expression and use of emotion language across different cultures, anthropologist Jean Briggs participated in field research among Inuit groups in the Canadian Northwest Territories. Her classic ethnography, *Never in Anger* (1970), described her observations among the Utku, where Utku adults did not express anger interpersonally or use anger or threats in child rearing. In contrast, it was clear that the Utku were troubled by Briggs' propensity to irritation and anger as she coped with the many frustrations of living as a stranger in a harsh climate. Her ethnography of the Utku focused on the apparent indifference of the Utku to anger because anger was not explicitly labeled in their conversation.

More recently, Briggs (1995) realized that her original assessment of anger as not a part of Utku life was an oversimplification. That is, anger does play a role in the emotional vocabulary in Utku life. She remarks that as she began a systematic study of Utku emotion concepts, discovering that "when I wrote *Never in Anger*, I had the emotional vocabulary of a four-year old; [and] that the Utkuhikhalingmiut had many emotional concepts; and that they talked about emotions all the time (Briggs, 1995, p. 204). Briggs' (1995) research has many implications for the multicultural mosaic classrooms of North America today. For example, given the culturally contingent definitions of emotions, what kinds of emotion words and labels should be taught in a classroom containing students from diverse countries and cultural backgrounds? Who decides what the standard "emotion vocabulary" will be for adolescents? Put differently, what will this emotional curriculum look like, and how will it be taught, and by whom? Who will ensure that the emotional curriculum will be sensitive to, and respectful of, the values and beliefs of students from diverse cultures?

Given that North American and most Western industrialized societies value the development of a unitary, coherent sense of identity and place much value on concepts of autonomy, individuality, and personal freedom, adolescents are often socialized to become independent and to know and use their voices. However, as researchers have shown, the connections among voice, silence, and power are culturally determined. As discussed earlier, in some cultures, silence does not indicate a lack of power, and can be viewed as a sign of complex thought.

To date, our understanding of the interface of culture and adolescent autonomy and experiences of silence have been limited to the documentation of and explanation of differences between cultures. Fuligni (1998) compared Mexican, Chinese, Filipino, and European adolescents living in the United States with respect to acceptability of disagreements with mothers and fathers, conflict, and cohesion. In contrast to the European adolescents, American adolescents of Mexican and Filipino heritage expressed more respect for parental authority, and Chinese-American adolescents expected to be granted behavioral autonomy later in life.

Besides the ability to express one's voice with parents, cultural variations also have been found in values and conceptions of the self, particularly regarding notions of independence and autonomy. In these studies, self-concept was often differentiated as autonomous, independent, and individualistic, or agentic versus relational or collectivist (e.g., Markus & Kitayama, 1994). In a recent study by Kashima et al. (1995), adults' conceptions of the self were placed on three dimensions: independent (agentic and assertive), relational (self as a relational being), and collectivist (self as a member of a group with group needs taking priority over individual needs). Findings showed that adults in Japan, Australia, the United States, Korea, and Hawaii differed on independent and collectivist self-conceptions, but differed most markedly in independence. That is, adults in Korea, Japan, and Hawaii reported being less agentic and assertive than individuals in the United States and Australia.

Given that the study of autonomy, silence, and self-concept as manifested in diverse cultures is in its infancy, many questions remain, including those regarding the antecedents and consequences of silencing among adolescents across cultures. For instance, the studies mentioned above have interesting implications for the development of silence and identity among youth across cultures. Based on Fuligni's (1998) findings, how did American adolescents of Mexican and Filipino heritage learn to express greater respect for their parents than the Chinese-American adolescents, and how does this parental respect influence the adolescents' experiences of silence and need for self-expression? How did the Chinese-American adolescents learn to expect behavioral autonomy later on in life compared to the American adolescents and how does this delayed timetable affect their experiences of silence (both public and private?) How do varied levels of autonomy and self-identity affect notions of voice and silence? In other words, how do adolescents learn to keep their true thoughts and feelings to themselves, or to share them with others? To what extent do adolescents incorporate oppressive social or cultural images into their voices and sense of self? How do some adolescents learn (or do they learn?) to question rather than adapt societal expectations to fit their personal voice? To what extent does the cultural voice or story become the personal voice or self-story of the adolescent?

Within Kashima et al.'s (1995) study, how did the adolescents with Australian and American parents learn that they needed to speak up for themselves because they learned that their society values agency and assertion? Overall, the metatheme gleaned from cross-cultural studies suggest that our identities and voices are constantly in process and may adapt to the particular context we live in. That is, adolescents may constantly create and recreate themselves through voice and the voicing of self may develop as adolescents become responsive to change and to creating new means of self-expression. Viewing identities and voices as continual works in process offers important opportunities for educators to challenge and perhaps change their assumptions about, and labels for, who we are and how we can express ourselves.

Regarding the use of silence as a means of power and self-expression during adolescence, silence can be used as a coping strategy in large-group situations such as schools. As vocalization is often connected to issues of power within the classroom, some students may feel more powerful than others and thus, more likely to use silence as a tool to convey this power. To examine silences and hidden literacies within adolescents, Margaret Finders (1997) conducted a yearlong, ethnographic study of adolescents' secretive literate practices in an American junior high. In her examination of the "literate underlife" of five 12- and 13-year-old middle- and working-class girls, Finders supported Baker and Luke's (1991) contention that literacy is a critical form of cultural capital that constructs and regulates identity and power. Thus, Finders' research is a rich illustration of how literary competence goes beyond reading and writing. Her research suggests that literacy is a social and cultural event that helps to construct social identities, positions adolescents amongst their peer groups, and demarcates social boundaries between adults and adolescents.

Finders's (1997) research demonstrated that the students were aware of the power of peer dynamics within the classroom as well as the social consequences of their classroom actions. Students were very aware of whom to include and whom to marginalize within the peer group; to raise one's status within the social hierarchy of the classroom, some students may choose to use silence as opposed to articulation. As one adolescent participant in Finders's study claimed, she did not feel comfortable in her classroom to use her voice and chose to remain silent. As Finders (1997) and other researchers have found (e.g., Brody, 2001), despite the attempts of their peers and educators to create a psychologically safe atmosphere, some individuals avoid self-disclosure as a means of self-protection. In Finders's study, those children who held the greatest social power (i.e., popularity) appeared to be the most comfortable and vocal in the classroom.

As many researchers have noted, in contrast to compliance or inequality, silence can also represent an act of resistance (e.g., Brody, 2001; Finders, 1997; Sangster, 2002). Both genders learn how silence can be used as a powerful social tool within interpersonal relationships (Jack, 1999). Drawing from her work involving 60 in-depth interviews with women of various cultural and financial backgrounds, Jack explored the definitions of aggression among women and found that most women were aware of the power of silence as a means to mask control, anger, and at times, the intent to hurt others. Drawing from her interviews, Jack created different types of silences as the voices of women helped her to unpack the complexities of the role of silence within relationships, including hostile, controlling, political silence, and safe silences. What follows is a brief description of each type as it relates to adolescents.

Hostile silence, according to Jack (1999) maintains a façade of nonaggression, although it can play a central role in a relationship in that silence can carry powerful emotional threats. This confusing, controlling aspect of hostile silence provides nothing specific to engage with. As a tactic of control, it refuses a dialogue that could resolve disputes. In children and adolescents, it creates anxiety about the security of attachment, because the silence may represent someone who is physically present, but mentally and emotionally absent. This type of silence fosters disconnection, not resolution and reconnection. In partnered relationships, women's angry silence is sometimes associated with their depression (e.g., Jack, 1991, 1999). Hostile silence many lead to less guilt and self-blame than ineffective explosions, but it rarely leads to dialogue and resolution. However, as many adolescent girls have claimed, silence may sometimes appear "safer" than "speaking out" because it stays within the stereotypic expectation of good femininity. That is, girls are often not encouraged to be verbally or physically aggressive.

Regarding adolescents, as Fordham (1996) suggests, the silent girl may protect herself from others' reactions and judgments, and thus preserves her secret sense of self. Based on her research, Fordham (1996) found that African-American girls described a good girl in terms of voice: good girls are not loud. Based on Fordham's participants' perceptions of middle-class, mixed-race neighbourhood, many adolescents claimed that the idea of a good girl is someone who doesn't talk back to adults, teachers, parents, or similar figure of authority. Although the idea of verbal loudness is sometimes associated with nonconformity and "badness," for African-American girls, verbal loudness may means presence. For some adolescents of particular ethnic and gender identities, however, the paradox may be that the louder they are, the more visible they are—and yet the more they are open to the judgment of others, the more they may be viewed as morally inferior or unacceptable.

Silence can also serve as an unhostile means of controlling others and expressing one's desires. Controlling silence is self-protective and regulates emotion in relationships without direct engagement. Silence can also be a form of positive resistance. It can be used to pry open a small space between compliance and rebellion, or to create a neutral ground within a relationships that is filled with smoldering hostility. For women raised in cultural and familial contexts that prohibit their verbal or physical aggression, resisting silence becomes a strategy to preserve their agency and sense of self.

Given the multicultural and multilinguistic contexts of North American adolescents' worlds today, many adolescents experience what Jack (1991) refers to as political silence within the classroom and beyond. Such silence may occur beyond intimate relationships and extend to political silence where adolescents of colour or ethnic minorities may strategically suspend their voices in white communities. Regarding gender-role orientations, some transgendered or lesbian adolescents may use silence as political tool to express their message within a community where the majority of the population is heterosexual.

When utilizing this political silence, the adolescents may return to their own safe communities to share what they have learned and to confirm the accuracy of their observations. Ultimately, the knowledge obtained by remaining silent is similar to a reconnaissance flight into enemy territory that allows for individual and group survival. Hurtado (1996) describes this tactical use of silence as "akin to camouflaging oneself when at war in an open field, playing possum at strategic times causes the power of the silent one to be underestimated" (p. 382). This political silence is different from the type of self-silencing that may lead to depression (Jack, 1999). Those who employ silence as an interpersonal strategy to keep a relationship or who use political silence without a community within which to share knowledge and political purpose more often end up depressed and self-alienated.

Finally, silence can be used for self-protection or preservation in situations in which adolescents may feel unsafe and fearful. Interestingly, quite often a happy, courageous, or blank expression—which suggests that on the surface the adolescent may appear compliant and pleasant—masks conflicting emotions and inner turmoil. As Sangster (2002) describes the experiences of adolescent Native American girls labeled as juvenile delinquents in Canadian training schools, for many of these girls, the ability to hide their emotions behind a façade of either silence or bravado acted as "safety valve" (p. 160) in that it helped the girls to cope with a hostile environment and as well as with traumatic memories. Thus, for some adolescents, this safe silence conceals as it communicates, hiding an adolescent's anger and/or fear behind a mask whose meaning she or he can quickly change if necessary.

Silence, then, often sends mixed or ambiguous messages to others. When controlled, silence can be wielded to protect the self or to create a space within relationships in which to formulate new directions and offer possibilities for movement and change. Thus, hostile silence, controlling silence, resisting silence, political silence, and safe silence can enhance possibilities for creating change in the self and in relational patterns.

However, silence may also send messages of alienation, despair, and hopelessness. By keeping confrontation and anger out of relationships, or leaking it into a relationship through belligerent, aggressive silence, such silence brings no change in the conditions that arouse it. Silence builds no bridges to others that could lead to dialogue, reconciliation, or new relational patterns. The hostility vented through silence affects others negatively. Given that silence may send mixed messages to others, it may communicate anger but contradicts the anger's call for a response. As Jack (1991) notes, such silence may represent an angry reproachfulness towards the other, who does not know what the anger is about, and it also suggests an unforgiving and critical harshness towards the self. Such silence is sometimes associated with chronic and sometimes major depression.

School experiences of racial and ethnic discrimination. In contrast to silence, loudness may also be viewed as a means of resistance. Lamb (2001) interviewed 120 girls and women between the ages of 6 and 70 from over 25 different American states, reflecting a variety of ethnic and financial backgrounds, regarding their secret lives involving relationships, sexuality, play, and so forth. Based on her interviews, Lamb found that many adolescents believed that speaking up for oneself was a way of taking up space and garnering attention. Although this may vary across cultures, in the majority of Western, industrialized countries, those individuals who are viewed as loud and take up a great deal of space are considered to be relatively masculine and may be viewed as pushy and unfair. For example, within our North American society, speaking up for oneself can be a form of self-protection and represents speaking one's mind and standing one's ground.

However, as Lamb (2001) notes, although speaking up may serve as a type of social glue to connect relationships, vocalization may also be viewed as individualistic strategy of fighting male and Western-European dominated institutions, which may prevent joining together with other like-minded persons to change the system. Furthermore, loudness may also be a strategy that supports a disconnection between other peers or their teachers. For example, as the majority of middle-class girls search for power in the school through the identification with teachers, loud girls look for a personal power that can never quite reach the level of power to change the environment that they deserve to have and deserve to change. Thus, Latina and African-American girls who were depressed had the best understanding of racism, sexism, and classism.

Researchers interested in the relatively poor academic performance of adolescents from some ethnic/racial groups have suggested that some classroom-based experiences regarding discrimination may play a critical role in adolescent development (Lee, 2003), particularly experiences of being silenced or marginalized in the classroom based on issues of race and ethnicity. Although this research is in its infancy, two types of discrimination have been discussed. One deals with the anticipation of future discrimination in the labor market, which could be viewed as undermining the long-term benefits of education. The second area deals with the impact of daily experiences of discrimination on one's mental health and academic motivation. Both types of discrimination are likely to influence adolescent development, and some researchers have found that anticipated future discrimination leads to increases in African-American youth's motivation to do well in school, which in turn leads to increases in academic performance.

In particular, some studies have found that anticipated future discrimination appeared to motivate the youth to do their very best so they would be maximally equipped to deal with future discrimination. With regard to experiences of silence, perhaps some of these students were preparing themselves for the potential to be silenced. In contrast, daily experiences of racial discrimination from their peers and teachers led to declines in school engagement and in confidence in one's academic competence and grades, along with increases in depression and anger (Eccles and Roeser, 2003).

Transcultural religious faiths and spirituality: Empirical evidence. Traditionally in Western European and North American culture, spirituality has almost always had a strong association with Christianity. However, Nye and Hay (1996) suggest that this spiritual awareness is found across various cultures, genders, and ages, and may influence perceptions and experiences of silence. Consistent with Levine (1999) and others, the cognitive underpinnings of spirituality need to incorporate various religious denominations as cultural contextualizations of that which we seek in the spiritual. One common thread underlying spiritual experience within Judaism, Christianity, and Buddhism is a form of prayer referred to as "contemplation." During these experiences, discursive cognition (which according to Piaget did not develop until formal operational stage, around the age of 11 years) is suspended so that the human knows by presence a union with the sacred. Within each of these religions, the spiritual experience of "presence" is focal, in which silence plays a key role.

Similarly, Hay (2001) found that relational consciousness expressed in the language, symbols, and stories of the children and adolescents interviewed was similar to the vocabulary used by adult theologians and mystics from various world faiths. Underlying themes across all cultural faiths focused on issues of individuality and relationality or connections with others, self, and beyond. Given space limitations, this chapter cannot outline all cultural traditions, although I describe briefly a few within the context of silence experiences within the classroom (see Loewenthal, 2000, for a summary of various faiths and the links to psychology).

In the Islamic tradition, the Sufi Ibn Arabil refers to a similar language of humankind's spiritual journey and involves balancing the duality of God's distance (*tanzih*) and nearness (*tashbih*) from the world, whilst living in the knowledge that in the ultimate relationship, God and humankind are in union (*tawhid*). In the Christian tradition, St. Teresa of Avila claims that the spiritual experience is ultimately a movement towards the intimate relation of union, the perception that "all things are seen and contained in God." Martin Buber of the Jewish tradition understood the religious life in terms of the "I-Thou relationship," a relationship between humanity and God that acknowledges the tension of separation but leads people to strive to relate more (Buber, 1970). Ramanjuja's Hindu theology proclaims that a dialectical relationship between humankind and the Godhead Brahman ends in the bliss of intimate relation. For the Mahayana Buddhist, realization of *anatman* (no-self) ends the differential that is *Samsara* and reveals that all human beings are related in sharing the Buddha nature (Harvey, 1996). Thus, the common ground across all religions and faiths is that a process of connections or relations characterizes spiritually meaningful experiences. However, given that silence and prayer play different roles in different religions and faiths, researchers need to explore the extent to which religious backgrounds of adolescents affect their experiences of silence within the classroom.

D'Andrade (1984) argues that beliefs are most likely to be distributed differentially in a cultural group, with some informants exhibiting more coherent or systematic beliefs than others. Interestingly, there was a relation between parents' beliefs and children's school attendance, but no relation between parents' beliefs and children's general interests in sports, reading, and collecting dolls or race cars. Parents who were more consistently creationists tended to have children who were more likely to attend a fundamentalist school, whereas children of non-fundamentalist parents were more likely to attend non-fundamentalist schools. As Evans (2000) asks, when a child or adolescent espouses religious and spiritual beliefs, is it because she or he has acquired them through communication, or have the beliefs been validated by some authority, such as a teacher, religious leader, or parent? Or is it because he or she acquired them through inferential processes similar to those that led to the original development of the belief? Both processes may operate in the emergence and transmission of origins of beliefs and may have an influence on how children and adolescents behave in the classroom.

Investigations regarding middle school-aged children and adolescents include studies by Hay & Nye (1996) and Nesbitt (1998, 2001). In particular, Nesbitt's ethnographic research on 8- to 14-year-olds from various religious denominations (Christians, Hindus, Jews, Muslims, and Sikhs) focused on exploring the children's experience of *bhakti* (religious development, the soul's yearning for God), to be integral to the spiritual development of young people. A study of 22 young Hindus aged 16 to 23 provided a follow-up. Consistent with past research (e.g., Hay, 1990), Nesbitt's research employed the term *bhakti*, which refers to a dreams, visions, or conversion experience and to the memorable sensations understood by the individual as encounters with the divine or with angels. As Nesbitt claimed, this religious experience is sometimes subsumed in spirituality.

In general, Nesbitt's (1998, 2001) research showed different aspects of religious experiences reflected cultural particularity: Christians reported a greater connection to their denominational conditioning, whereas no Protestant Pentecostals were healed by saints. In contrast, some experiences were less denominationally specific: reports of conversations with God and dreams involving heaven were reported across all denominations. In sum, discussion of the relevance of religious nurture to spiritual development more widely needs to engage transculturally with different paradigms of spirituality. As Nesbitt and others claim, future research needs to explore adolescents' spiritual experiences from diverse religiocultural backgrounds, and how such experiences shape their perceptions and behaviours around silence in the classroom.

In addition to studying the process and development of religious and spiritual concepts in children, researchers have recently begun to study the influence of parental religious beliefs on children's pretend play and fantasy life (Paley, 1999). More specifically, Taylor and Carlson's (2001) ethnographic research with young children, parents, and teachers from three religious traditions—Hindu, fundamentalist Christian, and Mennonite—showed religion-based attitudes about children's imaginary companions. Based on cross-cultural ethnographic evidence, Taylor and Carlson found that religious ideology contributes to substantial variation in adult reaction to and interpretation of childhood fantasy activities. In general, Taylor and Carlson found that there was a tendency to emphasize negative interpretations of fantasy behaviour based on religious beliefs. Such findings suggest that further systematic investigation is needed to explore how parents' religious beliefs may influence their adolescents' sociomoral and affective development, particularly within the context of the classroom regarding activities that include imagination, reflection, and creative/divergent thinking.

In sum, the cultural tales about the meaning of silence discussed in this section demonstrate the importance of understanding both the immediate (familial, peers, community) and the distant (cultural, political) contexts for silence and speech. Verbal communication is essentially the outcome of a higher-order cognitive process, the ability to make decisions. In unfamiliar societies and situations, the visitor or outsider must learn the social rules of speech particular to that culture or community. That is, the visitor needs to learn what kinds of speech are used in what kinds of situations. Adolescents learn about the meaning of silence in their community, school, and home, and the social repercussions of a dyad or group when someone remains or becomes silent. Even living within strict cultural rules, most adolescents claim a choice about when and where they speak what they know.

In any case, cultures across the globe emit particular messages or "cultural scripts" concerning how to behave, think, feel, and "be." Given such powerful messages, researchers need to continue to explore how adolescents learn these messages or scripts involving voice, silence, and power. How do adolescents apply these "cultural scripts" and how do such scripts or ways of knowing affect their emotions, thoughts, and actions regarding silence in the classroom? Given that gender may also help shape adolescents' experience of silence, the next section discusses gender-related experiences of silence among adolescents.

Gender, Silence, and Social Cognition

Gender is considered an integral factor in all aspects of human development, affecting both our mind and body. As Shields (2002) notes, new models of gender question the notion that gender is attained as a secure status throughout life, and agrees with Maccoby (1998) in that gender is considered more of a "culture" than a fixed trait. That is, gender is now viewed by some theorists as a fluid construct, one that must be negotiated in social relationships and challenged by changing social, cultural, and historical contexts (Shields, 2002).

As noted by Halpern (1992) and Miller and Scholnick (2000), most studies on social cognition and language tend to gloss over gender issues, or at least have not specifically aimed to investigate gender-related differences and/or patterns. As I discussed in Chapter 2, a psychocultural or "ethnopsychological" approach to ToM (Astington, 1996; Astington & Olson, 1995; Lillard, 1997; Yuill, 1993) provides a valuable form of inquiry to investigate the effects of gender on social-cognitive development. This approach to ToM asserts the notion that an individual's ability to understand mental states in others is largely relativistic and socially constructed. In support of this view, cross-cultural research has shown that the development of social-cognitive abilities, including ToM, may be dependent upon one's culture or social experience (McCormick, 1994).

A psychocultural approach to development suggests that individual differences in the ability to understand mental states in others may indicate that this ability is acquired in different ways for women and men. The process of learning to understand self and other within a social context may be contingent not on whether a child is female or male but on the way in which a child's gender interacts with her or his environment. Thus, if an adolescent is viewed as a "cultural invention" (Kessen, cited in Cahan, 1997, p. 205), gender helps to create a separate culture for that particular adolescent. This conception of gender as a social category or particular culture suggests that acknowledging the contribution of cultural milieu to a ToM may prove to be a fruitful avenue for future research on development of gender-role conception and behaviour (Maccoby, 1998; Nelson, Henseler, & Plesa, 2000).

A social-constructivist inquiry into the workings of the adolescent mind and its implications for social interactions would enable researchers to view gender in context (e.g., Shields, 2002), as it operates within a social milieu such as the classroom. In opposition to the more traditional sex-differences model (i.e., gender differences not mentioned a priori, only post-hoc statistical tests to indicate differences), such a gendered approach to research is in line with Hill and Lynch's (1983) gender intensification hypothesis. This hypothesis claims that during preadolescence, gender differences increase among girls and boys due to the increased pressure to conform to traditional gender-role stereotypes. For example, research has shown that during preadolescence, traditional gender-role behaviour and ascription (i.e., femininity = sociality, submissiveness; masculinity = autonomy, aggression) become intensified (Hill & Lynch, 1983; Tavris, 1992). In accordance with research that shows a link between traditional female stereotypic behaviour and depression among women (McGrath, Keita, Strickland, & Russo, 1990), intensification of gender identity among preadolescent girls may strengthen behavioural tendencies hypothesized to hold special relevance for vulnerability to depression, such as interpersonal sensitivity, an eagerness to please, and an increased concern for others (e.g., Zahn-Waxler et al., 1991). Thus, preadolescent girls who appear to be relatively competent in the ability to understand and be sensitive to the needs of others may be at risk for developing future self-concept disorders such as depression (Silverstein & Perlick, 1995).

In support of the gender-intensification hypothesis, many gender-related differences gleaned from research on social behaviour and social cognition in adolescence are usually consistent with traditional gender-role stereotypes. Concerning social behaviour, the majority of research findings show that girls are rated as more socially competent and popular by both their peers and teachers than are boys (e.g., see Maccoby, 1998). Similarly, research on teacher perceptions shows that girls are perceived by their teachers to be more compliant and prosocial than boys (e.g., Harter, 1996). Furthermore, studies on rejected and clinically depressed children have shown that, compared to boys, girls tend to display more internalizing behaviours such as unhappy, withdrawn behavioural patterns. In contrast, boys have been found to display more externalizing behaviours such as aggressive, antisocial behaviours (Underwood, 2002).

According to teacher expectancy research (e.g., Jones & Gerig, 1994), perceptions and labels of teachers may play a role in how adolescents experience silence and interact within the classroom, particularly if an adolescent is labeled as "quiet, shy," or "delinquent, troubled." Reflecting a self-fulfilling prophesy, this label may become integrated into the adolescent's identity. That is, once a teacher labels a student as quiet and shy, that adolescent may become to believe that she or he is quiet and shy, which in turn may cause the adolescent to exhibit quiet and shy behaviours. To validate the teacher's label, the adolescent may choose to speak less or to avoid and withdraw from conversation (either intentionally or unintentionally). Such behaviours may thus perpetuate the teacher's original label of quiet and shy.

Furthermore, the majority studies on teacher expectancies have shown that teachers' expectations of their students and subsequent student-teacher inter-actions have an effect on student behaviour and self-concept (e.g., Jones & Gerig, 1994). Given the crucial role teachers and peers play in both the gender-role socialization and co-construction of sociocognitive and linguistic abilities of adolescents (Denham, 1998), it is surprising that few researchers have studied how the links between teachers' and peers' perceptions of other students' social and academic behaviour, and the students' self-perceptions may shape silence experiences in the classroom.

Regarding social-cognitive abilities, research shows that boys score higher than girls on nonsocial spatial perspective-taking tasks (Coie & Dorval, 1973), whereas girls score higher than boys on social perspective-taking and empathy tasks (Jahnke & Blanchard-Fields, 1993; King, Akiyama, & Elling, 1996; Zahn-Waxler & Robinson,1995). Likewise, Offer, Ostrov, Howard, and At-kinson (1988) reported that across 10 countries, girls were more likely than boys to express a desire to help a friend when possible and thus gave evidence of a "more sociable and empathic stance" than did boys (p. 70). Gender-related differences have also been found in the social-cognitive area of person perception. In general, girls have been shown to emphasize such categories as interpersonal skills, psychological traits, and social relationships (e.g., Honess, 1981). In contrast, boys have been found to emphasize such categories as physical aggression, interests, and academic ability (Peevers & Secord, 1973).

Surprisingly, although researchers investigate social-cognitive abilities like the ones mentioned above, the exploration of gender-related differences among ToM abilities has just begun. Of the few ToM studies that actually do test for gender effects, most report nonsignificant results (e.g., Jenkins & Ast-ington, 1996). In contrast, some recent ToM studies have found evidence to support gender-related findings gleaned from the more general social-cognitive research area. More specifically, results obtained on young children show that girls score significantly higher on ToM types of tasks as compared to boys. For example, regarding preschool children, Cutting and Dunn (1999) investigated theory of mind and emotion understanding in preschoolers. Cutting and Dunn found that compared to boys, girls referred to mental-state verbs more frequently and their choice of emotion words was more sophisti-cated or developmentally advanced.

Although the research base in this area is thin, there is some correlational evidence that shows gender differences in the development of psychological understanding of self and others during adolescence. In particular, Hatcher et al. (1990) found that among 13-year-old girls, abstract reasoning was related to the understanding of others but not oneself, whereas the reverse was found for boys, abstract reasoning was positively related to self-understanding but not to the understanding of others. The authors claim that this finding suggests that girls are more likely to understand others than to understand themselves based on the tendency of modern Western culture to label interpersonal understanding and empathetic sensitivity as "natural" personality traits for females. The implications of these findings for experiences of silence are interesting, given that silence could provide some time for reflection and deepening one's self-awareness.

Given Hatcher et al.'s (1990) findings, perhaps for adolescent girls, increased amounts of silence may promote the understanding of other's inner lives as compared to furthering one's private world. In contrast, perhaps for boys, experiences of silence may promote the development of self-awareness and self-knowledge. Given the recent "boy turn" in research on gender and education (Weaver-Hightower, 2003), researchers will need to explore the gendered implications silence has for adolescents' self- and other-understanding.

Likewise, implicitly supportive evidence derived from investigations that suggest that a heightened awareness and understanding of the mental states and feelings of others may have negative consequences for girls' later psychoemotional functioning. For example, longitudinal studies investigating gender differences in developmental models of depression have found that as young girls, depressed adolescent females were more concerned with maintaining interpersonal relationships, more able to recognize the feelings of others, and more likely to include moral issues in their play patterns than boys (Block, Gjerde, & Block, 1991; Gjerde & Block, 1991). Further supportive evidence derives from the literature on the socialization of empathy and guilt, which suggests that high levels of empathy and guilt may serve as precursors for later depression in women (Bybee, 1998; Zahn-Waxler et al., 1991; Zahn-Waxler & Robinson, 1995). Similarly, in a study of 115 preadolescent girls and boys (8- to 12-years-old), Fraser and Strayer (1997) found that the most robust correlation between sensitivity and shame existed among the older girls (11- to 12-year-olds). Hence, such studies support the view that interpersonally sensitive individuals may be preoccupied with the psychological needs of others to the detriment to their own, which may eventually lead to a lack of self-definition (Park & Park, 1997; Silverstein & Perlick, 1995).

In sum, what do the past gendered findings on social cognition among adolescents tell us about their experiences of silences in the classroom? Based on the findings described above, compared to boys, adolescent females may be more likely to engage in solitary, social-relational activities that may affect their silence experiences. Compared to adolescent males, adolescent females may also be more likely to engage in thinking about the inner worlds of others rather than their own (Hatcher et al., 1990). Thus, researchers need to explore the implications of gendered social cognition for classroom silences among adolescents as the mental health of the adolescent is developing during this sensitive age.

Accordingly, connections between works on feminist epistemologies and psychoeducational research provides a valuable starting point for investigating the roles in which silence may play in the processes of understanding self and other in adolescents, and how this may influence their classroom behaviour (e.g., Belenky et al., 1986; Brown & Gilligan, 1992; Debold, Tolman, & Brown, 1996). Definitions and assessments of the processes that enable adolescents to understand social situations may offer some insight on gender-related research findings. Such a research agenda may help to shed some light on the wealth of findings from social-emotional studies that show around the age of 11, some girls (in contrast to boys) experience a significant decrease in positive feelings and thoughts of self-worth (e.g., Harter, 1999), an increase in self-consciousness (e.g., Simmons, Rosenberg, & Rosenberg, 1973), and an increasingly negative sense of self-worth despite high academic achievement, particularly among "gifted girls" (e.g., Silverstein & Perlick, 1995; Winner, 2000). Research on the ability to understand mental states in others and its links to self-concept and social relations may help to further examine the related phenomenon of why girls may be more at risk than boys to lose their sense of self or "inner voice" during early adolescence (Brown & Gilligan, 1992; Harter, 1999). Finally, as Weaver-Hightower (2003) suggests, if we as educators aim to understand gendered silences within the classroom, we need the curriculum, pedagogy, and research programs that explore gender in complex and interrelated ways, by looking beyond issues of gender inequity to examining problematic definitions of femininity and masculinity.

Gendered emotions. The mastery meta-language of the cognitive developmental view runs throughout the literature on children's and adolescent's play and recreation. This cognitive-developmental framework conceptualizes the youth's developing relation to her or his own emotional understanding and experience in terms of the goal of emotional self-regulation. That is, the endpoint of development is identified with the capacity for successful control or containment of emotion through self-understanding and the capacity for behavioral self-restraint. Hall (1986) stresses the significant role language plays in the child's successful development of self-control. Advocating that the child be encouraged to use words to "master strong emotions," Hall infers a progression from directly acting on the impulses generated by strong feelings of self-control through clarifying, tolerating, and containing feelings through language. Although Hall based his writing on his work with preschoolers, the underlying concepts of his theory can be applied to all ages, and may be especially relevant to adolescence, given that adolescence is a sensitive time for identity development. Of particular relevance to adolescence may be the strong sociocultural gender-typed messages received by our youth regarding what emotions to display and/or experience based on gender. Girls are still expected to comply, smile, and not show anger, whereas boys are expected to not be caring, and to be free to express anger and pride. Overall, these societal messages remain the same, and are being created and perpetuated by modern society.

Hall's perspective contrasts with Saarni's (1999) emphasis on emotional competence, which identifies emotional self-regulation as just one of several skills foundational to the achievement of emotional competence. There is a striking difference between treating emotional development as ever more sophisticated ability to contain or express emotion and one that incorporates emotion into the larger theme of social understanding and social cognition.

Doing emotion the "right" way, which is often a gendered way, serves as verification of the authenticity of the self. Not "I feel, therefore I am," but "I feel as I believe I ought to, therefore I am the person I believe I am." Gender may be marked by any of the other major categories of social identity such as age, class, or racial ethnicity, as well as other distinctive features such as attractiveness, status, disability, and so forth. Overall, the combination of gender and emotion is a potent identifier, and when we talk about the multiple components of an individual's identity, gender is always implicated.

Despite recent investigations of gender differences in sociocognition (Hughes & Dunn, 1998; Maccoby, 1998), results from such studies remain contradictory and inconclusive. Regarding mental-state understanding, as outlined earlier in this chapter, some studies have shown girls to possess higher levels of ToM and emotion understanding (e.g., Bosacki, 2003; Bosacki & Astington, 1999; Cutting & Dunn, 1999). In contrast, other studies have found either that boys possess higher levels of emotion understanding than girls (Laible & Thompson, 1998) or no gender differences (Astington & Jenkins, 1995). Unlike the research on psychological understanding, the self-concept literature has shown that in general, girls report lower levels of self-worth than boys (see Harter, 1999). Given the link between gender, understanding others, and self-worth (Finders, 1997; Hatcher et al., 1990; Veith, 1980), surprisingly little is known about these connections during middle childhood and early adolescence. Relatedly, some researchers suggest that gender differences need to be investigated in terms of interaction effects between biological sex and gender role (Geary, 1998). To support this view, results from my postdoctoral work with preschoolers showed parents' gender-role perceptions of stereotypic feminine behaviour were related to high levels of emotion understanding in both girls and boys (Bosacki & Moore, 2004).

Furthermore, a strong positive association was found between receptive language ability and emotional understanding for boys only.

Such links remain to be examined in middle school-aged children and adolescents in relation to psychological understanding, silence and language. For example, regarding adolescents, why do girls talk more about emotions than boys and how does this preference relate to the preschool findings? Is there a reason why boys are more "silent" about emotions in their conversations? Does a reliance on language competence influence the ability to develop and express emotion language? Or do adolescents feel silenced by their peers, teachers, and parents? In any case, although developmental and educational research on boys has increased during the past decade (Weaver-Hightower, 2003), further research is needed on the gendered emotional life and the sociocultural context of literacy among adolescents.

Given the lack of research on this area, the few studies on self-conscious, social emotions in children reveal contradictory findings. For example, compared to boys, girls have been found to exhibit a greater expression of pride (i.e., girls showed more positive expressions after success than boys) (Stipek, Recchia, & McClintic, 1992), and express greater emotional regulation and displays of shame and guilt (Kochanska, 1994). In contrast, some studies have failed to find such gender differences regarding emotions of pride, shame, and guilt (Griffin, 1995). Accordingly, given the complex interrelations among emotion expression, emotion regulation, and emotion understanding (Denham, 1998), more research is needed regarding individual differences in how adolescents experience silence in the schools given their ability to understand self-conscious emotions and how such understandings are connected to language development and self-concept within the classroom.

Given that cultural influence and emotion understanding are inseparable, how might emotion scripts merge with gender-role socialization? Given that the specific focus on the nature of the self is an extension of the ideas of many emotion theorists (e.g., see Frijda, 1986) emotions arise when events are relevant to the individual's concerns. Lutz (1988) contends that emotions reflect commitment to viewing the world in a particular way and refers to "what is culturally defined and experienced as intensely meaningful" (p. 8). These concerns and commitments converge in a view of self that structures ongoing experiences and the very nature of emotional experience.

According to the self-socialization hypothesis (Maccoby, 1998), during the preschool years, gender differences begin to increase among girls and boys due to parental pressure to conform to traditional gender-role stereotypes. For example, as mentioned earlier, research has shown that traditional gender-role behaviour and ascription (i.e., femininity = sociality, submissiveness; masculinity = autonomy, aggression) categorize the ability to be empathetic and emotionally expressive as a feminine characteristic (Hill & Lynch, 1983; Tavris, 1992; Harter, 1999). Maccoby contends that children self-socialize their behaviour by means of having their actual thoughts and emotion scripts socialized or shaped by their parent's expectations.

Following this gender-role development during the early years, according to the gender intensification process (Hill & Lynch, 1983), the next pivotal transition time occurs during early adolescence (9 to 12 years of age). According to the gender intensification process, preadolescents or preteens become exposed to the increase in societal expectations to follow stereotypic notions of femininity and masculinity. Given Maccoby's (1998) contention that children self-socialize their behaviour by means of having their actual thoughts and emotion scripts socialized or shaped by their parent's expectations, this could also be applied to preadolescents being influenced by parents, peers, and teachers in the context of creating multiple roles for themselves.

Furthermore, Maccoby's (1998) notion of self-socialization is in line with Elkind's (1967) description of adolescent egocentrism in that adolescents experience both the "personal fable" and the "imaginary audience." According to Elkind, adolescents play a role in their own understanding of who they are (create a personal fable) and also pay great attention to their audience (create an imaginary audience). Similar to self-socialization, the adolescents' developing sense of self may involve an interaction between how they present themselves to a particular audience, which may determine, in part, how they create their personal fables. Thus, given the theoretical claims that "self is dialogue contingent" (Bruner, 1990, p. 101) and the notion that "we are all co-authors of our own stories" (Freedman & Combs, 1996), in addition to the empirical claims that show ToM or the ability to understand the perspective of others further develops during the ages between 8 and 10 years (Saarni, 1999), adolescents may actually co-create their actual sense of selves with others' stories and the stories of their culture.

Gender differences in self-conception and social behaviour, then, may reflect differences in young adolescents' stereotypic gender-role ascriptions such as femininity and masculinity more than differences in biological sex (Harter et al., 1998). That is, guided by their own self-scripts that have been co-constructed through social interactions with their parents and others (e.g., siblings, peers, teachers), preadolescents' self-perceived competencies and social behaviour may reflect gender-role stereotypes, resulting in observable gender differences. Thus, the process of learning to understand one's inner world within a social context may be contingent not on whether a child is female or male, but on the way in which a child's gender interacts with her/his environment. That is, the types of "audiences" adolescents choose to "present" to, or perform in front of, may influence how they see themselves and behave. As Bruner (1996) suggests, "School judges the child's performance, and the child responds by evaluating herself in turn" (p. 37). What has a greater influence on an adolescent's sense of overall self-worth—the judgment of "other" (school) or the "self"—and what implication does this have for being silent or feeling silenced in the classroom? How does an adolescent learn the ability or the desire to be one's most harsh critic, and how is self-criticism and perfectionism related to silence experiences?

Drawing on Goffman's (1959) metaphor of theatrical performance as a framework for exploring the landscape of silence, social interactions, and self-presentation in everyday life, self-presentation differs according to the particular "audience" that the self performs to, or the particular context within which the performance occurs. Whereas everyone prepares for their "performance" (backstage), only the audience is allowed to see them perform "onstage." Within the context of adolescence and school, given that the self is co-constructed with others (Bruner, 1996), to what extent does the onstage character (that follows a particular script and performs for particular audiences) reflect the backstage character (or the real self/actor)? Also, in what way does the adolescent choose to represent her or his inner world on stage? That is, to what kind of audience will adolescents choose to express (or not express) their thoughts and emotions using verbal language, movement and dance, song, and so on? Also, what kinds of audiences create fear in adolescents and cause them to feel too scared to perform at all and choose to remain silent or to withdraw backstage? In contrast, what kind of audience creates an atmosphere of psychological safety that allows adolescents to express their "true selves?"

Within a school context, at what point does the script and performance prepared for the audiences (teachers, peers, parents) become the *only* script that the actor uses in real life (off-stage and outside the theatre)? Based on this notion of cultural scripts and self-scripts, research on adolescents' self-concept and social cognition needs to investigate how teachers' and peers' "scripts" influence adolescents' self-scripts and experiences of silence within the classroom. Regarding the self-script, which roles or voices remain silenced in that they remain unwritten and fail to reach the stage?

In general, despite the plethora of empirical evidence concerning gender-related differences in self-concept and social behaviour in preadolescents, the data remain inconsistent and fairly scarce regarding how silence and voice play a role in social cognition and behaviour within the classroom. Interestingly, given the important role language plays in which it acts as a major vehicle (and driver) through which self-concepts and self-behaviours are displayed, few studies explore the influence of language on gender orientation, self-concept, and social behaviours (see Harter et al., 1997, for an exception). In brief, past research has shown that across all age groups (preschool through adulthood), gender differences have been found in inhibition abilities and aggression, favoring females on delay of self-gratification tasks and relational aggression (e.g., Crick et al., 2001). As suggested by Crick et al. (2001), to explore how relational aggression is used differently by girls and boys—for what purposes and what goals (e.g., gaining access to potential mates)—more research is needed within the school context.

Gender differences in emotion understanding and experiences of silence, then, may reflect differences in children's stereotypic gender-role ascriptions such as femininity and masculinity as opposed to differences in biological sex. That is, guided by their own emotional scripts that have been co-constructed through social interactions with their parents and others (e.g., siblings, peers, teachers), adolescents' emotional competence may reflect gender-role stereotypes, resulting in observable gender differences. Thus, the process of learning to understand emotions within a social context may be contingent not on whether a child is female or male, but on the way in which a child's gender interacts with her/his environment or audience (e.g., Brody, 2001; Harre, 1986). Therefore, parents and teachers who endorse stereotypic gender-role expectations may have an indirect influence on the development of an adolescent's social-cognitive abilities, including her or his emotion understanding.

Given the crucial role parents play in both the gender-role socialization and co-construction of adolescents' social-cognitive and linguistic abilities (Denham, 1998; Haden et al., 1997), surprisingly few researchers have studied the links between parents' and peers' perceptions of gender role and children's emotion understanding and language ability. Regarding parents' socialization of their children's emotion understanding, the majority of studies have either 1) investigated parent-child conversations and not parental beliefs or 2) have studied parent's beliefs and expectations of their children's emotional development but not of gender-role behaviour (Hughes, Deater-Deckard, & Cutting, 1999). Although the majority of past research has shown that parents' beliefs and expectations about children's emotional development are gender specific (Brody & Hall, 1993), findings on parents-child emotion talk are mixed. Some researchers have shown that mothers tend to talk more about emotions with their young girls and focus more on emotion labels, whereas for boys, they focus more on the causes or explanations of emotions, and talk about emotions less overall (Fivush, 1989, 2000). In contrast, others have not found differences (Denham, Cook, & Zoller, 1992). For example, in a study of narrative structure in parent-child reminiscing (Haden et al., 1997), 40-month-old girls were found to produce more emotion words than boys, despite the fact that no gender differences were found in general vocabulary ability, and that fathers and mothers did not differ in how they structured past narratives.

In general, the empirical evidence concerning gender-related differences in emotion understanding remains inconsistent and fairly scarce (especially concerning adolescents' understanding of complex emotions). In brief, past research has found females to outperform males in emotion understanding tasks in young children (Cutting & Dunn, 1999; Parent et al., 1999), middle school-aged children and adolescents (Bybee, 1998), and adults (Brody & Hall, 1993). Although researchers suggest that girls seem to internalize earlier and more completely the message that it matters how people feel, some studies have found either no gender differences in emotion understanding (e.g., Banerjee & Yuill, 1999; Denham, Cook, & Zoller, 1992) or that school-aged boys outperform girls (Laible & Thompson, 1998). In sum, findings from emotion understanding and gender in younger children can help to inform researchers' explorations of emotions and silences among adolescents within the school.

Gendered silences and spirituality. In addition to research on emotional understanding, gender differences in self and spiritual moral development and religious involvement have also received an increasing amount of interest over the past ten years (e.g., Harter, 1999; Ream & Savin-Williams, 2003). From a developmental perspective, the question of to what extent adolescent females and males differ in their understandings and experiences of spirituality remains unanswered, perhaps given the unexamined complexities surrounding the term *spirituality* and how it connects to religiosity within the larger context of the self and silence. The widely observed greater religiousness of women has led to some studies of underlying religious differences between the sexes. These studies showed marked gender-related differences and implications for the difference of religious education (Hyde, 1990). For example, studies have found that girls and boys differ in their religious practices and that girls were more likely than boys to be more accepting of the supernatural (Randall & Desrosiers, 1980). Florian and Har-Even (1983) have found that girls feared death because it suggests a loss of identity, whereas boys feared death due its consequences to their family, friends, and of punishment following death.

Irrespective of gender, the religious or spiritual voice and support of the community may also influence adolescents' conceptions of religion, and whether or not silence plays a role in their religious beliefs and behaviours. For example, as Greer's (1972) work in Northern Ireland suggests, a strongly religious community may encourage adolescents to become more religious whereas more secular communities' children may be more likely to move away from religion. Although some research has been conducted on gender-role identity and religiousness, no studies to date have shown consistent gender differences in gender-role identities and religiousness and how such differences may have an influence on silent experiences (Bayer, 1982; Smith, 1982). Researchers interested in adolescence and silence could aim to explore similar topics or replicate past findings to see if similar results could be obtained with an adolescent sample. For instance, Smith (1982) found that more evangelical women were more likely than non-evangelical women to hold more traditional sex-role expectations, whereas no differences were found in the men's groups. Given Smith's findings, researchers could replicate this study with adolescents and see how their religious background influences their gender-role expectations and silence experiences.

As Hyde (1990) suggests, given the importance developmental psychology places on the developing sexual identity, it remains surprising that few studies exist on gender-related differences regarding experiences of spirituality and silence. Overall, as with most research that explores gender-related differences in childhood and adolescent development, the results remain mixed and inconclusive. Many results are contingent upon the culture and related to denomination and parent-child relationships (Nussbaum, 2000). Although Maccoby (1998) addresses the issue of spirituality in particular, she suggests further work needs to be conducted on gender-related issues regarding issues of morality and emotional development, including the connections among moral, emotional development, gender-role orientation, and stereotypic gender-role expectations.

Silence and sexual subjectivities. In adolescence, the link between agency and body becomes connected to adult genital sexuality. By sexuality, I mean the pleasure we get from our bodies and the experiences of living in a body. According to Martin (1996, p. 10), sexual subjectivity is an important component of agency, feeling that one can do and act. This feeling (agency) is necessary for a positive sense of self, including how one feels about her or his body. For example, if adolescents feel helpless, unable to act, as if they have no control over their lives, then they may feel negatively about themselves. Sexual subjectivities affect the ability to act in the world, and to feel that one can "will things and make them happen." Thus, one must experience a link between agency and body/sexuality. As this link (or lack of it) is established, girls and boys develop differing amounts of sexual subjectivity and therefore different levels of self-esteem. This alienation is particularly lethal because it is in large part from our bodies and sexuality that we derive agency and subjectivity throughout our lives.

During adolescence, gender differences become partially attributed to gender norms that become more rigid at adolescence. As gendered norms become intensified at adolescence (e.g., Finders, 1997; Hill and Lynch, 1983; Maccoby, 1998), less range is allowed in activity, appearance, and demeanor. The emergence of femininity, masculinity, and heterosexuality is seen as natural.

Teenagers are expected to act masculine and feminine; cultural norms about beauty, weight, appearance, and demeanor become more rigid. In particular, gender norms become more salient for girls. From early childhood, some boys are taunted with "sissy" for behaviour considered effeminate. However, some girls labelled as "tomboys" are often tolerated as children. But at adolescence, tomboys are expected to naturally transform into feminine beauties. The expectations that girls will become appropriately feminine and boys appropriately masculine at adolescence also affect boys and girls differently because as some literature suggests (e.g., Leaper, 2000), the gender norms for women are more unattainable, more enforced, and more oppressive than those for men. Thus, the effects of intensified gender norms, relations with parents, experiences of puberty, and experiences of sex all overlap and build on each other and shape adolescent selves.

During early adolescence, this gender-role intensification sometimes leads to what many refer to as gender ambivalence (e.g., Martin, 1996; Silverstein & Perlick, 1995). This gender ambivalence, which can occur in both girls and boys, occurs when adolescents realize that they possess characteristics or personality traits that are in conflict with the gender stereotypic norms (Maccoby, 1998). Such an ambivalence towards one's own gendered self can lead to what Aptheker (1989) has referred to as an "internal corrosion," described as a loss of self-esteem, loss of self-confidence in one's knowledge, and an inability to give expression to experience; it may result in experiences of self-silencing.

As I discussed in Chapter 1, adolescence is a time of exploration and experimentation, both of oneself and others. In particular, early adolescence is a time of experimentation of sexual realities, of incorporating sexuality into one's identity. The majority of adolescents eventually manage to develop a mature sexual identity, but most have periods of vulnerability and confusion along life's sexual journey (e.g., Lips, 1997). During this crucial time in the development of sexual identity and gender-role orientation, preadolescents are faced with ambiguous and paradoxical sexual values and messages.

As adolescents explore their sexual selves, they engage in sexual scripts. These scripts are stereotyped patterns of role prescriptions for how individuals should behave sexually (Santrock, 1993). Differences in the way females and males are socialized are expressed in the sexual scripts adolescents follow. Discrepancies in male/female scripting can cause problems and confusion for a developing sense of self.

A psychocultural perspective on gender and literacy allows us to integrate the cultural, social, and historical with the psychological. As Best and Thomas (2004) remind us, cultural mechanisms responsible for developmental change need to account for both within-culture individual differences and between-culture variation across cultural groups. To help explain the role culture plays in development, Simon and Gagnon (1986) describe three levels of scripting or storying that can assist us to understand the gendered experiences of girls and boys. They argue that for behaviour to occur, scripting must occur on three distinct levels: cultural scenarios, interpersonal scripts, and intrapsychic scripts. Cultural scenarios are the instructional guides that exist at the collective level. They are the broad cultural guidelines or norms to social life and behaviour. However, they alone are too broad and are subject to interpretation by individuals. Therefore, in line with Goffman's (1959) notion of self-presentation, social actors must improvise in social interaction. Thus, adolescents create interpersonal scripts, where they become "partial scriptwriters" and make cultural scenarios for the specific context of their interactions. Finally, actors engage in intrapsychic scripting in which reality is symbolically reorganized in ways that make it complicit in realizing more fully the actor's many-layered and sometimes multivoiced wishes. Thus, the internal corrosion that some adolescents experience may be a product of cultural discourses (about bodies, sexuality, gender relations), social interactions (with parents, peers, teachers), and their internalization of each of these. Such corrosion may then lead to self-silencing. That is, some adolescents may either no longer wish to express their voice or they may lose sight of their voice altogether.

For example, a girl who enjoys competition, doing things for herself, and speaking her mind may find that these stereotypic "masculine" traits are not encouraged in early adolescence because the more traditional "feminine" roles of passivity and focus on caring for others as opposed to oneself is more culturally desirable, especially if one wants to be accepted by the peer group, and attractive to the opposite sex. Thus, such girls may feel ambivalent towards these gender roles which, in turn, may lead to a drop in self-worth and an increase in negative self-cognitions and emotions. This low self-worth may then manifest itself into various behaviours such as withdrawal, depression, and other self-harming behaviours (e.g., disordered eating, substance abuse).

Although the majority of research focuses on girls' notions of gender ambivalence, boys can also experience this and, thus, experience the "internal corrosion" or inner conflict as well. For example, as boys approach adolescence, they soon realize that cultural scripts or norms do not value stereotypic feminine characteristics such as compassion, sensitivity, caring for others, or emotionality in young males. As stereotypic cultural norms encourage boys to incorporate "masculine" traits, this may lead to inner conflict or to the "internal corrosion" described above. Thus, similar to girls, boys may learn to "silence" any aspect of their self-concept that does not "fit" the stereotypic male gender-type. As Weaver-Hightower (2003) suggests, the recent focus on exploring the inner world of boys within the educational context may help us to learn more about their perceptions of gender-role stereotypes and related issues.

Gender, autonomy, voice, and silence. Sometimes the term *silence* is linked to the notion of a "loss of voice" as used by Gilligan (1982), Harter (1999), among others. This loss of voice has been defined as the suppression of opinions, emotions, thoughts, or behaviours of the authentic self and some researchers have found that girls experience this "silencing" as they enter adolescence. During middle childhood, Gilligan holds that girls are generally self-confident and able to express clearly and openly what they believe and what they feel. However, according to Gilligan and others (e.g., Pipher, 1994), when some girls enter adolescence they adapt the cultural prescription of the female persona of the "good woman," meaning one who is nice, is polite, and who adapts herself to what others want her to be. She also takes on the role of serving others' needs rather than her own. In the process of making these adaptations, girls' true voices are lost and go unheard.

Gilligan (1982) also refers to as what she calls a relational impasse for girls, stemming from the notion that females, more than males, value connectedness to others. Girls value social connection; to avoid judgment and possible alienation, they may decide not to speak their mind (or their heart). However, recent research findings have contradicted some of Gilligan's findings.

For example, to understand the changes that occur in boys' and girls' voices and sense of selves when they approach adolescence, Harter et al. (1997) studied large samples of both male and female adolescents, from the sixth grade through the twelfth. The researchers asked the adolescents whether, and how often, they spoke openly and frankly with certain others (parents, teachers, male classmates, female classmates, and close same-sex friends) as distinct from speaking guardedly and not saying what they really felt or observed. In general, adolescent girls and boys did not differ with respect to the loss of "voice." For young people of both genders, about one third said that they disguise their true thoughts and feelings when dealing with certain categories of others, but the majority of both sexes did not report doing so.

According to Harter et al. (1997), when young people did speak cautiously to guard their inner worlds, they did so mainly in the context of interacting with classmates of the other sex. Both girls and boys reported that they were less confident when talking with age-mates of the other sex than they were when talking with their teachers, parents, or same-sex classmates or friends. They seemed to be aware that their same-sex interaction styles might not have been appropriate for situations where romantic interests might have arisen. Adolescents of both sexes said that they were careful not to embarrass themselves or to "look stupid" in front of the other sex. In particular, Harter and colleagues found that there has been no systematic documentation of the alleged fact that females suppress their voices more than males do. Harter found that recognition of false-self behavior escalates during adolescence for both genders (Harter, 1999), and that average levels of voice for female and for males were similar among middle and high school students.

Adolescents' experience of "doing gendered emotion" is influenced by the sites in which the practice takes place, and also by the number of emotional exchanges in their lives. Developmentally significant sites are those in which adolescents practice emotion and language in play and in competition. In Chapter 4, I provide some strategies to help teachers utilize events that entail play, cooperation, and competition to help further the development of emotional competence. The integration of emotional education in gender practice with adolescents underscores the dynamic complexity and continuity of the formation of a social self. Thus, educators need to consider the ways in which emotional practice is affected by language, gender, and ethnicity (and vice versa) within the adolescent peer group during the school hours. To help us learn about the inner world of the adolescent, we need to explore how play within the peer group may illustrate performance of emotional scenarios. In turn, these emotional scripts may serve as a framework for practicing gender and for addressing issues of silence and voice.

Socioeconomic Status and Silence

Differences reflected in the jobs and income levels of children's family backgrounds are represented as unequal socioeconomic status (SES). Many aspects of development are affected by the child's family's socioeconomic status, or the general social and economic standing in society that encompasses family income, occupation, and education level of the child's main caregivers. On average, children and adolescents from low-SES backgrounds achieve at lower levels than young people from middle-SES backgrounds, and the gap between the two groups widens as children develop (Jimerson, Egeland, & Teo, 1999). The majority of past research also suggests that compared to middle- or high-income children and adolescents, some low-SES adolescents exhibit more frequent and severe behaviour problems at school and are more likely to drop out prior to high school graduation (e.g., Ackerman, Brown, & Izard, 2004).

Regarding emotional and language development, children and adolescents from low-SES backgrounds are more likely to live in chronically stressful situations and function less effectively when under stress and anxiety (e.g., Bolger, Patterson, Thompson, & Kupersmidt, 1995). In addition, adolescents from low-SES backgrounds are more likely to be subjected to parent and adult maltreatment and to encounter violent crimes in their neighbourhoods (e.g., Bolger & Patterson, 2001). Such experiences may have a detrimental effect on an adolescent's sense of self and competence in various academic areas, including social and language development. Silences can also result as a consequence of maladaptive peer relations. Although in its infancy, researchers have started to explore the influence of socioeconomic status and adolescents' experiences of peer harassment, particularly psychological and emotional bullying and victimization experiences (Brennan, Hall, Bor, Najmam, & Williams, 2003).

Given that children develop an understanding of the inequalities of wealth at a very early age, although initially at a fairly superficial level, some children choose to use this knowledge as a harmful tool to hurt and silence others. For example, Leahy (1981) reported that when children aged 6 to 11 were asked to describe what makes someone rich or poor, the majority of the children emphasized peripheral characteristics such as appearances, possessions, and behaviour as opposed to life chances or class differences. By around age eight, children become aware of the link between social differences and income, and relate the differences in wealth to earnings from work (Jahoda, 1959). Leahy also found that there was an increase, with age, in references to the role played by earnings in equalities of wealth.

Cross-cultural research findings on adolescents' conceptions of socioeconomic status are rare, although the extant research has revealed variations in adolescents' thinking about social class according to nationality. For example, a comparison of Algerian and French children found that the most prevalent explanation for both poverty and wealth in Algerian children was the personal characteristics of the individual (Leiser, Sevon, & Levy, 1990). In contrast, for French children, Leiser et al. found that children and adolescents viewed poverty as a consequence of the socioeconomic system, and attributed fate to wealth as opposed to poverty. Overall, Dickinson and Emler (1996) argue that youth from different socioeconomic backgrounds develop in very different social worlds, and that this results in varying beliefs about the extent, the causes, and the justifications for economic inequalities in society.

Regarding the issue of verbal loudness and social class, as many researchers have suggested (e.g., Fordham, 1996; Lamb, 2001), cursing and verbal loudness are sometimes associated with those who have less power, be it one of the following status variables: lower-class financial backgrounds, ethnic minority, or gender orientation. Luttrell (1993) discusses how the image of white, working-class femininity conveys characteristics such as touch-talking, feminine, and responsible nurture at the same time. Loudness is also sometimes associated with telling the truth, and it may represent a division between the private and public life (Lamb, 2001). For some individuals, loudness, and "telling it like it is," or "speaking one's mind," are seen by those who cultivate a more private life as a lack of class or restraint. However, those who have the opportunity to cultivate a private life can do so without fearing that their beliefs, visions, and opinions will go unheard, particularly if their opinions are preserved in the dominant society. As noted earlier, Markus & Kitayama (1994) suggest that for some cultures, both ethnic and gender identity may be combined. For example, depending upon their cultural heritage and upbringing, some adolescents may believe that being good means suppressing disagreements. That is, the louder one disagrees with others, the harder it is to be viewed as being good.

Building on this work, Fordham (1988, 1996) found that loudness suggests that "I am here and I will not be made invisible." Based on her research on high school students in the northeastern United States, Fordham (1996) found that some African-American girls who were academically successful were also willing to silence themselves. Fordham worried that some girls silence themselves too much, and that "loudness" had become a major metaphor for African-American women's contrariness and resistance to cultural images of their "nothingness." As another example, Fordham found one third-grade Asian-American girl sent to the closet for misbehaving was so quiet that she was invisible—and her teacher forgot she was there for the entire day.

Given that adolescents are capable of understanding the inequalities of wealth, to what extent does this knowledge affect their sense of silence in the classroom? Alternatively, to what extent do adolescents use silence as a tool in their social interactions with others? Some adolescents may perceive this knowledge about themselves as silencing; thus, their socioeconomic status may have an influence on their experiences of silence within the classroom. More specifically, some adolescents may find that the financial background of their family plays a role in their self-concept and inner voice. For instance, some studies suggest that social class has a negative influence on how adolescents view themselves in the classroom (e.g., Harter, 1999).

Although in its infancy, recent research has begun to explore the relation between adolescent bullying/victimization experiences (psychological and physical) and the socioeconomic status of their parents (Rigby, 2002). Sometimes adolescents may be victimized (psychologically and/or physically) or treated differently because of their socioeconomic status. For example, some studies have found that bully/victim problems are significantly more likely to occur in schools in relatively disadvantaged and inner-city places (e.g. Junger-Tas, 1999; Whitney & Smith, 1993). In contrast to this view, some studies have found no connections between social class and bullying/victimization experiences (e.g., Almeida, 1999). Thus, whether social class is a factor in bullying and victimization among adolescents appears to vary among countries and will be worth examining in the future, particularly with respect to silence and voice.

Developmental Exceptionalities: Special Needs and Silences

Aside from the silences produced by status variables in the classroom, differences in learning abilities can also create silences around the adolescent. Interestingly, although the World Health Organization (WHO) estimates that 10% of the world's population has some type of disability that interferes with social functioning and full community participation (WHO, 1999), definitions of "disability" are constantly changing across communities and cultures (Diamond, 2002). More specifically, given the prevalence of adolescents with exceptionalities in the current school system, surprisingly little research exists on how adolescents with exceptional needs experience silence within the classroom setting. Furthermore, with respect to ethnicity and learning problems, there remains a dearth of developmental, educational, and clinical research on ethnic minority children and their families (Capaldi & Shortt, 2003).

Definitional problems surrounding terms such as "special needs" and "learning disabilities" could be one complicating factor that may account for the dearth of literature, in that the terms are inconsistent and contingent on context (Wolfendale, 2000). Such definitional issues are important for theoretical as well practical reasons, particularly for diagnosis issues. For instance, according to Swanson (2000), the number of students classified as having learning disabilities has increased over the last thirty years. Research on the social experiences of exceptional adolescents also includes students with developmental exceptionalities and include a range of difficulties such as mental retardation, behavioral disorder, attention deficit disorder, visual or hearing impairment, learning disabilities, autism, and developmental delay (e.g., Gresham & MacMillan, 1997).

Over the past few decades in North America, there has been an increasing emphasis on including adolescents with exceptionalities in activities and environments designed primarily for adolescents. Sometimes referred to as "mainstreaming," various approaches to education for exceptional students exist, and they all have important social and personal ramifications. Given these educational developments, researchers and educators have recently started to explore the social and emotional experiences of these exceptional adolescents, including their perceptions of silence experiences.

Normalized school experiences for adolescents with exceptionalities are contingent upon the cultural context, which includes cultural expectations of success and competence. For example, notions of equity in opportunity and treatment reflect distinctly Western cultural values (Harry, Rueda, & Kalyanpur, 1999). Also, because of the value that Western, industrialized societies place on independent living, much of the research on the social and self-competence of exceptional students has occurred in Western Europe and North America. Thus, from a psychocultural perspective, as researchers and educators, we need to explore how adolescents with exceptionalities make sense of silence, and how their experiences of silence may differ according to their family background.

In particular, special communicative needs may play a crucial role in how an adolescent communicates with teacher and peers. As I have mentioned throughout this book, adolescence is an important time in self-development, and adolescents often experience an increase in self-consciousness (e.g., Harter, 1999). Thus, any defining characteristic that the adolescent may have (e.g., hearing aid, glasses) that brings attention to any physical or cognitive special need may lead to either strategic (imposed by others) or structural silence (self-imposed). Regarding strategic silence, as a self-protection mechanism, adolescents with special learning needs may silence themselves to avoid ridicule or ostracism from the social group.

Regarding structural silence, the classroom may be physically organized to silence the student (e.g., placing the desk in the back by a computer) or the student may be withdrawn from the regular class for a period of time to work with a specialist (e.g., speech pathologist). Similarly, the difficulty adolescents with exceptionalities experience in classroom and small-group interactions also may extend to less structured contexts. For example, children with exceptionalities are often isolated at recess, moving from playgroup to playgroup or spending a lot of time doing little or nothing. For example, studies have found that during recess, adolescents with language impairments spent significantly more time than typical children exhibiting withdrawn behaviours, and high amounts of reticence and solitary-active withdrawal (e.g., Fujiki, Brinton, Robinson, and Watson, 1997). However, the inability to participate using spoken language did not fully account for the failure of these children to become part of group interaction; Fujiki et al. (1997) found that children with Specific Language Impairment (SLI) were not easily integrated into nonverbal aspects of group activity either. Fujiki et al.'s findings suggest that perhaps researchers need to explore reasons for social exclusion beyond impaired communication skills.

For adolescents with exceptional needs, successfully participating in school and community settings with peers and developing age-appropriate social behaviours are an important challenge. The majority of research provides evidence that suggests adolescents with exceptionalities display lower levels of social competence than typically developing peers. For example, peer relationships have been reported for adolescents with mild mental learning deficits (Juvonen & Bear, 1992), communication disorders (Guralnick, 1999), and sensory disabilities (Erwin, 1993). Social competence problems have also been found for adolescents with significant mental, physical, and behavioral exceptionalities (Staub, Schwarz, Gallucci, & Peck, 1994) and chronic health problems (Wallander & Varni, 1998). Furthermore, adolescents with exceptional needs have been found to elicit a number of behavior patterns that make them vulnerable to poor social relationships (Martlew & Hodson, 1991). Compared to their typically developing peers, adolescents with exceptionalities reported forming significantly fewer friendships with school peers, both in and out of school.

Socioemotional Development of Youth with Exceptional Needs: Empirical Evidence

Overall, adolescents with learning exceptionalities may experience social-emotional challenges (e.g., Capaldi & Shortt, 2003). As a potential source of social marginalization, adolescents with learning exceptionalities may experience greater structured and strategic silences. Regarding feeling silenced by others, there is considerable evidence that adolescents with mild cognitive deficits are less popular and more likely to be rejected and neglected than their typically developing peers (e.g., Ochoa & Palmer, 1995). Furthermore, research in inclusive play groups has consistently demonstrated that children with exceptionalities are included in social interactions with their peers much less than children without exceptionalities. Moreover, their social play has been found to be less cognitively sophisticated than that of their typically developing peers (Guralnick, 1999).

Regarding maladaptive social interactions, researchers have started to explore bullying and victimization experiences in adolescents with exceptionalities, also referred to as peer harassment. Bullying is a particular type of peer victimization that can be defined as "the abuse of physical and psychological power for the purpose of intentionally and repeatedly creating a negative atmosphere of severe anxiety, intimidation, and chronic fear in victims" (Marini, Spear & Bombay, 1999, p. 33). School bullying can be conceptualized as a particular type of abuse, one perpetrated by peers, where the behaviours can be pervasive, severe, and have long-term ramifications (e.g., Marini, Dane, & Bosacki, 2002; Olweus, 1993).

Given that bullying in school children is a well-established area of research in social development, it is comparatively underdeveloped in the exceptionality population. Surprisingly little empirical evidence exists on bullying in adolescents with exceptionalities, although the extant literature reveals a pattern where the incidence of reported bullying is higher in students with exceptionalities than in those without. For example, Sabornie (1994) found that young adolescents who were labeled as learning disabled also experienced patterns of victimization and reported lower levels of social competence. Similarly, Doren, Bullis and Benz (1996) found that over half (54%) of the 221 adolescents diagnosed with a developmental problem reported in their interviews that they had experienced some types of peer harassment (teased or bothered, stolen from, hit or beaten up). Research findings have also shown that adolescents with learning exceptionalities are at least twice as likely to be victimized as the general population (Baladerian, 1994).

Furthermore, Whitney and Smith (1993) examined a number of antisocial behaviours in adolescents with exceptionalities and a typically developing (mainstream) sample. They examined name-calling, taunting, playing pranks, spitting, and kicking. The results indicated that in the young adolescent group (junior/middle school), significantly more adolescents with exceptionalities experienced bullying compared to mainstream students. Similarly, within the older adolescents (secondary school), compared to mainstream students, a significantly larger percentage of the exceptional students were bullied sometimes or more frequently. Similar findings have been reported by other researchers using a variety of approaches, such as peer nominations (Torrance, 1997) or a combination of individual interview, teacher questionnaire, and direct observations (Martlew & Hodson, 1991). In sum, past research suggests that adolescents with exceptionalities are more likely to experience peer harassment as their typically developing peers, which in turn may lead to experiences of lower self-esteem and consequent silencing of oneself (Capaldi & Shortt, 2003).

The umbrella term of "learning exceptionalities" also includes adolescents who are categorized as academically talented or "gifted." Although adolescents who score relatively high on standard IQ tests may not experience a cognitive deficit, they may experience problems in other areas of development. In particular, past research has suggested that gifted children, particularly adolescent females, are more likely to experience self-concept difficulties and social-emotional challenges (e.g., Silverstein & Perlick, 1995; Winner, 2000). Thus, similar to those adolescents who are diagnosed as developmentally delayed, those adolescents who are developmentally advanced or sophisticated may also experience peer harassment and social exclusion and/or neglect from their peers. Similarly, studies have shown that despite their academic competence, gifted adolescents may also experience low levels of self-worth and negative self-concepts and may be more susceptible to internalizing disorders such as depression and disordered eating (Silverstein & Perlick, 1995). Given the sparse research on the social emotional development of gifted adolescents, future researchers need to explore the silences experienced by exceptional adolescents with various competencies.

Combined with Chandler's (1987) assertion that the development of relativistic thought is linked to the emergence of generic self-doubt (implying a decrease in self-worth), one could hypothesize that the development of higher-order cognitive abilities such as recursive and reflective thought may negatively impact an adolescent's sense of self (Dabrowski, 1967). Furthermore, given that girls develop their sense of self through their connections with others and are more likely to internalize their social problems (e.g., Chernin, 1985), classroom silence may have a more negative effect on adolescent girls' self-concept as compared to boys' (Silverstein & Perlick, 1995). For example, a more sophisticated understanding of others' mental states may also be related to a greater psychoemotional sensitivity that may lead one to feel psychologically isolated and vulnerable.

Dabrowski (1967) refers to this experience as "overexcitability," which he claims is often accompanied by feelings of isolation and vulnerability. In turn, such negative emotions may lead to a decrease in one's sense of self-worth and an increased feeling of being silenced from within (Park & Park, 1997). As discussed in the previous section on helpful and hurtful silences, the possibility that classroom silences may have a deleterious influence on an adolescent's sense of self requires further exploration. Educational implications regarding adolescents' oversensitivity to classroom silence, particularly concerning gifted adolescents, need to be addressed from a psychocultural approach. Thus, to investigate the possibility of maladaptive social-emotional responses as a consequence of developing an advanced understanding of others' minds, more applied research is needed on the role silence plays in gifted adolescents' cognitive and affective processes.

Language proficiency is extremely important to peer interaction. In addition to severe hearing impairments, adolescents may also suffer from Specific Language Impairment (SLI). Unlike adolescents with profound hearing loss, there is no context in which adolescents with SLI will find both a viable alternative to spoken language and membership in a cultural community that does not view language impairment as handicapping. For example, as Brinton and Fujiki (2002) suggest, an adolescent with profound hearing loss may be fluent in ASL (American Sign Language) and may interact freely with other members of the hard-of-hearing culture. In contrast, for an adolescent with SLI growing up in a society that values verbal fluency, there is no equivalent community.

The isolation that adolescents with SLI may feel at school and the difficulty they have with classroom social tasks could be expected to affect the way they are viewed by their peers. Although studies on the personal and social experiences of SLI children are rare, extant literature suggests that compared to typically developing adolescents, SLI adolescents experience greater loneliness, and SLI adolescents are not perceived by their peers as very desirable playmates as early as preschool (Gertner, Rice, & Hadley, 1994). More research on how exceptional adolescents see themselves, their thoughts on classroom silences, and how they are accepted by their peers is needed. Although intervention is helpful and essential, manifestations of language impairment may be likely to persist into adulthood. For example, a recent longitudinal study illustrates how the social adjustment of some young men with SLI may be influenced later on in life (Howlin, Mawhood, and Rutter, 2000).

Overall, the research on the social competence of adolescents with profound hearing loss has been complicated by a myriad of factors that influence social-cognitive development. For example, adolescents with profound hearing loss demonstrate varying levels of language development, a wide range of communicative opportunities within the home, and different opportunities to interact with peers who share the same language system. Such variables are often not systematically controlled across research studies, and research findings must be evaluated with these factors in mind (Brinton & Fujiki, 2002).

Although language ability plays a crucial role in social interaction, it is not the only factor that determines social functioning. For example, visual or physical impairments may also influence adolescents' social interactions and self-concepts. Compared to other research on adolescents with exceptionalities, little research exists on the social and personal experiences of adolescents who are visually impaired. Loeb and Sarigiani (1986) studied children and adolescents with hearing loss and compared them to hearing peers as well as to peers with visual impairments. Teachers perceived the students with hearing loss as being more shy and having lower self-esteem than other groups. Furthermore, compared to students with visual impairments, students with hearing losses perceived themselves as less popular and more shy. Overall, results suggest that adolescents with visual impairments are more isolated from peer interaction, have more frequent contacts with adults, and participate in more solitary activity than do their sighted peers (Warren, 1994).

Various studies involving adolescents with chronic illnesses and physical disabilities have also shown that adolescents who suffer from these syndromes appear vulnerable to peer relationship problems because opportunities for social interactions may be limited by absenteeism from school, physical limitations, and parents' concerns. Research that examines specific cognitive processes and social development, such as the work on theory-of-mind skills in adolescents with autistic spectrum disorders, has found that these adolescents suffer from an underlying disorder in interpersonal perception and communication. In turn, this difficulty may interfere with the adolescent's ability to experience others as individuals who are important in the social environment. Consistent with Guralnick's (1999) model, adolescents with autistic spectrum disorders show deficits in foundation processes (including both emotion regulation and psychological understanding) that are critical for socially competent behaviour. For example, Lord and Magill-Evans (1995) found that autistic adolescents produced significantly fewer initiations to peers than did children with language disorders or typically developing children.

Consistent with the other research on exceptionalities, research is only beginning to examine the personal and social experiences of adolescents who experience physical and chronic exceptionalities. Given that researchers who investigate autism focus on the connection between affective and cognitive processes, the research on autistic adolescent's social and personal experiences may be particularly helpful to researchers who are interested in exploring the complex inner worlds and silences experienced by these exceptional adolescents.

In sum, adolescents with exceptionalities may experience particular classroom silences that are different from their typically developing peers. The results of recent studies suggest that characteristics of the social setting, including the availability of typically developing peers and supportive adults, are important in the development of adolescents' social skills. Guralnick's (1999) general model of social competence suggests that abnormalities in cognitive skills may also be associated with deficits in other areas of social development. More frequent interactions and higher levels of social competence have been reported for adolescents when they participate in activities with typically developing peers. Research is only beginning to examine the role of adults and peers as well as child and setting characteristics in the social development of adolescents with exceptionalities.

Recent research that examines social-cognitive processes such as work on theory-of-mind skills in adolescents with autism are beginning steps towards understanding the ways in which adolescents' specific competencies affect social relationships. Understanding which characteristics of the social context are important in supporting social interactions of adolescents with exceptionalities is also an important focus of research. Finally, there is evidence that typically developing adolescents may benefit from interactions with peers with exceptionalities (Diamond, 2002). Research that examines the ways in which these interactions foster the development of socially desirable characteristics (such as altruism) in adolescents without exceptionalities provides an important focus for future research.

For adolescents with language loss, SLI educational programs have wisely targeted language development as a major objective. It has become clear, however, that increased educational emphasis on social and emotional functioning is warranted. Educators need to look for more effective, efficient ways to facilitate language and social skill simultaneously. It is time to help adolescents bridge the gap between the exceptional and normal children, and to help those adolescents with exceptional needs to cross the border into the adolescent social world. Given that the incidence of abuse and peer harassment of adolescents with exceptionalities far exceeds the incidence of victimization in the general population, researchers and educators need to explore the social and personal experiences of these marginalized adolescents. For example, what does silence mean to adolescents labelled as "exceptional" in the classroom? As warranted by Sobsey and Mansell (1997), for meaningful change to take place, we must find ways of empowering people with exceptionalities so that they can control their own educational journey. We need to provide opportunities for them to share their experiences with others and we need to listen. For example, as part of an empowerment strategy, there is a need for researchers to understand how adolescents play a role in the victimization process and how these behaviours can best be identified. As Marini, Fairbairn, and Zuber (2001) suggest, the multidimensional approach to the identification of bullying provides a way of intervening in a more precise manner in the designing of targeted preventative strategies aimed at the development of "resistance" to peer harassment in adolescents with exceptionalities.

Furthermore, a psychocultural approach to social understanding in adolescents may help to demonstrate that the dynamics of social understanding differ for girls and boys and may increase educators' awareness of the different ways girls and boys interpret and come to understand both self and social knowledge. In relation to giftedness (e.g., Winner, 2000), assisting educators in achieving an explicit understanding of the adolescent mind may also help to illustrate that advanced social-cognitive ability may have different consequences for girls and boys. As I describe further in Chapter 4, such understanding may encourage educators to recognize both the social-emotional and cognitive needs of their exceptional students. Due to the lack of empirical work relating ToM to schooling, it cannot yet be said whether or not a more developed theory of mind has any educational implications. However, a growing number of studies and claims (Astington & Pelletier, 1996; Bosacki, 1998) suggest that there is some connection between ToM and schooling, including the relation between ToM development and social behaviour, which may subsequently have implications for the classroom.

Given the empirical evidence, adolescents with exceptionalities share a common challenge in social development. Their classroom peer interactions often entail exclusion, and they must learn to establish and maintain relationships when they cannot easily share their feelings with others. Although language ability plays a crucial role in adolescents' development of social behaviour and self-concept, the interaction of impaired language with other cognitive, social, emotional, and behavioral processes is complex and may vary from adolescent to adolescent. Given this problem, what can educators do to prevent such silences from occurring within classrooms that contain students with exceptionalities? How can educators and researchers uncover the silences experienced by exceptional youth, and how can educators help adolescents to cope with these silences? As I will describe in detail in Chapter 4, I recommend that educators need to consider a more holistic, inclusive approach to education, which in turn may help adolescents with exceptionalities to cope effectively with their silence.

Summary

The aforementioned cultural stories about the meaning of silence demonstrate the importance of understanding both the immediate (familial, community) and the distant (global, cultural, political) contexts for silence and speech. Verbal communication is the outcome of a decision-making process and reflects our mental states. Newcomers to unfamiliar situations must learn what kinds of speech and speech acts are used; they must learn the rules of psychological pragmatics. That is, they must learn not only the language content but also how to use the language to structure their nonverbal behaviours. Given the complex cultural rules, most people claim a choice about when and where they speak what they know. Thus, Roman Emperor Claudius' 1,000-year-old statement "Say not always what you know, but always know what you say" (Claudius, Roman Emperor, 10 BC–AD 54, source unknown) remains wise advice to this day.

Drawing on the broad array of social-cognitive literature on adolescents outlined in the above sections, empirical findings are mixed concerning the link between social understanding, self-concept, and social relations. Although the investigation of self-concept and social understanding in adolescents began over forty years ago (Bruce, 1958; Flapan, 1968), researchers and educators remain puzzled and intrigued as to how adolescents learn to make meaning from their social experiences. As already noted, although there exist a large number of studies on social cognition in adolescents, they either examine specific components of social cognition and social relations or the interrelations between two constructs.

In sum, this chapter reviews a vast array of research on social cognition and social relations in adolescence, which holds many educational implications. Thus, the following chapter addresses some of the practical issues that may be drawn from the research on classroom silences. Thus, based on past literature, the next chapter aims to provide some educational ideas and strategies that may encourage both educators and researchers who work with youth to continue to explore and address the sensitive issue of silences within the classroom.

·4·

PRAGMATICS OF SILENCE: HOW CAN WE "SCHOOL THE SILENCES?"

It is wise to listen.
(HERACLITUS)

Introduction

Despite the increasing recognition that schools play a crucial role in adolescent development, researchers have just begun to explore beyond the cognitive domain regarding the extent to which the school experience affects the inner life of the adolescent. That is, to what extent does school life affect the adolescents' feelings, self-beliefs, and behavioural choices, particularly around the issue of silence? Although the majority of developmentalists have focused on the peer and teacher-student relationship, educational researchers have focused on the impact of schools on the cognitive rather than the social, moral, and emotional outcomes. There remains a need for an interdisciplinary and holistic approach to the impact of schools on adolescents (Eccles & Roeser, 2003). As researchers in educational, psychology, sociology, anthropology, and similar fields have tended to work independently of one another, utilizing a variety of different methodologies, such diversity has made it difficult to build a coherent body of knowledge about the connection between the school and private life of the adolescent. In this chapter, through the lens of a psychocultural approach, which views schooling as a discursive space, I outline various ways in which researchers and educators can consider how various aspects of the school experience may influence the adolescent's sense of self and experiences of silence. Particularly for educators, I suggest some educational strategies that aim to promote the benefits of silence through focusing on the social and emotional factors surrounding the silence experience.

Apparently, schools that emphasize ability (e.g., academic, athletic, etc.) may alienate and/or silence some students who cannot perform at the highest levels. Such alienation may lead to anxiety, anger, disenchantment, and self-selection out of the school context (Finn, 1989). Overall, as Simmons and Blyth (1987) suggest, the key to optimal development and a sense of happiness in education is a good fit between what goes on in the school and the needs, beliefs, and cultural values of individual adolescents. The question for educators remains, how do we achieve the ultimate person-environment fit? That is, to maximize learning and development in adolescents, we need to achieve a good fit between the needs/characteristics of the learner and the characteristics of the environment.

Who determines what a "good fit" consists of—the teacher or student? Or is a "good fit" co-created together? Such questions remain, and the ideas outlined in this chapter attempt to provide some strategies for educators to achieve this "good fit"—which, according to some researchers, is necessary for happiness and self-fulfillment (e.g., Noddings, 2003).

Pedagogical Directions: Creating the Caring, Connecting Curriculum

A psychocultural approach to schooling views schools as both a discursive space in which identity and culture are negotiated (Yon, 2000) as well as formal social organizations that have their own characteristics, including values, norms, activities, and everyday routines. Such routines and rituals may influence adolescents' intellectual, social-emotional, and behavioral development in that they provide the discursive space in which adolescents can negotiate their identities and cultures. Various researchers have investigated how the school climate or psychological atmosphere affects students' lives. For example, a school-level emphasis on different achievement goals promotes an atmosphere of cooperation and connectedness, rather than competition and social comparison (Aronson, 2004; Capaldi & Shortt, 2003). Thus, schools that focus on personal mastery/tasks rather than school-level achievement may place some students at risk for fear of failure.

Accordingly, some students within these competitive academic schools may feel silenced by the school atmosphere, and this may have a negative influence on their mental health. For example, in a series of studies by Roeser and Eccles (1998) adolescents' beliefs that their school is ability-focused lead to declines in students' education values, achievement, and self-esteem, and increases in their anger, depressive symptoms, and school truancy as they moved from seventh to eighth grade.

Casting Call: Classroom Relationships

As educators and researchers concerned with the promotion of an overall healthy psychological and emotional state in adolescents, we need to focus on programs and activities that promote not just positive self-thoughts but useful techniques that can be taught that may help adolescents to learn how to deal with emotional pain and self-doubt. We need to borrow from the spiritual literature and from clinical psychotherapy work to create self-comforting techniques that promote self-trust and acceptance, including relaxation techniques, visualization, art therapy, play therapy, and psychodrama. In addition, we need courageous, reflective teachers to serve as role models in our schools, teachers who are interested in furthering their own self-understanding as well as promoting this ability in their students.

A psychocultural approach to education cannot be reduced to any single technique. It is the art of cultivating meaningful human relationships. It is the dialogue between teacher and learner within a caring community. The focus is on dialogue, connection, and the mutual co-creation of meaning. There is no one technique for doing this, because it stems from being authentic, being who you really are. Teaching and learning reflect our identities and what we need to learn. Thus, as educators and researchers wishing to promote a psychocultural educational approach, we must begin with openness and trustworthiness, and open up to ourselves, feel our experience, and explore the inner landscape of our lives. Although openness begins as an inner, personal discipline, it has the potential to evolve into a dynamic, interactive experience. Our own openness has the potential to collapse or dissolve boundaries between ourselves, others, and the world. By offering genuine engagement to our students, they can begin to experience interconnection and wholeness, which in turn allows them to co-create environments where they interact with their peers in similar ways. As co-participants in learning communities, we can begin to teach and model together the practices of openness, awareness, tolerance, respect, kindness, and trust.

Consistent with past research (e.g., Finders, 1997; Martin, 1996), I agree that both educators and the adolescent learners are responsible for their learning and exploration of their experiences with silence. As mentioned earlier in the book, teacher expectancy research findings (which suggest that teacher ratings of adolescents' behaviours may shape adolescents' self-perceptions) support the holistic vision that both the adolescent learner and the adult teacher hold implicit theories and are equally capable of envisioning themselves as "intersubjective theorists" (Bruner, 1996). Thus, the teacher and students share the role of learner and co-constructor of knowledge. The research mentioned in this chapter might also encourage both teachers and students to think of themselves as collaborators, constantly learning from each other. Once students adopt such a perspective and realize that they have an equal opportunity to learn/teach and to create knowledge, potential teacher/student power struggles that are common to early adolescent classrooms may be reduced (Paechter, 2000). Both the teacher and the learner must work towards the same goal, to become reflective practitioners and learners together.

For example, encouraging students to participate in curriculum development may provide students with a sense of personal power and ownership of their own learning. That is, by contributing to such objectified knowledge as the class curriculum, students may begin to envision themselves as connected knowers (Goldberger et al., 1996), ones who are active participants in the construction of objectified knowledge. Furthermore, given the elimination of traditional teacher/student roles, adolescents may develop a greater sense of agency based on a greater belief in their ability, which in turn may lead to greater competence in all areas of school (Acker, 1994). If adolescents learn that they are responsible for their education, they may be more likely to engage in classroom activities.

Given that past research gender differences often reflect gendered stereotypes (e.g., Maccoby, 1998), educators need to be aware of their use of gender labels. Teachers of adolescents need to examine their own definitions and behaviours of gender roles, particularly to avoid promoting self-fulfilling prophesies within their classrooms. The specific gender patterns found among the teacher ratings, and the children's perceptions of their gendered selves and competencies, suggest that differential patterns of treatment by educators may reinforce biased assumptions about gender-appropriate roles for girls and boys. Given past findings that suggest teachers perceived feminine boys as less physically aggressive, more compliant, and competent in art suggests that educators need to reexamine their definitions of masculinity and femininity and be cognizant of the use of particular gender labels within the classroom. Although stereotypes may be useful to educators as cognitive frameworks for person-related information (Lips, 1997), they have the potential to be detrimental to a student's sense of self-worth. For example, regarding stereotypic notions of femininity (e.g., compliance), masculinity (e.g., athletic ability), labels such as "sporty girls" or tomboys and "artsy boys" or sissies may have a direct influence on adolescents' sense of self, particularly if they incorporate such labels into their self-stories or scripts. The finding that both girls and boys who perceived themselves to be feminine also perceived themselves as more "well-behaved" suggests that self-fulfilling prophecies may have already started. That is, perhaps they have already "storied" their teachers, parents, and culture's notions of feminine as compliant and passive into their personal life narratives.

Furthermore, an educator who stereotypes a child as "quiet and shy" might also ignore that child's distinctive personal qualities and her/his positive contributions to others and to society. Also, the teacher expectancy research suggests that teachers' stereotyped expectations such as the "talkative, social girl" and the "nontalkative, athletic boy" may actually help shape that targeted child's self-perceptions (e.g., Brophy, 1983). As Bruner (1996) contends, "School judges the child's performance, and the child responds by evaluating himself or herself in turn" (p. 37). Recent related research has also suggested that teachers find shyness to be a positive attribute for girls, but a negative attribute for boys (Rubin, Burgess, & Coplan, 2002). Hence, educators need to be aware of the effects of gender-role socialization on preadolescent girls and boys and attempt to minimize their damage through the avoidance of gendered metaphors. Moreover, educators of preadolescents need to challenge and redefine their definitions of femininity and masculinity and attempt to understand how gender-role stereotypes may affect preadolescents' self-perceptions and consequently shape their behaviour.

Compared to younger children, adolescents begin to understand the "subtext" or hidden messages of their peers' and teachers' talk. As I have mentioned throughout this book, given that adolescence is a crucial time in all stages of growth (e.g., Harter, 1999), harmful attitudes such as sarcasm may have potentially long-lasting effects on the students' own developing sense of self and spirituality. We need teachers of both genders who have the courage and emotional strength to speak their mind with all of their heart. Such courage will enable teachers to show that they are not afraid to show their sensitivities. When teachers transcend society's stereotypic roles, they may further develop their own spiritual dimension that enables them to be in tune with their authentic self. Thus, they will learn to teach who they are.

Furthermore, I agree with Kessler (2000) and others (e.g., Bruner, 1996; Haynes, 2002) who suggest that educators of adolescents need to be courageous in the sense that they need to address their own assumptions, beliefs, and feelings towards sensitive topics such as spirituality, gender, race/ethnicity, or social class. Educators need to take an active role to address their own personal silences and examine how silences in the classroom make them feel. They need to explore their own past experiences with silence and create ways in which they can promote a psychologically safe learning environment for adolescents to engage in authentic enquiry and dialogue that promotes critical discussion and reflective thought. After all, if educators do not address their own feelings and thoughts about silence, they may inadvertently perpetuate a culture of fear and silence within their own classrooms. Such dangerous cycles need to be broken if educators wish to create a caring and supportive learning community, one that encourages critical dialogue, enquiry, and self-growth.

Considering some of my own and others' research findings on adolescent's self-concepts and spirituality, the fact that young adolescents are willing to discuss such multifaceted issues points to a complex web of gendered selves, sexual subjectivities, and spiritual growth that is grounded in relationship—to the world, others, and oneself. Adolescents require relationships that offer comfort and meaning, while simultaneously providing space for negotiation of freedom and independence. Within a holistic educational framework, one that addresses the whole child, the use of story is perhaps the ideal way to address the complexity of the preadolescent. As Paley (1999) suggests, stories have a spiritual quality in that they lift our spirits and define all aspects of humanity, including who we are and the various roles we play in life. Thus, adolescents need to explore themselves in stories through both verbal and written forms of storying and dramatic or visual arts. In the next section, I outline some ways in which both teachers of adolescents and adolescent learners can develop into authentic, caring, reflective, and compassionate individuals of society.

Setting the Stage: Communication Ensures Psychological Comfort

Based on both psychological and educational literature that outline similarities among the roles of teachers, students, researchers, and psychologists (e.g. Beatty, 1996; Haynes & Marans, 1999; Selman, 2003), educational programs that are situated within a psychocultural foundation view both the group facilitator/teacher and the participants/students as co-learners who come to share beliefs, goals, and intentions to subsequently form a culture or a caring community of learners. Such educational programs aim to encourage both the group leaders and the participants to learn from each other and thus support the holistic principle that claims teaching and learning are mutually reinforcing processes. Thus, as suggested by Collin (1996), some participants may need encouragement to engage in a collaborative, dialogical relationship, respecting the fact that each co-learner is a knowledgeable individual of her or his own situation.

Equitable relationships experienced by learners in both non-school and school settings may help to alleviate the risk of "psychological exposure," which possibly plays a key role in precluding both students who feel silenced and students who acts as silencers from participating in educational programs (Okely, 1987). If "an idea is a sound from the heart" (Patterson, 1991, cited in Barbieri, 1995, p. iii), the learning environment or classroom culture needs to be warm, caring, and emotionally supportive so that both teachers and students learn to trust themselves and others in order to feel secure enough to speak from both their heart and their brain (Noddings, 2003). Consequently, this psychologically safe environment provides opportunities to experience "connected teaching/learning" (Belenky, Clinchy, Goldberger, & Tarule, 1986), which occurs when two co-learners engage in the co-construction of knowledge as they learn from their shared self-disclosures. Thus, in aiming for what Elbow (1973) claims to be a "yogurt class" that fosters a culture for growth as opposed to a "movie" class where students are viewed as passive observers and recipients of information, connections with both self and other may be strengthened.

Encouraging educators to view curriculum from a psychocultural perspective has the potential to create a psychological-social curriculum that deals with both self-reflective, metacognitive skills or the ability to "go meta" (Bruner, 1996, p. 88), and social-communicative skills such as empathetic sensitivity (e.g., Tomasello et al., 1993). Educational activities that focus on both self-reflection and critical discussion can help promote both critical consciousness and social awareness among preadolescents (Giroux & Penna, 1979). Although reflexive thought or the "best kind of thinking" (Dewey, 1933/1966, p. 3) has been mentioned by various educators/psychologists in the past (Piaget, 1981; Vygotsky, 1978; Bruner, 1990), the majority of critical reasoning curriculum remains within the domain of gifted education (Winner, 2000).

In addition, given that many researchers claim that language plays a critical role in social cognition and self-development (Astington & Pelletier, 1996, 1997; Harter et al., 1997), activities that involve literacy are crucial for the development of self-knowledge within the adolescent years. Various writers and curriculum designers have noted the importance of narrative and metacognition for the curriculum (e.g., Astington, 1993; Bruner, 1996; Kuhn, 1989; McKeough, 1992; Olson, 1997; Ontario Ministry of Education and Training, 1997). According to narrative theory (Bruner, 1986, 1990), children learn to make sense of their social world as they acquire the ability to tell stories about it. The use of writing and reading stories can help adolescents develop their abilities to understand and to integrate multiple perspectives. That is, adolescents can use narratives to integrate what they and others think, feel, and do. Accordingly, educators of preadolescents need to encourage silent reading, book sharing, and "story-time" with books that focus on the private, subjective experience of the adolescent. For example, Margaret Atwood's (1988) *Cat's Eye* and Judy Blume's (1982) *Then Again Maybe I Won't* are excellent examples of books that explore the private world of adolescent girls and boys respectively. Thus, by examining the thoughts and emotions of characters in a novel, adolescents can learn to clarify and develop their own perspectives.

Many researchers claim that the value of language activities is that they encourage dialogical reasoning and critical reflection and may encourage teachers to engage students in activities that promote interpretive understanding and intentional creativity (Jackson & Davis, 2000; Schank & Cleary, 1995). For example, in line with various educators' claims that metacognitive and meta-linguistic activities need to be integrated into the classroom (e.g., Keating, 1990; Kuhn, 1989; Olson, 1997; Paley, 1999), activities that utilize metacognitive abilities such as journal writing, bibliotherapy, and psychodrama allow a kind of experimentation within the self that may promote a greater understanding of one's own mind and how it relates to others. Thus, the use of metacognitive activities that are frequently referred to in the gifted literature (e.g., Lovecky, 2004; Swanson, 2000; Winner, 2000) should be made available to all children and need to be rigorously used within the classroom of the adolescent.

Related findings from social cognitive research suggest that metacognitive understanding may be linked to aspects of social and self-understanding. Thus, based on past research that has shown exposure to metacognitive and meta-linguistic verbs may increase the use of such verbs among children, which in turn may lead to a greater understanding of mental states (Astington, 1993; Astington & Pelletier, 1996), both teachers and curriculum developers should also be encouraged to increase their use of metacognitive or mental language in both classroom talk and curriculum materials. Within a holistic educational framework, educators can increase their usage of metacognitive and psychological language by talking about their own thought processes and emotions. Thus, by making their own implicit, psychological theories more explicit, educators may foster the growth of metacognitive understanding in their students (Astington & Pelletier, 1996). The use of such language, then, may help to promote both individual growth and a united classroom consciousness.

Educational programs for the gifted can also provide some answers for students who may be at-risk or particularly vulnerable to feelings of low self-worth and social incompetence. Results from some of my past findings on ToM and adolescents suggest that girls with a relatively sophisticated ToM and boys with a relatively less complicated ToM may suffer from social-emotional difficulties. These findings support the view that the core educational issue remains the adolescent's perceived worth as a person. Thus, educational programs that strive to increase the learner's self-worth need to be a priority in the adolescent classroom. Thus, drawing on relevant holistic educational models (e.g., Waldorf schools) and psychoeducational programs that aim to foster self-development and social competence (e.g., Davis & Phillips, 1994; Selman, 2003), various activities can be used to increase the self-confidence of such children. In particular, an arts-based program that focuses on self-expression and understanding can be used to foster a coherent sense of self that is necessary to effectively connect with others.

Consistent with recent research on personal and emotional intelligence (e.g., Goleman, 1995; Matthews, Zeidner, & Roberts, 2002), findings from social-cognitive research can help lay the groundwork for a holistic educational program that focuses on the metacognitive abilities of both social and self-understanding. Drawing on findings from my past research and holistic and transformative educational principles and goals (Bosacki, 1998; Miller, 1993), and borrowing from various affective educational programs and curriculum documents (Ontario Ministry of Education and Training, 1997; Richardson & Evans, 1997; Vernon, 1997), I have developed a framework for a metacognitive emotional education curriculum for adolescents (see Table 2). In general, the main goal of the program is to foster both personal and social growth through arts-based activities designed to improve adolescents' understanding of their own feelings and behaviour and those of others. The activities listed in Table 2 aim to provide adolescents with an understanding of the social world, and to help them recognize the differing beliefs, desires, and feelings that different people can bring to the same situations. Based on the constructs of social and self-understanding, Table 2 lists the corresponding metacognitive skills followed by the educational goals and suggested activities.

Although space does not permit the discussion of all of the suggested activities listed in Table 2, two are worth brief mention, as they are particularly relevant to self-development in adolescence. First, Rudolf Steiner's (1976) concept/method of eurhythmy or "music and speech expressed in bodily movement" (Holland, 1981, quoted in Reinsmith, 1989, p. 87) is an educational concept/method that especially speaks to the issue of the body-mind connection. An integral part of Waldorf Education, this form of movement education focuses on learning through rhythmic experience by moving to music (Richards, 1980). Such an activity can provide preadolescents with a personal sense of mastery by enabling them to create rhythmic movement. Consequently, this sense of competence can promote the preadolescent's ability to love and accept one's mind and body. Such an activity, then, may help to immunize both girls and boys against self-concept disorders where mind and body become psychologically separated.

The second activity mentioned is that of guided imagery and group/classroom meditation that promotes the concept of mindfulness or the ability to be aware in the present (Goleman, 1995; Miller, 1993). In such activities, the teacher asks the children to imagine a particular scenario, one that is comforting and has personal meaning for those involved. The goal of visualization or guided imagery is to develop preadolescents' awareness of their thoughts, physical sensations, and emotions simultaneously. Activities that focus on

TABLE 2. The Connecting Curriculum: Curriculum for the Psychological and Social Lives of the Adolescent

Overall aims: 1. to foster the understanding of self and other as psychological beings; 2. to further personal and social growth; 3. to foster the metacognitive abilities that underlie the ability to understand one's private and social worlds (i.e., foster "emotional literacy" skills).

Metacognitive Skill	Educational Goal	Educational Activity
I. Social Understanding		
interpersonal understanding	— develop ability to attribute mental states to others	— read and reflect on novels that focus on the psycho-emotional aspect of interpersonal relationships (peers, family, teacher/student)
1. Conceptual Role-Taking	— understand multiple perspectives — understand the beliefs and intentions of others	— dramatic role-playing (psychodrama), painting and writing from multiple perspectives — classroom debates, cooperative games, peer teaching
2. Empathetic Sensitivity	— understand the emotional states of others	— dramatic role-playing, creative writing, conflict mediation
3. Person Perception	— to view others as psychological beings (i.e, understand personality traits)	— creative writing/video, bibliotherapy, painting others' portraits, people sculpting, create comics, characters
4. Alternative Thinking	— create alternate solutions (divergent thinking skills)	— critical media analysis (tv, radio, magazines, film, etc.)
II. Self-Understanding		
intrapersonal understanding	— develop ability to attribute mental states to self	— read and reflect on novels that focus on the psychoemotional aspect of intrapersonal relationships (e.g., self-discovery, self-journeys)
1. Affective	— develop ability to trust, care, and accept oneself	— guided imagery focused on body/mind connection, teacher-led meditation/mindfulness, eurhythmy, face/body (e.g., using various media such as clay-self-sculture, paints, paper-maché, film/video, music), masking (creation of masks)
2. Cognitive	— understand workings of one own's mind — gain knowledge of how one thinks	— bibliotherapy, journal writing, dream work (both narrative and visual), self-portrait of the mind (using various mediums), self-narration, autobiographical writing

Notes. Activities within each domain (social and self, respectively) are interchangeable. Activities can be applied to a variety of psychocultural themes (gender, ethnicity, social status/popularity). Social understanding activities can serve as both individual and cooperative group assignments.

mindfulness, then, promote connections within all realms of the self, including body-mind, thought-emotion, and logic-intuition. Furthermore, such activities could be also be viewed as relaxation techniques used to teach children cognitive strategies that can later be used as a coping mechanism to deal with real-life emotional stress, such as academic and social anxiety.

Although the activities presented in Table 2 may be adapted to include any theme, given the research and literature on sociocultural factors, a curriculum that is meaningful and relevant for adolescents should include the themes of status, such as social class, ethnicity, or gender. To encourage adolescents to challenge and redefine gender-role stereotypes and expectations, valuable activities could include critical analysis and discussion of the portrayal of such stereotypes in the media (see Daley et al., 1994, for a comprehensive curriculum guide on gender-related issues). Furthermore, such activities may encourage students to replace dualistic thinking with a more healthy, global, and holistic perspective by encouraging them to view things on a continuum (Noddings, 2003). For example, critical group discussions of dichotomous terms such as masculine/feminine, fat/thin, good/bad could prove beneficial by inspiring preadolescents to both challenge and escape the tyranny of societal expectations that glorify linear, dichotomous thinking.

Self-connections can be further strengthened by adapting the ecological and spiritual perspective towards the self and education. Classroom silences speak directly to the issue of spirituality and emotionality in the classroom, and it my hope that this book will serve as a catalyst by encouraging educators to develop curricula that attend to such crucial issues. In agreement with progressive educators who advocate for the development of a spiritual and ecological understanding (e.g., Coles, 1990; Donaldson, 1992; Gardner, 1985; Goleman, 1995; Hutchison, 1998), this model also promotes Sternberg's (2003) suggestion that we need to teach for wisdom, in that we should promote the application of successful intelligence to our everyday lives for a common good. The integration of such competencies into mainstream education deserves greater discussion and study in educational and psychological circles. In particular, we need to suggest ways to integrate silence into the curriculum in a positive sense. That is, we need to include a spiritual/emotional dimension to curriculum, one that incorporates aspects of silence into the everyday routine. Such a curriculum will outline ways in which a holistic curriculum can help to eliminate fear (in both teachers and learners).

Across all aspects of social cognition, educators can draw on activities from the language arts, particularly drawing on a wealth of books written for children that promote moral and social development. For example, regarding racial and ethnicity issues, many books available today involve the understanding of multiple perspectives across various cultures: books such as *First Person, First*

Peoples by Andrew Garrod and Colleen Larimore (1997) and *Souls Looking Back: Life Stories of Growing Up Black*, edited by Andrew Garrod, Tracy Robinson, and Robert Kilkenny (1999) are examples of books that will encourage youth to think about the perspectives of people from diverse cultures and to understand issues such as prejudice, power, marginalization, and identity. Books by Toni Morrison such as the *Bluest Eye* (1994) may also add to the classroom library.

Children's books may also be one of the most effective ways to send a message to adolescents regarding important "life lessons" that need to be addressed in the school social curriculum. Some example of young children's books that can be read to adolescents include Ed Young's (1992) *Seven Blind Mice*, Freymann and Elffers' (1999) *How Are You Peeling: Foods with Moods?* and Leo Lionni's (1970) *Fish Is Fish*, as all of these books can be used to promote human values of respect, cooperation, kindness, and the notion that we need to "read beyond the cover" and be tolerant and kind towards other human beings, irrespective of physical appearance or personal agendas.

Regarding practical tools for educators, further exploration of various experiences of silences and their socioemotional and spiritual consequences suggests the need for useful assessment tools and interventions. Given past research, which suggests that psychological understanding is related to school experiences (Astington, 1993; Bruner, 1996; Bosacki, 2003), we could teach "psychological language" to adolescents, focusing on self-reflection and self-acceptance (Rhedding-Jones, 2000; Tannen, 1994). As educators, we can encourage adolescents to develop a "mental state vocabulary of the self and others." Such initiatives support educators who advocate the importance of narrative and metacognition in education.

According to narrative theory (Bruner, 1996), children learn to make sense of their social world as they acquire the ability to tell stories about it. Thus, writing and reading stories can help children to develop their ability to integrate multiple perspectives (Pajares, Miller, & Johnson 1999). Curriculum development that utilizes narrative may thus enhance children's ability to understand themselves and others in a psychological sense. Books that describe people's psychoemotional worlds can be used in the early grades to encourage children's mental-state understanding. For instance, excerpts from Sylvia Plath's (1996) *The It-Doesn't-Matter Suit*, Judy Blume's (1972) *Tales of a Fourth Grade Nothing*, and Doreen Cronin's (2003) *Diary of a Worm* could be used to illustrate the landscape of adolescents' private worlds and inner voices. Moreover, in line with work on the "emotional" intelligences and literacies (Finders, 1997; Goleman, 1995; Salovey & Sluyter, 1997), and my recent work on holistic education and spirituality (Bosacki, 2001), future research in this area may provide a framework for a holistic curriculum aimed to foster both inter- and intrapersonal competencies.

Interestingly, although the books mentioned above are categorized as children's books, from my personal perspective as a university professor teaching courses in a graduate education program, I have often integrated children's texts into my graduate course curriculum. For example, one year when I was teaching a course on global and holistic approaches to teaching and learning, I read Young's (1992) *Seven Blind Mice* as an example of how story can be used to illustrate complex reasoning skills, such as the ability to understand and develop multiple perspectives. Similarly, in my graduate education course that explores developmental and educational issues in children and adolescents, I have also read Leo Lionni's (1970) *Fish Is Fish* to graduate students to illustrate the importance of social acceptance, identity, and cultural context.

Also, as many of my graduate students are adult learners in service professions (e.g., many teach at various levels including elementary, secondary, postsecondary), I encourage my students to challenge themselves and to read "children's texts" from the critical perspective of a young learner and an adult educator. Following the reading of such texts, the class often engages in a critical group discussion of the underlying messages of the book, and discusses the imagined intent of the author. By incorporating such practices into my own classroom, I also aim to provide my students with a model of teaching. I encourage them to draw on the activities that we engage in together during our sessions and to apply them to their own professions. For example, I encourage students to use the children's stories to address the particularly sensitive issues within their classroom that are usually kept silent, such as dealing with issues of power and dominance, racial and ethnic diversity, and so forth.

In line with Kessler (2000), who discusses how educators and students need to consider and feel comfortable with silence in their own lives before they can effectively integrate periods of silence into their classroom, I often note a change in the atmosphere of the classroom whenever I read children's texts to a graduate class. I realize that all students have started to listen, and they become engaged in the story and in the subsequent conversation. Is it possible that story and silence are linked by some socioemotional connection? As Kessler asks, how can we as educators incorporate aspects of silence into our classroom if we do not feel comfortable with our own experiences of silence?

In sum, through the integration of ideas from both cognitive psychology (metacognitive activities) and holistic curriculum models (language and art-based activities), a psychocultural educational program may provide a valuable contribution to preadolescent education. Such an educational program could be used to enhance the provincial curricula standards in that it would help to balance the distribution of affective and cognitive activities. However, it should be noted that due to the self-exploratory nature of some of the activities, the program is not intended to provide psychotherapy for serious emotional problems. Educators would thus need to be aware of such children and to provide them with the proper psychological resource, if needed. The complex relation between education and therapy is discussed later in this chapter.

The Connecting Curriculum: Psychocultural Educational Strategies

The concept of balance or the ability to maintain various energies and qualities in the correct proportion underlies all aspects of holistic education (Miller, 1993; Steiner, 1976). This "education of balance" strives to assist children in their self-development by the integration of body, mind, and soul. From this view, the intellectual development of the child is kept in appropriate relationship to the child's social, emotional, physical, and spiritual development. Thus, holistic education sees mind and body as connected and interrelated, advocating a balance between cognition and emotion—and, more specifically, between the use of rational/logical-scientific and intuitive/narrative thought.

In contrast, the traditional models of both psychology and education value the mind over the body and thus emphasize the importance of cognition over emotion (Bruner, 1996; Kessler, 2000). Although the notion of a split between mind and body dates back to at least Aristotle in fourth century BC, which states that only men possessed the mind/soul and reason that ruled the body and emotions (Wiltshire, 1989); the cognitive-behavioural or transactional approach to learning may reflect the ongoing gender bias that exists in modern Western culture (Miller & Scholnick, 2000). In particular, this gender bias fosters the mind/body split by equating the former with the stereotypically masculine traits (i.e., independence/autonomy, success) and the latter with stereotypically feminine traits (i.e., dependence/sensitivity, failure). Adolescents may thus learn that women are associated with an irrational, lower self, requiring mastery or the "world of the body," whereas men are associated with the rational, higher self, possessing power or the "world of the mind" (Coole, 1995).

Adolescents living in the 2000s may be especially susceptible to such stereotypic gender-role expectations through their constant exposure to conflicting sociocultural messages (Ward, 2004). Researchers on adolescents claim that between the ages of 10 and 13, girls and boys experience an increase in societal pressure to conform to gender-role stereotypes of the "perfect body" (e.g., Chernin, 1985). For example, although the majority of schools support a traditional, cognitive-based education (valuing the intellect), messages from the media (i.e., TV, magazines, films) value the physical body, encouraging adolescents to not accept who they are and to constantly strive for perfection. One of the headlines on a recent issue of *Teen Vogue* (December 2003/January 2004) states, "Make me over: 50 ways to rethink your clothes, bedroom, makeup, hair, workout." Thus, traditional models of education may be a contributing factor to the recent research findings that show an increase in identity/self-concept disorders among adolescents (e.g., Harter, 1999).

However, although adolescents are exposed to the paradox of school's over-emphasis on intellect and society's obsession with the body, girls may be particularly susceptible to the possible damaging effects of such conflicting messages. For example, a syndrome of self-concept disorders including anxiety, depression, and disordered eating (anxious somatic depression) has recently been argued to be the result of the "cost of competence" in young women who aspire to achieve academically in a society that values woman's bodies over their minds (Silverstein & Perlick, 1995). Accordingly, holistic programs emphasizing personal integration and social awareness need to be implemented in the late grades of elementary school or early grades of junior high school to promote a body/mind unity and to provide preadolescents with coping strategies that can be used to combat conflicting sociocultural messages.

Holistic educational activities that may help to promote spiritual development include self-comforting techniques such as relaxation techniques, visualization, and journalling, to name a few. Furthermore, programs adapted from Waldorf schools that promote the aspect of wonder and mystery in learning could also be incorporated into a curriculum for preadolescents that promotes a sense of balance and inner peace or coherence (Steiner, 1976).

To bridge the divide between theory and practice, I propose some ideas for holistic educational activities suitable for adolescents in the sections below, drawing heavily on the use of arts education and on a variety of literatures (e.g., cognitive science, feminist theory, holistic education, psychotherapy). More specifically, I group the classroom activities based on Miller's (1993) conception of holistic education as a series of connections or relationships among self (mind/body, cognition/emotion, rational/intuitive), community, and earth.

Developing a Curriculum for the Inner Self

Within educational programs, self-inquiry and forms of inquiry become intertwined, thus maintaining Dewey's (1902/1966) notion "that the child and curriculum are two simple limits which define a single process" (p. 11). Similar to various holistic curriculum models (e.g., Bruner, 1996; Drake, 1998; Miller, 1993), the individual person is at the source of the learning and is believed to participate in a cyclic journey of self-growth, where the recursive property of the curriculum provides opportunity to both self-reflect and to participate in the co-creation of the curriculum. Moreover, holistic approaches to address social and personal issues in the classroom also incorporate the holistic notion of emphasizing the importance of the attainment and application of personal knowledge by focusing on the learning process and what it means to each individual (e.g., Steiner, 1976). For example, the first session of a holistic, psychoeducational program for adolescents could ask the students to provide a personal definition of learning by outlining their goals and commitments that would assist them on their personal journey of learning. Such an activity encourages the student to take ownership and responsibility for her/his own learning. As Bruner (1996) suggests, we cannot force another person to learn; the motivation and appetite for learning must begin from within, although it may be "sparked" by outside sources.

The notion of developing a curriculum for the inner self could prove to be extremely valuable in holistic education for adolescents. Given that adolescence is considered to be time of both self-definition and self-differentiation, (e.g., Blos, 1979; Gilligan, 1982), holistic curriculum models that emphasize the importance of self-integration through the sharing of one's personal story seem particularly relevant (e.g., Drake, 1998; Steiner, 1976). Such models that focus on the creation of a personal curriculum provide an opportunity to self-reflect and analyze one's own thoughts and feelings which, in turn, may help preadolescents to construct self-knowledge and to alter or challenge their existing cognitive constructions of self and other.

The prerequisite for acquiring self-knowledge, however, is the ability and motivation to listen and reflect upon one's own voice. Unfortunately, the majority of traditional educational programs encourage children to listen to others, thereby neglecting their own voices from within. Reflecting on my traditional Canadian (southern Ontario, elementary and secondary school) experiences, I learned to listen and show compassion to others, but I was not taught how to listen and learn about myself. The educational system I experienced as a young adolescent in the early 1980s fostered the interpersonal skills used to nurture and be sensitive to others, regardless of whether or not I learned the intrapersonal skills of nurturing and being kind to myself. Thus, schools today need to provide adolescents with holistic, educational experiences that will help them to develop Gardner's (1985) notion of "personal intelligence" or the ability to understand both self and other as psychological beings.

Self-connections. In accordance with a growing number of holistic educators (e.g., Kessler, 2000; Miller, 2000), an arts-based, holistic program designed for preadolescents can be used to foster the development of a positive relationship between body and mind. Reflecting on my experiences with elementary grade-school students and graduate students at the university level, many of my most memorable classroom activities (irrespective of the academic content, whether it occurred in a fourth-grade science lesson or a graduate seminar on educational research) were related to the arts or humanities and would have particular relevance in an adolescent classroom. In particular, the use of narrative or storytelling, visual arts, dance, movement, drama, and journalling can be used as a vehicle to foster self-expression, aiming to develop a greater self-understanding in both a psychoclinical (non-school) and school setting.

For instance, adolescents could participate in role-playing activities that include a student who feels silenced or marginalized /ostracized from the classroom learning community. The reason for the marginalization can reflect particular themes relevant to the class at the time (e.g., social class, ethnicity, etc.) because the key is that the student believes and feels that he or she is marginalized. Once this role is established, students could be asked to play the role of the "ostracizers" or "silencers" and a scenario could be acted out to illustrate issues of power and control among various group members, I use this technique in my own class work with my graduate students, as I find the use of dramatic expression useful because it helps students to develop higher-order thinking skills, including the ability to see things from different perspective, build interpersonal skills, and promote a positive sense of self by providing an opportunity to become competent in the dramatic arena. In addition to drama, self-expression was promoted through the use of drawing self-portraits with particular emphasis on the body. Within a school context, the use of art could encourage preadolescents to explore different aspects of themselves, which in turn could help to discover their true or "big Self" (Miller, 1993).

Building on the notions of holistic curriculum theorists who advocate the use of narrative in education (e.g., Bruner, 1996; Lightfoot, 1997; Noddings, 1984, 2003; Steiner, 1976), the use of personal storytelling and self-narration (i.e., journal writing) can be a valuable vehicle to self-development in preadolescents. For instance, Susan Drake's Story Model (1992) represents a transdisciplinary approach that provides a framework that can be used to study a particular theme in its real-life context. Once a theme has been chosen by the students (e.g., silencing), the story model is used to co-create a new story by incorporating the students' and the teachers' personal, cultural and global story. Thus, conceived as a metanarrative or a story that provides a foundation for other stories used to help adolescents to examine past and current patterns in both their beliefs and behaviours, Drake's Story Model can help adolescents create a personal guide or inner curriculum to self acceptance and personal integration.

Self-connections can be further strengthened through group/classroom meditations, guided imagery exercises, and discussions on mindfulness or the ability to be aware in the present (Goleman, 1995; Miller, 1993). For example, to help children understand the powerful emotional effects that the process of ostracizing and marginalization or socially excluding another peer may have, students could be asked to engage in a guided imagery exercise. For example, educators could ask students to imagine a scenario where they are deliberately ignored or left out of a social group in which they would like to belong, and to ask them to become aware of what they are thinking and how they are feeling (emotionally and physically). This use of visualization/guided imagery could easily be adapted to other uses in the classroom where teacher-led visualizations could include themes of social class, ethnicity, and peer popularity.

In accordance with Steiner's (1976) educational goal of a mind, body, and spirit integration, such an exercise could help to develop adolescents' awareness of their thoughts, physical sensations, and emotions simultaneously. Thus, the use of visualization/guided imagery is an activity that promotes connections within all realms of the self, including body-mind, thought-emotion, and logic-intuition. Furthermore, through teaching relaxation techniques such as guided visual imagery, educators of preadolescents assist in the development of cognitive strategies that can be later used as a coping strategy to deal with real-life emotional stress. Such activities can provide preadolescents with a personal sense of mastery by presenting them with the opportunity to create rhythmic movement to music. Consequently, this sense of competence can promote the adolescent's ability to love and accept one's mind and body and thus may help to immunize both girls and boys against self-concept disorders where mind and body become (psychologically) separated. Similar to social ostracism, one can develop the beliefs and feelings of being ostracized from one's own body.

A holistic approach to a curriculum for adolescents needs to include activities that inspire girls and boys to both challenge and escape the tyranny of societal expectations that glorify linear, dichotomous thinking. Similar to approaches used in psychoeducational programs, educators of adolescents can provide activities that encourage their students to replace dualistic thinking with a more healthy, global, and holistic perspective that enables them to view things on a continuum. Given preadolescents' metacognitive abilities or the ability to think about thinking (Gardner, 1985), classroom discussions that encourage students to critically discuss dichotomous terms such as masculine/feminine, fat/thin, and good/bad can prove beneficial to students by assisting in their development of interpersonal and intrapersonal understanding. Thus, the integration of ideas from both cognitive psychology (metacognitive, critical reflection activities) and holistic curriculum models (mindfulness, guided imagery) can contribute to a holistic education that is appropriate for adolescents.

Community connections. Adapting the ecological perspective towards the self and education can further strengthen self-connections. Building on the principles of eco-spiritualism (Caine, 2003), perhaps educators of youth can encourage adolescents to direct their thoughts, feelings, and actions towards the big picture or the web of life (Capra, 1996). According to various writers who explore the ecological factors in human growth (e.g., Cajete, 1994), eco-spirituality subsumes any conception of a higher power of creation within all living beings such as plants, animals, humans, earth, rocks, water, etc. Eco-spirituality celebrates our connection with nature, not apart from nature, and asks us to embrace a connection with all other species. Cremin's (1976) ecological approach to education and Rozak's (1992) concept of ecological self, a perspective that emphasizes humans as part of nature and our communality with all living things, would enable preadolescents to develop a positive relationship with their minds and their bodies. Within this framework, adolescents can be motivated to examine their connections to society and how various sociocultural factors influence their thoughts, emotions, and behaviours.

Concerning adolescents, a classroom activity aimed at exploring the paradoxical messages found in the media regarding stereotypical body images and the portrayal of woman and men would promote the use of both cognitive and affective abilities. For instance, girls and boys could be asked to critically analyze and deconstruct various magazine advertisements or television commercials that perpetuate both gender-role stereotypes, and appear to "silence" particular social and ethnic groups (i.e., people of colour, various body types, etc.) and contemporary, feminist values (i.e., all women must have a university education; caring, sensitive stay-at-home father). Hence, a holistic approach to this activity would not only ask the adolescents to define conflicting media messages and hypothesize why they exist but also how such an experience makes them feel.

Earth connections. From a broader perspective, an emphasis on a "world core curriculum" (Muller, 1984) and corresponding universal themes such as respect for the earth and caring for nature, can encourage preadolescents to see "the big picture," and at the same time, to feel a sense of connectedness or part of the global family. Holistic curriculum models such as Waldorf Education emphasize the connection between the individual and the earth by focusing on environmental issues. More specifically, various activities used in Waldorf Education such as physical activities with the environment (i.e., gardening and cooking with organic foods) can promote adolescents to see themselves within the larger framework of the ecosystem and nature. As Caine (2003) suggests, eco-spiritual education encourages educators to extend curricula beyond the classroom to integrate nature within natural settings. For example, adolescents can be introduced and asked to critically discuss the ethics and practices of veganism, which suggests that one should lead a lifestyle that avoids animal and nature exploitation.

In a similar vein, building on Miller's suggestion (1993), the integration of Indigenous People's literature such as the Indigenous concept of the medicine wheel (e.g., Shilling, 1986) could provide the basis for various discussions on other cultural stories (Drake, 1998). Exposure to such stories can assist preadolescent learners in creating and adapting their own personal stories by recognizing the numerous global stories that exist around the world. For example, during a group discussion on North America's obsession with aesthetic perfection, preadolescents can be questioned why emotional and anxiety disorders are rarely found in underdeveloped or Third World countries. This question can act as a catalyst for a lively discussion on why civilized, advanced societies choose the perfection of physical appearance, including thinness, as a symbol of personal success and social status whereas in Third World countries extreme thinness usually represents personal failure and poverty (e.g., Chernin, 1985).

Discussions involving different cultural perspectives can provide students with the opportunity to broaden their own worldviews and realize that various psychological disorders are largely a sociocultural phenomenon (e.g., Silverstein & Perlick, 1995). In general, the development of a more holistic and caring attitude towards other cultures and environmental issues may help to de-emphasize the egocentrism that occurs during adolescence (e.g., Gilligan, 1982). Consequently, as adolescents learn to develop a more holistic perspective towards their own connection to the world, they may learn to view themselves and others from a more inclusive and accepting lens.

Classroom Strategies for Fostering Silence Sensibilities

The theories and research findings reviewed in the previous chapters have implications for those who work with adolescents within an educational context. Once educators become aware of their own assumptions and experiences concerning silences, they may also become actively engaged in developing educational activities for youth that will aim to promote both affective and cognitive goals in the aim of developing a healthy mind and heart. Given that the majority of children and adolescents spend much of their mental energy engaged in social cognition (or thinking about people, including themselves, and society), in addition to the holistic education strategies, outlined below are some suggestions for fostering greater understanding of self and others. Furthermore, given that adolescents need to develop the capacity to respond both intellectually and emotionally, I offer some suggestions that may help to develop the adolescents' "silence sensibilities." It is my hope that such activities may encourage adolescents to engage in critical enquiry and dialogue concerning classroom silences that may involve complex and sensitive issues such as morality and spirituality/religiosity.

Self and Social Understandings

To further promote the development of self-knowledge and the awareness of mental states in both self and others, educators can engage in the following strategies:

- Encourage discussion (promote both dialogue and inquiry) about psychological and philosophical phenomena and other people's perspectives in age-appropriate ways.
- Regularly include references to mental states (thoughts, feelings) in daily conversations with children and youth.
- Provide opportunities for adolescents to encounter multiple, and often equally legitimate, perspectives and ask adolescents to share their perspectives with one another and to consider the perspectives of people they don't know.
- Pay special attention to adolescents with exceptional cognitive and social-emotional needs.
- Provide opportunities for "play" or unstructured activities where the teacher would not be present or not be formally evaluating anything, such as an artist's corner in the corner of the classroom where one could find all the art materials needed.
- Provide a drama group or classroom space where costumes and scripts can be created and/or developed.
- Provide opportunities for healthy competition, such as developing a team or group approach to the completion of some tasks, where the entire group is rewarded for the efforts of all group members.

Although these activities do not address particular group members who wish to be silent, they may provide some comfort for those who do not wish to speak in the front of the class. For example, they may find an alternative action to speaking in order to participate and contribute to the group and thus feel included.

Societal and Cultural Understandings

Adolescents' abilities to navigate effectively in their social world depend not only on their understanding of themselves and others but also on their understanding of society. Below are some suggestions to foster young people's conceptions of social institutions and social groups:

- Invite adolescents to participate in the world of work, commerce, and government.
- Invite society's institutions into the classroom (e.g., invite guest speakers from social service professions including health care practitioners, law enforcers, etc.).
- Critically examine society's inequities concerning "status variables" such as gender, ethnicity, and social class.
- Provide opportunities and support that enable children and adolescents to make a difference in their community.
- Combat prejudice by working to break down stereotypes by encouraging children to look for the individual differences that exist within groups of people. Encourage children to see people as human beings and individuals with their own unique strengths and weaknesses, rather than as members of particular groups.
- Encourage the critical consumption and review of how popular media portrays other countries by a class discussion using current newspaper articles, videotape news programs from around the globe, and watch as a class and compare/contrast the different newscasters and the delivery of the news (e.g., what are the similarities, among CNN, BBC, and CBC? Do they differ according to how they addressed the stories, guests, etc.?).

Moral Understandings

Children's and adolescents' understanding of self, others, and society support their developing ability to consider others' rights and needs—that is, their growing sense of morality or the general set of standards about right and wrong including such traits as honesty, compassion, and respect for other people's rights and needs (Nucci, 2001). According to Noddings (2003), happiness is connected to moral goodness, but exactly how do adolescents learn this "moral goodness?" How do schools and educators/youth workers promote this aspect of humanity in adolescents without overaccentuating the notion of being too perfect, or overvirtuous? As Noddings claims, one of the most challenging tasks of education is to encourage students to tolerate ambiguity so that it will not paralyze them or prevent them from making social commitments. As educational programs, particularly those that claim to involve "character education," aim to help our children and youth become and remain "happy," how can such programs also fulfill the government mandates to promote academic excellence and superior performance across standardized tests? Such an issue is relevant to both Canadian and American schools, as educators and youth workers both struggle to answer the question of how to encourage adolescents to be "caring scholars." That is, how can current educational programs and educators promote both academic excellence and intellectual virtue together with virtues such as courage, persistence, honesty, and kindness?

Given that children's and adolescents' beliefs about moral and immoral behaviour affect their actions at home, at school, and in the community at large, below are some suggestions to foster young people's understandings of morality.

- Clarify which behaviours are acceptable and which are not, and help adolescents understand the reasons for various regulations and prohibitions.
- Expose adolescents to numerous models of moral behavior through modeling appropriate moral and prosocial behaviour.
- Encourage critical dialogue and inquiry surrounding moral issues and dilemmas through group discussion and viewing of popular media (newspapers, TV news shows, etc.).
- Challenge adolescent's moral reasoning with slightly more advanced reasoning and expose them to diverse views about moral issues.
- Remind adolescents that standards for what is moral and immoral differ from one culture to another.
- Encourage adolescents to understand the perspectives and justifications of individuals who choose to follow a moral, virtuous life, and to understand the perspectives of those who did *not* choose this lifestyle. For example, adolescents should be encouraged to question why some people who are educated and deemed intelligent choose to perform acts of violence and hatred. Although such exercises may be unpleasant, adolescents need to be encouraged to try to imagine the perspectives of all kinds of individuals— those who wish to follow their moral responses and those who do not, setting out to deliberately hurt others.

In sum, morality is never simple, and complex issues require complex dialogue. Many developmentalists and care theorists agree that children and adolescents need to develop the ability to recognize the complexity and ambiguity of issues such as moral dilemmas. During adolescence, issues involving friendship and peer relations may help youth to understand the perspectives of others and such dilemmas could provide guided questions to encourage one to think about decision making. For example, issues surrounding the concept of loyalty could be used to illustrate how individuals need to think through moral issues and reflect upon their own thoughts and feelings in addition to those of others.

Spiritual and/or Religious Understandings

As the dialogue between science and religion continues to escalate, social science researchers and educators have become increasingly interested in the role that the school plays in the development of children's understanding of spirituality and religion. According to Sri Swami Satchidananda, "the purpose of any religion is to educate us about our spiritual unity and to help us achieve inner peace" (cited in Matousek, 1998, p. 48). Similarly, if one defines spirituality as the ability to wonder about and to celebrate the mystery of life, and the need to feel connected to something larger than ourselves, one would assume that schools would aim to promote this spiritual aspect of development. Recent debates on the topic of religion and education claim that schools in both North America and Britain are failing to provide sufficient nourishment for the growth of a child's soul or spiritual sense of self (e.g., Sweet, 1997; McLaughlin, O'Keefe, & O'Keefe, 1996).

For instance, in *God in the Classroom: The Controversial Issue of Religion in Canada's Schools*, author/journalist Sweet (1997) examines the role that Canadian schools play in the development of what she refers to as "religious literacy." Sweet traveled across Canada and interviewed various teachers, parents, and children about the issue of religion and spirituality in the contemporary Canadian classroom. Sweet aims to provide the diverse Canadian population an opportunity to voice their opinions on issues of religion and education. Unlike Sweet, who attempts to cover the vast majority of religions found in Canada, McLaughlin, O'Keefe, and O'Keefe (1996) compiled a comprehensive collection of essays by both British and American educators that explored various aspects of identity and diversity in *The Contemporary Catholic School*. Both McLaughlin et al. and Sweet suggest that schools in today's society need a language to express spirituality other than traditional, organized religious language. Such literature illuminates the importance of language in the development of a curriculum that will promote the spiritual aspect of development in children.

Sweet (1997) maintains that Canadians should neither ignore religious differences in public schools nor heighten them by segregating children in religiously based schools. In Sweet's overview of how Canadian schools treated religion in the past, she distinguishes between religious education and education about religion. Sweet refers to the former as indoctrination and the latter as illumination. However, Sweet does not discuss the differences between the terms spirituality and religion, using the terms interchangeably (e.g., "religion or the spiritual quest," p. 6). In line with Sweet (1997), among others, schools need to promote religious literacy. Future researchers will need to discuss the term "religious literacy" in more depth, particularly among multicultural school contexts.

Although Sweet (1997) attempts to address multiculturalism by incorporating the various religious beliefs held by Canadians, she (like many writers, as I mentioned in Chapter 2) focuses on the Christian versus non-Christian debate. Aside from addressing the rich tapestry of various religious faiths, educators also need to further the discussion concerning Catholic schools, given that it remains a controversy, particularly in Canada. For example, differences *within* the Catholic system are rarely addressed, such as the distinction between Roman and Ukrainian Catholics. For example, within the Canadian school system, given the relatively large number of Ukrainian-Canadians, differences among the learning and teaching experiences and the curriculum remain to be explored. The creation of a developmentally appropriate curriculum that is sensitive to the diverse ethnicities and faiths of the learners and teachers will remain a challenge for future educators and researchers.

Although many writers and educators may raise awareness in parents and educators concerning spirituality and education, solid, practical answers remain to be seen. For example, in contrast to global statements such as "Dialogue is essential if we are to create an education system capable of fostering religious literacy in our children" (Sweet, 1997, p. 251), modern schools require policies that foster a healthy pluralism in a complex society. Educators and social science researchers need solid curricular recommendations founded in robust empirical evidence if schools are to attain Sweet's (1997) hope that one day, "it will be possible for all of our children—Buddhists, Muslims, Sikhs, Hindus, Christians, Jews, secular humanists, and so on—to play together in the school yard and to study together in the classroom, without fear of either religious compromise or religious harassment" (pp. 252–253).

McLaughlin et al. (1996) outline the differences and similarities between British and American Catholic schools. For example, the authors explore the question of what it means to be a Catholic student in Britain as opposed to the United States. Similar to Canada, in the U.K., Catholic schools are increasingly concerned with a diverse population. In the U.S., compared to state schools, Catholic schools have a more positive effect upon the achievement of pupils. According to McLaughlin et al. (1996), Catholic schools appear to offer an alternative, more humanistic vision of schooling. In general, one can glean from the two chapters that both nations are interested in the wider contribution they could make to education for a pluralist society and the debate of the nature and justifiability of separate religious schools.

Future curriculum needs to examine issues of diversity and future educational implications for addressing spirituality in the classroom. As I was writing this book, I envisioned a future volume that would include a larger number of countries—not only Canada but also countries from all over the world, such as Eastern Europe, the Orient, and the Middle East. Future work in adolescent development and education should aim to include the maximum number of voices from around the globe, to ensure that everyone has the opportunity to share spiritual/educational experiences. Many holistic researchers purport that, as industrialized countries become more diverse and pluralistic, there is a need for a coherent educational policy regarding religion and spirituality in the classroom. To promote "meaningful and inclusive" pluralism, such a policy needs to include the partnerships of various people in the community—educators, parents, social science researchers, and so forth. Educational guidelines need not only to focus on children's intellectual competencies but also to foster critical thinking and reflective skills that enable children to search for "the truth" as opposed to "the answer."

As I discussed in Chapter 2, Myers (1997), among others (e.g., Miller, 2000; Goldstein, 1997), suggests future research should focus on spirituality within the school system. Although many holistic educators and developmentalists stress the importance of language in educating children about spirituality, we must continue to draw on literature from psychology and education that discusses the role narrative plays in education. As Kessler (2000) suggests, we need to draw on the vast amount of literature to hone our abilities to use narrative as a vehicle to explore possibilities of teaching and learning (Bruner, 1986). The main point of language has an inescapable moral dimension and thus provides organization to our moral sense (Postman, 1995).

Regarding the link between psychology and education, there are few examples of psychological research that explore issues of adolescents' language, religiosity, and spirituality within an educational context. A comprehensive discussion of spirituality in education needs to include examples of psychological research from areas such as epistemology, self-concept, morality, identity formation, and social understanding. For instance, we need to draw on works of researchers and educators such as Robert Coles (1990) and his book on the spirituality of children or other numerous works that explore links between holistic education and children's spiritual, emotional, and moral development in the classroom (e.g., Donaldson, 1992; Miller, 1993, 2000).

In addition to the scarcity of psychological research, there is a lack of critical discussion amongst the literature concerning the issue of gender in the classroom—especially surrounding the notion of adolescents' self-concept and the link to religion, language, and education. Aside from James Day's chapter on moral education, which suggests that future research needs to look at issues of self-esteem and depression in Catholic females (McLaughlin et al., 1996), current research needs to investigate gender issues in relation to spirituality and education, particularly why so many people continue to remain silent about such topics. Future work on spirituality in schools needs to focus more thoroughly on issues of gender, power, and identity within the context of various cultures (for further discussion on gender, spirituality, and knowledge, see Goldberger, Tarule, Clinchy, & Belenky, 1996).

Future work on spirituality in education also needs to include an elaborate discussion of the influence of technology and the media on children's development. Given the increasingly important role technology and pop culture play in the majority of children's lives, future research needs to explore these issues. For example, Postman (1999) warns that technology and pop culture might have a detrimental affect on the spiritual and moral development of children. Furthermore, it is imperative that educators and parents of youth remain up-to-date on the current status of the notion of spirituality within the context of pop culture. For example, in a recent issue of *Teen People* magazine, an article entitled "Choosing My Religion" outlines interviews with five American teenagers on what spirituality means to them (Adato, 1998/1999). With definitions of spirituality ranging from an unquestioning belief in God's word (17-year-old Orthodox Jew) to one's own personal set of beliefs (19-year-old agnostic), educators and parents need to be aware of how such media messages can influence the development of children's spirituality and religious beliefs.

In sum, many writers promote the notion that schools must realize that spirituality and religion are not synonymous. Educators and policymakers need a language other than that of traditional religious language to foster spirituality in adolescents. The two terms may be related, but not equated. For instance, an educational program designed to teach students *about* different religions in other cultures may help to promote spirituality in children, but it does not ensure that children will experience a feeling of self-understanding and/or a connectedness with others. Thus, as researchers continue to explore issues of spirituality and religiosity (e.g., McLaughlin et al., 1996; Sweet, 1997), they provide a starting point that educators and researchers can use to develop educational programs that foster the development of self-acceptance, and emotional and spiritual meaning. As other holistic educators have noted (e.g., Miller, 2000), schools must endorse holistic programs that focus on the development of the whole child and the interconnectedness among mind, body, and soul.

As with all aspects of development, adolescents' spiritual and philosophical convictions evolve over time, including such topics as religion, spirituality, and the meaning of life (Haynes, 2002). Interestingly, personal, social, and moral education often do not include ways to include broader issues of understanding such as the understanding of the spiritual, religious, or magical. Although there are some cognitive developmentalists who are beginning to explore the understanding of the metaphysical (e.g., Harris, 2000), few psychoeducational programs address issues of religiosity and spirituality. Bruner (1996) recommends that schools are valuable because they help to nurture the "reasonable person," which includes more than rationality. According to Bruner, for schools to nurture the "reasonable person," schools need to adopt philosophical enquiry and promote dialogue, listening, enquiry, and play across the curriculum.

Although matters of church and state are required to be kept separate, public school teachers can discuss religious and spirituality within the context of curricula about history, culture, or other appropriate academic topics. Religious understandings and understandings about the spiritual and the unknown can provide an important source of diversity among children and families. The contemplation of meaning and self-identity (including the philosophical enquiry and dialogue) can also provide a sense of connection, trust, and belonging with others, aspects of nature, and oneself (Gollnick & Chinn, 2002). To help adolescents develop and maintain such connections, schools need to encourage adolescents to develop a spiritual vocabulary, which in turn may help adolescents to build a repertoire of spiritual activities. Such activities will encourage children to be aware and present in the now (not past or future). This notion of "mindfulness" may encourage adolescents to be appreciative of their current surroundings, including their own physical selves. As many educators and researchers suggest (Haynes, 2002), such experiences can be both individual and personal or social or common. For example, to promote the virtues of caring and responsibility, group activities could be planned to promote the caretaking of nature (gardening, animal caretaking) and followed by personal reflection time (providing children with opportunities to express their private thoughts and feelings regarding such activities such as journal writing, sculpture, painting, etc.).

As many writers on spiritual aspects of education discuss, given that spiritual experiences can be considered both intensely social and personal, opportunities to reflect upon such experiences are critical in that all individuals will respond differently to each activity. For example, two adolescents may participate in a tree-planting ceremony although each child will experience the event differently and each will have his or her own need to express his or her thoughts and feelings about the activity. Some children may wish to write about the tree planting in their journal, whereas some may prefer to paint or draw a picture. The common element to such activities is that they all include time and silence, or a lack of verbal expression and a focus on "listening," as silence may encourage some children to listen to themselves and their own thoughts and emotions. The inclusion of music may also become an important aspect of these activities, as music has been referred to as the "language of emotions" (Goldberg, 1997). To enhance the student's personal development, Reid (1995) encourages the integration of music with other subjects. For example, students can listen to music and then write or draw in their reflective journals.

The founder of Waldorf education, Rudolf Steiner, claimed that art is essential to self-development and thus must be an integral part of the entire curriculum (Richards, 1980). Educators of adolescents, therefore, need to create curriculum aimed to foster the development of adolescents' capacity to observe, distinguish, and reflect upon vital forces in nature and in themselves (Miller, 2000). Thus, the inclusion of art in the curriculum can provide various ways to encourage learners to become completely engaged with "what-is-there" (Buber, 1970, as cited in Noddings, 2003, p. 169).

Overall, Waldorf education is a comprehensive example of how the arts can be integrated into the school program. As Miller (2000) suggests, educational programs can learn from the Waldorf schools and adapt some of the Steiner approaches to any classroom. Given that the development of enquiry and dialogue surrounding issues of the unknown and metaphysical can provide a positive guiding force in some adolescents' lives, outlined below are some ways to promote religious and spiritual development within the classroom:

- Develop awareness of religious diversity in your community.
- Integrate the arts into all aspects of the curriculum (e.g., dance, music, painting, etc.).
- Foster a climate of religious tolerance; many school districts and other government institutions have policies that prohibit any name-calling that denigrates others' religious beliefs, practices, and affiliations.
- Cultivate productive communication with families about controversial issues.
- Develop a more in-depth appreciation for, and create stronger connections with, nature through the use of gardening, preparing meals and sharing food, caring for animals, etc.

Culture and Cognition in the Classroom: Educational Programs

What does the "connected and caring classroom" mean in today's multiethnic, multilingual, and increasingly technologically advanced world (Noddings, 2003)? A psychologically safe and sacred place is necessary for children and adolescents to explore and learn. They cannot be "afraid" to be silent and/or to articulate their questions. Research shows (e.g., Harter, 1999) negative affect, including negative self-beliefs, may have a deleterious effect on learning. Also, as Lopez (2003) asks, for those youth who are considered to be "mixed" racially or ethnically and to identify as such in North American society, their self-identity is different today as compared to other times in history. For example, take my own heritage: my Canadian-born father is from a Polish background (second generation) and my Ukrainian mother, although a Canadian citizen, was born in Germany. Although both of my parents can minimally speak their ancestral language, my parents decided to raise my sister and me as Canadian. That is, we attended Canadian schools and were not taught Ukrainian or Polish. Thus, as an adult, both my Ukrainian and Polish voices have been "silenced" to a certain extent, to achieve the goals of my multiethnic parents who wished to raise "Canadian daughters."

Within the complex web involving language, identity, cognition, and emotion, I often wonder to what extent some of my emotions and cognitions have been silenced, given the absence of my parents' original languages. Regarding North American youth today, what are the academic, social, moral, and spiritual implications of integrating individuals' self-stories with the larger cultural stories? As Lopez (2003) points out, the identity of mixed-heritage youth has changed from previous times when it was considered to be an entirely marginalizing experience, or one in which people who live "in-between" are psychologically tormented (Nakashima, 1992). In contrast, contemporary researchers suggest that today's youth of mixed heritage often possess a particular "cultural competence" and "successful intelligence" in that they express pride in being unique, illustrate social competence, and have the ability to appreciate multiple perspectives (e.g., Lopez, 2003; Sternberg, 2003). However, despite the advantages of identifying with multiple racial-ethnic identities, some researchers suggest that the power of psychological harassment, including derogatory comments regarding ethnicity or race, may have a greater negative impact on an adolescent's emotional life compared to more physical acts of harassment (Crick et al., 2001).

As educators, we need to explore the emotional worlds of mixed-heritage youth in that we need to question how their experiences of silences differ from youth raised in uni-ethnic and/or uni-linguistic homes. The increasing prevalence and asserted presence of mixed-race youth demands a critical examination of our ways of talking about and studying race and ethnicity in schools. Educational and research programs need to allow for fluidity and multiplicity regarding racial-ethnic identification. For example, within the educational context, universal standards for human rights need to be promoted. Notions of respect and compassion for oneself and others are necessary to provide an authentic, safe, learning environment for children and adolescents of all ages.

The promotion of "the golden rule" (e.g., "treat others the way you wish to be treated") is necessary to promote genuine dialogue and enquiry among the students.

Given that culture can be situated as something we need to understand about others (Lee, 2003), educators need to embrace a more dynamic view of culture and cognition as located in history, in belief systems, and as carried through institutional practices (Flanagan, 2002). Many scholars agree that culture is never static, and that the belief systems and practices associated with cultural groups are always under negotiation with new generations and social conditions. As Gutierrez and Rogoff (2003) suggest, educators and researchers should strive to create "repertoires of practice" that maintain that individuals develop and communities change.

A culture or climate of mutual respect, caring, and sensitivity is one that helps to promote prosocial attitudes and behaviours, including acceptance of and respect for differences. The tacit and explicit social norms and rules that govern sociolinguistic behaviours in the school setting help to define what are acceptable and unacceptable treatments of individuals. Such a respectful and caring atmosphere invites dialogue and may encourage some adolescents who are normally more reticent to break their silence and to contribute to the conversation.

Given that school life affects all aspects of human development, and given that our world is becoming increasingly global and diverse, children are more likely to meet and interact with others whose race, ethnicity, and family backgrounds differ from their own (Haynes & Marans, 1999). In addition to race and ethnicity, other differences such as gender, social class, physical characteristics, and sexual orientations may serve as focal points for conflict and intolerance among adolescents. As many researchers have noted (e.g., Bruner, 1996; McKeough, 1992), there is a need for the creation and implementation of developmentally appropriate curricula that promote tolerance and respect for difference among adolescents in schools in this increasingly multiethnic and democratic society.

The school culture or climate also represents the nature of the interpersonal relationships (student-student, student-teacher, teacher-teacher/parent) that exist in the school and how involved parents are in the daily activities and decision-making processes in the school. The emotional or psychological tone that is set in the school establishes expectations for standards of interpersonal relationships among the students both within and beyond school walls. That is, to promote a larger culture of authentic understanding and empathy, the classroom and school need to reflect the larger community (and vice versa). Furthermore, educators and researchers must learn to address emerging tensions between ethnic and school or academic identities in educational practice (Nasir & Saxe, 2003).

To address the need to promote acceptance and respect for self and others, various holistic educational programs have been created to help promote children's and adolescents' learning, and to transcend status variables such as ethnicity and social class. For example, Haynes and Marans (1999) developed a holistic, educational program that follows a cognitive, emotional, and behavioral framework. Their program draws on psychocultural principles of development and promotes tolerance for differences by understanding the developmental contributions to attitudes towards diversity by examining the cognitive, emotional, and behavioral ways in which these attitudes are expressed. The cognitive component refers to knowledge, expectations, and beliefs about others; the emotional component refers to children's affective reactions; and the behavioral component includes the observable actions towards others who are different.

Similarly, Comer's program of school reform emphasizes the crucial role school culture plays in the promotion of holistic approaches to development and education (Comer, Haynes, Joyner, & Ben-Avie, 1996). Involving over 700 schools in the United States, the Comer School Development Program aims to help schools provide supportive, organized, caring, peaceful, and respectful environments that teach children empathy and respect for differences. Furthermore, to provide young people with guidance and skills that may prevent them from making potentially harmful decisions that could hurt themselves and others, the Resolving Conflict Creatively Program (RCCP) demonstrates strategies for incorporating a comprehensive and systematic approach to integrating social and emotional learning through the lens of conflict resolution and interpersonal relations.

In particular, the program aims to foster resiliency and promote the development of caring and sensitive, socially responsible young adults (Lantieri, 2001). For example, to promote RCCP's models of "peaceable schools," it is essential to include a curriculum component that focuses on key skills such as active listening and assertiveness, professional development and administrator training, peer mediation, and parent training. Furthermore, given that peace is regarded as a dynamic process in which everyone works towards and believes in, peaceable schools need to include the promotion and practice of cooperation, caring communication, expression of emotions, appreciation of diversity, responsible decision making, and conflict resolution (Feuerverger, 2001).

In addition, one of the most widely accepted notions of peace education reform in North America is the school conflict educational strategy of peer mediation training. Such a program encourages students to manage conflicts constructively using negotiation procedure and peacemaking skills. The Community Board Program and Anti-Violence Program in the United States are examples of how students can take responsibility for changing the level of violence within the landscape of racial and ethnic diversity in their schools and communities (e.g., Mathews, 1994, cited in Feuerverger, 2001, p. 87). Key features of these programs include the development of models that promote conflict mediation, nonviolent leadership, and respect for differences.

Consistent with these North American models of peace programs, additional educational programs from other countries aim to promote peace. Some programs include recent grassroots educational innovation in that attempt to turn around the destructive patterns of intergroup conflict and war resulting from the ongoing struggle between Jews and Arabs in Israel and the Middle East. Informal and formal sociolinguistic projects encourage Jewish-Arab coexistence in a growing number of Palestinian and Jewish schools in some parts of the country.

More specifically, Grace Feuerverger's book (2001), *Oasis of Dreams* describes the Neve Shalom/Wahat Al-Salam School, a bilingual/bicultural/binational elementary village school developed in 1984, and officially recognized in 1997 by the government as an experimental school. She also discusses an educational program entitled "School for Peace," which has been operating since 1979 within a cultural context of war and conflict. As Feuerverger suggests, both the elementary school and the specific educational program exemplify an authentic attempt at partnership between two peoples whose cultures are in conflict.

Given that schools need to be viewed in their historical, societal, and relational contexts, effective schools should be sites of linguistic, political, and cultural negotiation that encourage teachers to situate and scrutinize the borders of their own ideological discourses. As Feuerverger (2001) suggests, before we develop peaceful schools and programs to promote peace over conflict, we must first listen to the voices of those who are experiencing the conflict. The underlying message of the elementary school and the School for Peace program is the overriding importance of maintaining personal, social, and national identity for both Arabs and Jews within an egalitarian perspective. Both the village school and the educational program attempt to deconstruct the traditional school discourses in Israel that, according to Feuerverger, perpetuate the dominant/subordinate status of Hebrew and Arabic, respectively, within the curriculum. The village school provides the possibility for Arab and Jewish educators to learn together on a daily basis in a full Hebrew-Arabic bilingual, bicultural, binational setting. Coordinated by a teaching team of Jewish and Arab educators to promote inclusiveness and mutual understanding in formal and informal school activities, both languages are utilized. Overall, the program aims to provide a psychologically safe environment to encourage those who feel silenced to feel connected and invited to participate in the conversation.

The School for Peace conflict resolution program is geared towards bringing Palestinian and Jewish adolescents from all over Israel and the West Bank together for workshops conducted by well-trained facilitators in the village. The model of the program was co-developed with members of the psychology department at Tel Aviv University and is derived from seminal work on intergroup conflict and cooperation; group-dynamics theory; models of small-group interaction; motivation/cognitive processes and their influences of intergroup attitudes; stereotyping and the formation of prejudice; and majority/minority group experience of "otherness" within the dynamics of conflict resolution. The program focuses on emotional and cognitive processing of the different aspects of conflict and their influence on each of the participants.

The structure of the School for Peace workshops is guided by principles of equality and the three-day workshops are all conducted in both Hebrew and Arabic. As conflict resolution and peacemaking are inextricably intertwined, peacemaking is the process towards conflict resolution (Feuerverger, 1995). To help the adolescents who find that they may deal with the complex, self-conscious emotions such as shame and fear, the facilitators aim to provide ways to process and understand these feelings during the program, and to help them thus to cope in more healthy, constructive ways with the Jewish-Palestinian conflict.

Irrespective of educational programs, to encourage adolescents to express their voices, schools should provide a learning culture or climate that promotes a sense of mutual respect, connection and caring, compassion, and inclusion. The climate in schools must reflect the collective values and standards of the interpersonal relationships and interactions that prevail. The climate is a measure of the essential nature of how individuals are regarded and treated. It is an imperative that educators and psychologists help students develop a set of values and standards that would eliminate insensitive and intolerant behaviour in the classroom and beyond. Thus, a climate of mutual respect and regard for all, regardless of group and individual differences, is crucial to developing Bruner's (1996) notion of "reasonable people" and promotes the idea of good work (Gardner, Csikszentmihalyi, & Damon, 2001). Such programs may help children to develop into competent and caring adults who are experts in their chosen careers and also socially responsible. As the 21st century becomes more complex and technologically advanced, educators and researchers need to take the time to be critical of the programs and examine the gaps and silences to promote the ideal connection between ethics and excellence and culture and cognition.

Similar to school programs that promote cultural competence, there are relatively recent advances made in the area of "youth development" that create programs within the area of sports and leisure (Bloom, 2000; Danish, Taylor,

& Fazio, 2003; Smith & Smoll, 1996). Such programs are designed to help adolescents learn both sport and life skills, and are built on the assumption that teaching life skills (e.g., leadership, problem solving, goal setting, emotion regulation, coping abilities, time and stress management, collaboration, etc.) is similar to teaching any new skill. The basic process remains the same: name it, describe it, provide a rational for its use, demonstrate both correct and incorrect uses of the skill, and provide opportunities for supervised practice of the skill with continuous feedback.

Such programs are also based on the assumption that participation in sports can be a significant factor in the development of an adolescent's identity, self-esteem, and competence. Also, because sports are important to youth, it is an environment where they spend time of their own accord. That is, most adolescents willingly participate in at least some level of athletic or physical activity. An example of an integrated sports and life skills program includes the SUPER program (Sports United to Promote Education and Recreation) (Danish, Taylor, & Fazio, 2003). As an overview, the SUPER program is a series of sports-based life skills that are taught within sports clinics and form the basis of a program. For example, sessions involve three sets of activities: learning the physical skills (e.g., golf), learning life skills related to sports in general and how these skills are applicable outside of sports, and playing the sport. Some of the life skills taught include how to dream, turning dreams into reachable goals, developing plans to reach the goals, overcoming goal roadblocks, developing social support, emotional management, and learning positive self-talk.

In addition to life skills, adolescents are also taught research skills such as observational techniques. More specifically, adolescents are taught to use the Sport Observation System (SOS), which involves the careful observation of the participatory process, as opposed to how well they perform. This observational technique helps adolescents to develop the higher-order cognitive skills, including critical evaluative observation and recording techniques, that can easily be applied to real-world situations. Although the life skills program described above has been taught to adolescents who live in their country's dominant culture, the SUPER program has also been adapted by indigenous populations. For example, the Hokowhitu Program (Heke, 2001) is a life skills, sports-based drug and alcohol program designed by, and developed for, the Maori, an indigenous population in New Zealand.

Clinical and Therapeutic Implications: Ethical Concerns and Cautions

To address the culture of classroom silence, both the adult and the adolescent must take the risk to explore their inner worlds, and reflect upon who they are as human beings. For some individuals, such reflection and introspection may be associated with negative emotions. Accordingly, adults who work with youth on issues of classroom silence, including therapists, researchers, and educators, need to take the time to develop a trusting and respectful relationship.

Similar to the high school classroom, the educational therapist aims to work with the adolescent in a respectful, open and curious atmosphere (Griffith & Griffith, 1994). Given that both therapists and educators need to develop an authentic relationship with the adolescent, once trust has been established, such an accepting atmosphere can help to eliminate negative emotion in therapists and adolescents. Regarding the school context, issues involving classroom silence are likely to be emotional and sensitive, educators and researchers need to take heed when exploring such issues with adolescents. Similar to researchers, therapists and clinicians must also be aware of ethical issues when working with adolescents on issues such as confidentiality and the risk of psychological and emotional harm. The psychological and emotional safety of the adolescent must be ensured at all times.

Given that both therapeutic and educational dialogues involve self-growth and development (Freedman & Combs, 1996; Jack, 1991), a psychocultural educational approach can be applied to clinical, therapeutic, and educational settings. A psychocultural approach to learning and development suggests that both therapy and education involve the cognitive and emotional contributions of the adult educator/therapist and the adolescent learner/client, in that knowledge is co-constructed through dialogue and enquiry (Gergen & Walhrus, 2001). Accordingly, when working with adolescents regarding issues of silences, one can never be sure if the adolescent views the dialogue as either educational, therapeutic, or both. Given this ambiguous theoretical divide between therapy and education, adults who work with adolescents in the area of silences and self-concept must be extremely wary of ethical issues that may develop.

For example, activities that involve self-disclosure such as bibliotherapy may be both educational and therapeutic. Similar to narrative therapy, the educational activity of bibliotherapy can be applied to both a classroom and a therapist's office. Although a high school teacher may have specific curriculum objectives to achieve, both the educator and therapist aim to promote the development of a healthy self-concept in the adolescent. That is, both the educator and therapist require the adolescent to engage in a conversation about silences and the self. Such learning activities (irrespective of whether or not implemented within the therapeutic or educational context) involve extreme care regarding the therapist (and educator, researcher).

As educators and researchers concerned with the promotion of a healthy overall psychological and emotional state in adolescents, we need to focus on programs and activities that promote not just positive self-thoughts but useful techniques that can be taught that may help girls and boys to cope with class-room silences in a healthy and constructive manner. Borrowing strategies from spiritual and clinical psychotherapy, activities that promote self-comfort and self-acceptance—such as relaxation techniques, visualization, art therapy, play therapy, and psychodrama—may help adolescents to explore their inner worlds.

Furthermore, the use of metaphor may be useful in therapeutic settings in that it may help promote the access of an unconscious sensory system within the adolescent. During therapy, narratives are offered that present examples of ex-periences that are parallel to, but not identical with, those experiences that are problematic for the client. Metaphor may also be useful in that it may help the child or adolescent to conceptualize an abstract concept in a concrete manner. For example, through holistic education methods such as guided imagery/visu-alization and meditation, painful emotions such as embarrassment or shame could be represented by an object that the child can visualize and address di-rectly, such as a particular colour or shape or object (e.g., stone, weed, etc.). Fo-cusing on a neutral object can thus help the client to reflect upon the painful ex-perience or thought in a manner that is more comfortable and familiar.

According to various holistic educators (e.g., Hutchison, 1998; Kessler, 2000; Levine, 1999; Miller, 1993; Winston, 2002), the use of literature and art during adolescents' cognitive therapy is effective as the structural organization of literature mirrors adolescents' spontaneous cognitive processes, which al-lows for accessing unconscious resources. The result is that through the inter-pretive process, the adolescent in therapy is tapping unconscious knowledge that can offer creative ways to resolve problems and enhance growth. Given that adolescents' cognitive abilities may help to promote creative healing, cog-nitive abilities may also help to unfold the unconscious resources. For in-stance, as already noted, bibliotherapy can serve as a therapeutic vehicle in that the literature offers material in both context and form that allows for ease in applying the child's cognitive abilities. Thus, bibliotherapy with adolescents is a valuable method because the form of the therapy is isomorphic to the cog-nitive skills for adolescents.

In a similar vein, another example of an educational and therapeutic activity that addresses classroom silence involves dream work. In addition to self-disclosing conversations, adolescents' dreams can also be explored through sim-ilar concepts with the use of visual art, drama, narrative, and metaphor. Given the importance dreams play in adolescent psychological development (e.g., Kagan, 1984), therapy that helps to promote adolescents' understandings of dreams may also lead to further growth in self-development and self-knowledge. Growth in self-knowledge may also encourage social connections to develop with both peers and adults as well, leading to a greater sense of spiritual awareness, or as Hay and Nye (1998) claim, relational consciousness. In sum, to encourage adolescents to engage in authentic dialogue regarding classroom silences, educators and researchers need to be aware of the ethical issues surrounding such sensitive activities.

Future Directions: Silence, Media, and Technology

Given modern society's hectic and fractured pace, silence and stillness are often looked at as "wasting time." Noise, speed, and constant stimulation define modern life for most children and adolescents. Given the technologically advanced classroom, and the availability of televisions and computers in most homes, many children find that both their school and home worlds are filled with noise and various machines (e.g., TV, computer, radio). For many children, solitary play or time alone may have been a time when she or he enjoyed some "quiet time" to themselves, but research shows that an increasing percentage of children and adolescents are spending their solitary and/or leisure time either on the computer or using some electronic device (Ward, 2004).

This dependence upon technology may play a role on adolescents' psychological and emotional development. As Moore (1992) states, "Soul cannot thrive in a fast-paced life" (p. 286). But why is slowing down so foreign to our young people? How can silence, stillness, and solitude be considered frightening? What are teenagers afraid of if they are asked to sit with themselves for a few moments with no external stimuli and asked to be still?

As Ho (2001) asks in his discussion of the notion of spirituality or mystery sensing, do adolescents today have the room and the necessary mental dispositions for solitude, idleness, and silence? Ho reflects on his observation of his colleagues in China, that in Hong Kong, a common sight in schools and public places is people talking on their mobile phone. This action can be found in schools and universities across North America as well. Although I have yet to see it in grade schools, many high school students and university students walk the halls engaged in a conversation on their cell phones. As Ho asks, what are they missing out on, and what motivates this need to avoid being "idle" or "waste time?" When did "time" become so precious to us that we need to be "productive" or "accountable" for every minute of the day? What lessons do adolescents learn about the use of personal time and life habits, including the balance between work and play? More importantly, where do adolescents learn these lessons and how are they learned?

As Kegan (1994) and Postman (1999) suggest, with modern technology, there is no more need for waiting, whereas it could be argued that waiting and patience are behaviours and characteristics that need to be promoted in the classroom. Are students being "held hostage" by new technologies? Are educators? Do the increasing "technologization," globalization, and related multitasking characteristics of our society hinder our ability to show a dedication to meaningful work? Does our ability to be efficient multitaskers make us happier in the end, or does it prevent us from defining our identity? Are academically successful students also able to consider the possibility of a profound sense of meaning, which may be one of the hallmarks of spirituality?

For example, in Pope's (2001) portrayal of five academically "successful" high school students, she encourages the readers to think of adolescents who would be considered "successful" and ask the following questions, such as: what kind of behaviour does our current educational system promote? Do our schools promote an atmosphere of collaboration, kindness, and integrity, or do they breed competition, cruelty, and deception? As Sternberg (2003) wonders, will today's high school graduates be prepared to become productive, happy, and honest citizens who are able *and* willing to apply their knowledge to promote a common good? Thus, as Gardner et al. (2001) suggest, will adolescents be able to find the balance between ethics and excellence in the sense that they will engage in "good work?" Both Pope (2001) and Sternberg (2003) suggest that, as educators and researchers, if we wish to promote a psychologically healthy definition of "success," we need to continue to actively listen to the voices of adolescents. I would further suggest that we also need to look at ourselves as role models for youth. Do our behaviours contradict our words? Are we walking self-contradictions? What values do our behaviours reflect? Are we as educators and researchers satisfied with modern society's definition of "success?" If not, what are we willing to do about it?

While writing this book, I experienced a taste of living with no electrical power when the largest power outage in history occurred (August 14, 2003). Although my community was only out of power for 22 hours, in my view, the most noticeable environmental change was the silence. The silence was loud. The silence was both shocking and soothing. Such silence inspired me to think about how life would have been without the constant bombardment of noise, and how our senses are constantly overloaded and overstimulated. I wondered how this constant and chronic noise exposure affects our minds, bodies, and hearts! What is this noise doing to our children and adolescents? What are the long-term psychological, emotional, spiritual, and physical consequences of such environmental noise? And more importantly, what can be done, and is there anyone else who is worried about it?

Some Western educators are discussing the socioemotional impact of our technologically advanced society (e.g., Meehan, 2002; Myers, 2000; Noddings, 2003). As Noddings suggests, perhaps the information overload is wearing us down emotionally and spiritually. Is it all about efficiency? As Noddings notes

(2003), if we are so efficient and productive, why are adolescents so unhappy? For example, the headline and subsequent article in the Canadian weekly news magazine *Maclean's* (2004) "Teen trouble: Drugs, sex, depression: Canadian experts on how to help kids survive trying times" suggests that we need to look beyond the "behaviours" such as drugs, alcohol, and disordered eating, as these are just masking the emotional difficulties teens experience. Thus, adults need to be concerned about the emotional lives of adolescents and what they are not talking about, and explore why they are silent. Similarly, as Postman (1999) contests, how do we encourage children and adolescents (and adults) to discern meaning from information and create knowledge? How do we encourage children and adolescents to develop wisdom from knowledge? Can faster computers and more advanced websites and Internet servers help children to feel more emotionally secure? More happy?

As Myers (2000) asserts, one of the greatest paradoxes of the 21st century (within technologically advanced countries) is that we are spiritually hungry in a world of technological and electronic food. As we create our curriculum and schools for the 21st century, we need to ask ourselves if we wish to produce students who are willing to be valuable members of society and excited to do "good work" (Gardner et al., 2001). That is, are we—as responsible adults who work with adolescents—teaching for wisdom in the sense that we encourage adolescents to balance ethics with excellence? As Pope (2001) asks, following findings from her ethnographic study with five American high school students who were high achievers, are we as educators willing to provide a classroom culture that promotes intellectual excitement, integrity, and cooperation, or are we fostering a culture that promotes anxiety, deceit, and competition?

Technology and Popular Media Influences

Given our technologically advanced society, and the increasingly important role the media play in the lives of children and adolescents via television, Internet, film, radio, and so forth, surprisingly little research exists on the link between media and/or technology and adolescents' sociocognitive and psychosocial development (Rossiter, 1999; Strasburger & Wilson, 2002; Sweet, 1997). As noted by many educators and researchers, the number of people in the world who are on-line or have access to either a computer or the Internet continues to grow exponentially. For example, a Time/CNN (Children and the Internet, 1999) survey of teenagers revealed that 82% use the Internet and 44% have seen X-rated content.

Interestingly, in a report on media use in the home, a Kaiser Family Foundation (1999) study found that 69% of children live in homes with one or more computers, and 45% of these homes have some form of Internet access.

In a recent survey by the Kaiser Family Foundation (1999), children and adolescents in the 9- to 17-year-old range were also regular users and that youth prefer their computers to more traditional media such as television or phones. Overall, the use of the Internet has increased 50% a year since 1990; between 1999 and 2002, there was an expectation of a 155% increase in use among 5- to 12-year-olds and 100% among teens (Paik, 2001). Also, the Internet was considered more important than fathers (Kaiser Family Foundation, 1999).

In general, the Internet is rapidly becoming an extension to our social universe and to our schools (Elliott, et al., 2002; Strasberger & Wilson, 2002). Over the Internet, people participate in activities traditionally considered social, such as competition, shopping, gambling, conversation, meeting new acquaintances, attending concerts, and so forth. Unlike traditional media such as TV, radio, and print, the Internet provides children and adolescents access to a variety of content; this interaction has created a new dimension for researchers to consider when they examine the effects of both problematic content (violence and sex) and educational content. Compared to traditional media such as television, an increasing number of researchers claim that the Internet is the most interactive of our current media, and suggest that the Internet and related electronic media such as video games may have a stronger influence on adolescents' developing minds (Paik, 2001; Tarpley, 2001).

Such widespread use of technology has implications for the school classroom and the larger culture education. Take the example of "wireless classrooms" and "laptop schools" that are becoming a growing phenomenon in North America and other parts of modernized countries across the globe. The recent educational movement has integrated laptop computers into elementary schools and high schools, where all students and faculty own and work on a laptop computer. Building on this idea, the "wireless school" goes a step further by changing the entire campus into a wireless Internet-access zone. For instance, students at the Packer Collegiate Institute in Brooklyn, New York, are currently undergoing this experience as the entire campus is wireless and all students will own a laptop computer that can access the Internet because they are in constant high-bandwidth contact with the school and one another (Grossman, 2003). In other words, another campus has been created in the school, a cyber or virtual school campus, that may not necessarily reflect the societal rules and processes in the real-life world. Such rules and regulations are constantly in creation and being negotiated as educators attempt to confront new issues such as cheating on-line.

In wireless schools, all assignments, handouts, work sheets, and so forth are distributed electronically. Students take their notes in class on their laptops, then take their laptops home and do their homework on them; to turn in an assignment, they drag and drop the file into the appropriate folder where the teacher can wirelessly retrieve it. Interestingly, the paperless classroom has yet to exist. For example, to avoid cheating and plagiarism from the Web, Brooklyn's Packer middle and high school requires children still to take their exams on paper. At the university level, to avoid plagiarism, some professors in North America are requesting that their students submit their papers to websites such as Turnitin.com, which ensures that their work is original and not a copy of an already existing published paper.

Another issue that arises from engaging in on-line learning is that adolescents still need a space for "play" and "privacy" away from the prying eyes of educators and parents. Strategies such as video games, downloading music, e-mailing, and instant messaging or "IM-ing" are ways in which adolescents are avoiding schoolwork. To address such issues, many schools have put into place monitoring devices within the computer to monitor what the students are working on, or have school rules that limit or do not permit the use of games and e-mails during school time.

Socioemotional Implications

Despite the benefits such as instant connections across the globe at a split of an instant and increased access for children and adolescents with learning and physical challenges, a wireless society has some moral and socioemotional implications as well. Larger, more troublesome societal and psychological issues underlie the immediate, surface-level benefits of a wireless school. For example, to what extent is the school really "connected" if youth consider IM-ing to be synonymous with talking? Is such technology strengthening the relationship between the educator and learner if the learner is using her or his imaginative and creative skills to think of ways in which to deceive teachers and inflict psychological harm on others? How does technological progress affect moral and emotional progress? Do the two develop in tandem or independently of one another? For example, is a child more likely to send a disparaging remark via e-mail as opposed to saying it face-to-face or on the telephone? Are students more likely to break into someone's personal computer by stealing her or his password than physically stealing her or his backpack? Finally, will "wireless" classrooms invite respectful conversations and/or create new silences?

To answer such questions, researchers are now beginning to explore some of the sociomoral and emotional consequences of technological progress and Internet use. The sheer number of students using the Internet and the increase in wireless schools demand the attention of educators and social scientists, given that most adolescents use the Internet for some form of communication, using one or a combination of options—e-mail, IM, chat rooms, or MUDs (multiuser dungeons, which involve fantasy role-play). Despite the active and interactive use of the Internet (as compared with the passive activity inspired by TV), Kraut et al. (1998) found that individuals who made more use of the Internet for just a year or two were more likely to become lonely and depressed. As a result of frequent but shallow interactions, they claim the quality of interaction decreases, resulting in feelings of loneliness, depression, and a lowered sense of belonging.

Unfortunately, given that the Internet has the potential to be an effective and powerful communicative tool, some adolescents have chosen to use the Internet as a psychological weapon to hurt others. Cyberbullying has become increasingly popular among adults and adolescents, using the Internet and e-mail as a way to psychologically harass others (e.g., sending an insulting or threatening e-mail; creating a website with derogatory, personal comments about a particular individual; posting unflattering photos without permission on websites, etc.). Examples of cyberostracism are also on the increase, as ignoring or not responding to e-mail correspondence may have deleterious psychological ramifications (Williams, 2001). For example, Rintel and Pittman (1997) found that Internet users often perceive that they are being ignored. The researchers viewed chatters' responses to noninteraction as particularly difficult, because of the chatters' need to defuse carefully the "hostility of silence" (p. 510), while gaining the attention of another interactant. Rintel and Pittman acknowledged the particularly ambiguous nature of silence over the Internet relay channel, in that the silence can be interpreted on a spectrum from deliberate to nondeliberate. Therefore, depending upon how one uses her or his imaginative skills, chatters may feel they are being ignored whether or not they really are.

Regarding learning and teaching, will a wireless and virtual society help adolescents make sense of the overload and continuous flow of information? Is technology a mere tool that will enable students to further their own learning by allowing them to build on their thoughts? Alternatively, does the use of technology actually change their way of thinking and feeling? As Postman (1999), among other concerned educators, asks: as computers can provide us with easier access to larger amounts of information across the world, and facilitate our communication with one another by transforming the problems of geography, who will help the adolescents to transform the information into knowledge and eventually wisdom? Who will create a caring and reflective computer, and is the creation of such a computer feasible? Hypothetically, if the task is doable, we need to ask ourselves why would we want such a computer? How would our society benefit from such a creation? Where would the caring computer's motivation to do "good work" and to further the common good of society stem from? As many educators and students have noted, the culture of the classroom is changing due to increased technology and not everyone may be comfortable with the changes. Both educators and research-ers need to continue to explore the influence of technological progress on the inner lives of adolescents and the implications such growth may have for the larger society.

Although past research suggests that the media and popular culture have a shaping influence on children's beliefs, values, and actions (Strasburger & Wilson, 2002), much research needs to be conducted on how popular media affect adolescent mental health (Bensen, Donohue, & Erickson 1989; Spilka, Hood, Hunsberger, & Gorsuch, 2003; Ward, 2004). For example, regarding the development of values and beliefs, the use of television as a vehicle to pro-mote religious beliefs has been used since the 1950s with religious celebra-tions portrayed via satellite. It would be interesting to study the influence of Pope John Paul II's visit to Toronto in 2002 and to investigate whether or not those children and adolescents who attended or viewed his visit via the televi-sion screen differed from those who visited the site in person.

Given the increasing violent and sexual content reflected in popular media in today's society (e.g., Strasburger & Wilson, 2002), many educators and re-searchers question the social, moral, and religious implications of our ad-vanced technology (e.g., Ho, 2001; Kessler, 2000; Postman, 1999) and suggest more research needs to be conducted on how media such as television, Inter-net, electronic games, and movies influences children's and adolescents' val-ues, beliefs, and behaviours towards human beings (Flory, 2000; Ream & Savin-Williams, 2003; Strasburger & Wilson, 2002).

For example, educators of adolescents need to promote the use of critical thinking and encourage students to become critical consumers of popular media, and to develop a healthy skepticism by encouraging students to ask questions and to engage in conversations regarding the moral, emotional, and ethical implications of some of the popular media, including TV shows and video games. Within the framework of a critical media literacy program, ado-lescents need to be encouraged to ask questions about the experience of silenc-ing. For example, how are particular minorities, disabled persons, and similar groups "silenced" from the popular media? What sample of the population are portrayed by the majority of TV shows, films, magazines and why?

Within the framework of a holistic curriculum that encourages critical thinking skills and literacy skills, educators can encourage adolescents to write letters to editors of newspapers, magazines, TV executives of popular TV pro-grams, and advertising agencies to ask for their policies and reasoning behind their choices of representation in the popular media. As noted earlier in my discussion of holistic education and related programs, such activities that pro-mote inquiry and dialogue aim to provide adolescents with a sense of agency and control in that they have some control over what gets broadcast or published in the popular media. That is, such activities may help adolescents realize that they have the ability and power to question the creators of popular media and they do not need to view themselves as "passive recipients" of media and technology. Recent studies suggest that connections exist between media exposure and the likelihood of experiencing depression and disordered eating (e.g., Field et al., 1999). In sum, more work needs to be done on how the media may play a role in sociomoral development.

In contrast to the possible negative influences of the media on childhood and adolescent religiosity, given the importance of personal relationships and connectedness to others, the Internet may have the potential to improve social connections across the globe and may thus have a positive influence on religious experiences (see Mares & Woodard, 2001, for a description how the Internet may have prosocial effects). As Paley (1999) reminds us, although the computer can help us to gain information from multiple sources, it cannot help us to reflect, to care, and to be kind and productive citizens.

Towards a More Psychocultural Approach to Adolescent Education

Based on Western, industrialized society's current fixation with external, physical beauty and the intolerance of physical imperfections, I fear for the future emotional lives of today's adolescents. From the perspective of both a teacher/ student and an educational researcher interested in exploring issues of self-esteem and social-cognition among adolescents, I believe that a multifaceted, holistic approach that attempts to integrate all aspects of a child's sense of self is the most effective way to prepare preadolescent girls and boys for the complex and chaotic century that lies ahead. Thus, through the implementation of activities that promote balance, inclusion, and relationships within a psychologically safe environment, children may learn to develop a positive sense of self and to form trusting, secure relationships with themselves and others.

As a cautionary note regarding the emphasis of language in holistic education, language-related activities are only one method to encourage adolescents to express their inner worlds in the classroom. In particular, some emotional and spiritual experiences in particular may become distorted or misinterpreted through writing and/or verbalization (Wierzbicka, 1989). In contrast, more accurate representations of one's inner landscape may be obtained nonverbally through the use of images and/or movement. Holistic educational activities that aim to promote spiritual development nonverbally (including relaxation techniques, visualization, art therapy, play therapy, psychodrama, and mask-making, etc.) may also foster children's ability to self-comfort and learn to respect and trust themselves. For example, to strengthen self-connections, guided imagery and group/classroom meditation can be used to promote the concept of mindfulness or the ability to be aware in the present (Goleman, 1995; Miller, 1993; Winston, 2002).

Also, as examples of nonverbal activities at the postsecondary level, I have often incorporated the use of various objects such as blocks, puppets, fruit, sculpting clay, or crayons in my own teaching to help students further their understandings of complex and sensitive psychoeducational issues. Given that some individuals may feel "silenced" about some educational issues and concepts that are sometimes very sensitive and complex, sometimes activities that do not entail a large amount of dialogue in the beginning are the most effective activities to unlock adult learners' thoughts. For example, to address the multileveled and complex issue of power and status variables among individuals, in contrast to beginning class with a discussion of the relevant academic readings, I would begin class by bringing a variety of fruit to class and ask each class member to choose a fruit. Working collaboratively in groups of four or five (depending upon the size of the class), the task of each group is for each group member to choose one fruit and to create a story involving issues of power and control with a peaceful solution. Although sometimes the students choose to narrate their dramatizations, often times, the "fruit stories" are enacted in silence. I have found that quite often students find such activities particularly meaningful as they have been asked to challenge their assumptions and previous ways of knowing and to engage in what they consider to be risktaking activities in my class.

As Winston (2002) mentions, drawing on examples from moral education, drama may help to contribute to spirituality in terms of experience and development through the use of drama curriculum that promotes an understanding of ritual as performance and the relationship between drama and ritual. The use of drama in the classroom can also be used to promote transcultural competence in that it can help expose children to various types of performances, including dances, dramas, and plays found throughout different cultures. As Haynes (2002) suggests, to further enhance critical thinking skills and more complex mental reasoning, educators need to promote enquiry and dialogue. For example, current media literacy programs could be applied to encourage children and adolescents to view television and the media through a critical lens and to question how media portray sensitive social issues such as morality, identity, spirituality, or sexuality.

At the graduate level, I always aim to incorporate aspects of the current media into my curriculum, as students need to continue to question how the media portray educational research and issues related to adolescents. For example, in my developmental and educational issues in children and adolescent education course, I dedicate one class session to the critical examination, enquiry, and dialogue surrounding how popular media portray the adolescent self. In this class, we usually critically examine and question popular magazines, television programs, websites, and video games that adolescents are currently engaged in. Again, as in my other classes, I encourage my students to see things from multiple perspectives, such as the perspective of the television producer, educator, or youth.

In conclusion, reflecting on my past educational experiences as an adolescent, I question why many educational programs continue to focus on the promotion of academic competence in lieu of Sternberg's (2003) notion of "successful intelligence" or one that balances the inter, intra, and extrapersonal—especially when recent psychoeducational theories and research suggest that it is now the latter construct that is being claimed to be the key to adaptive functioning and psychological well-being (e.g., Gardner, 1985; Goleman, 1995). Hopefully now, a generation later, the dialogical discourse between psychologists and teachers will encourage educators to become more cognizant of the role psychosocial development plays in the academic life of young adolescents and hence, decide to embark on (or continue) the journey of the holistic curriculum. A holistic approach to both psychology and education can promote awareness of both preadolescent development and complex societal phenomena such as emotional and psychological disorders (e.g., depression, anxiety disorders, etc.). Thus, as we approach the increasingly complex and ambiguous world of the 21st century, the need is great for both educators and psychologists to continue to work together and co-create a caring "curriculum of hope" that teaches children and adolescents to learn to listen, love, and accept both their brains and their bodies.

Summary

Overall, this final chapter has explored some of the pragmatic issues of silence in the classroom. That is, this chapter discussed some strategies that educators of adolescents may find useful once they have acknowledged silences in their classrooms and in their own lives. It is hoped that this chapter has provided educators and researchers with helpful pedagogical and empirical directions that will encourage the concept of silence to remain an important aspect of the adolescent curriculum.

CONCLUSION

Silence Speaks: Closing Thoughts and New Questions

Every time we ask a question, we're generating a possible version of a life.
(DAVID EPSTON, *cited in Cowley & Springen, 1995, p. 74*)

Overall, programs that are holistic, systemic, and responsive to adolescents' developmental and cultural needs are needed. Holistic is used here in the sense that such programs need to take into account the multiple dimensions of intolerance and development. The approach is also developmental and culturally sensitive in that it considers the physical, cognitive, emotional, and spiritual changes that children and adolescents experience as they develop their own sense of identity in the school world. Given the power of language, educators need to redefine existing race-based classification schemes and create programs that reconceptualize race and ethnicity in educational research and practice (Lee, 2003).

Through the implementation of a balanced curriculum that includes both affective and cognitive components within a "psychologically safe" classroom climate, educators can create a learning environment that will maximize the growth of both intra- and interpersonal functioning. As I have argued throughout this book, a psychocultural model of social and self-understanding for adolescents may help to bridge the gap between the fields of education and social cognitive research. In the end, I hope that this book deepens educators' and researchers' awareness of the different ways in which girls and boys interpret and understand social and self-knowledge, thus furthering the discourse in social-cognitive psychology and holistic education.

Furthermore, as suggested by Harter et al. (1997), future research needs to investigate the links between the multidimensional self-concept and its relation to adolescents' ability to articulate their subjective experience or their level of "voice" (Gilligan, 1982). That is, in addition to studying the influence of verbal and nonverbal ability, future studies need to create ways to assess whether adolescents feel that their emotional voices or true selves are being "psychologically" heard by adults. Thus, the investigation of adolescents' emotional worlds may assist researchers in answering the question of how and why adolescents develop social insight and how this mentalizing ability relates to their ability to get along with others.

Although large scale, cross-sectional studies that occur within one population are the most economically feasible, such studies provide culturally biased information and do not allow researchers to examine the development of attitudes over time. Given the strong sociocultural influences on adolescent self-identity, following the method of Barbara Kerr (1994), it would be interesting to follow a group of children (girls and boys) and interview them at pivotal times in their development about psychoemotional issues, perhaps focusing on experiences of silences throughout their lives. Ideally, a cross-cultural, longitudinal study on the links between social understanding and social relations would provide an excellent sketch of how adolescents in various cultures view and understand both themselves and others.

To investigate properly the complexities of the adolescent mental and social life, the ideal method is to employ both "thick" and "thin" methodologies (Geertz, 1973). Future research needs to use techniques from both the etic (outside-in) or more objective perspective drawn from cognitive research (e.g., standardized tests, controlling for verbal/nonverbal IQ) and the more emic (inside-out) or subjective techniques gleaned from social and anthropological research (e.g., visual-drawing tasks, narrative techniques, action research, autobiographical work). The use of such a multitasked approach may provide data that is richer in content and more valuable in the end to both educators and researchers.

Overall, regarding research and practice within the school and clinical context, inquiry regarding the inner world of the adolescent must be grounded in an understanding of adolescent "voices" and "faces" across all cultures. Adolescents' experiences of silence and the individuals associated with them need to be viewed as fluid, internally complex, and changing. Regarding promising areas of psychological research, two in particular may offer exciting new possibilities to help researchers explore adolescents' experiences of silence. In particular, the research areas of developmental social cognition, or cognitive science, and the positive psychology movement may promote the creation of new questions surrounding the private worlds of the adolescent. Regarding the cognitive science area, the particular focus of theory-of-mind research suggests promising links between spiritual, moral, emotional, and social development with cognitive growth. As mentioned earlier in the chapter, ongoing investigations with the theory-of-mind literature are starting to explore children's and adolescents' understandings of metaphysics, spirituality, religiosity, and the magical and supernatural (see Harris, 2000). Issues of spirituality, morality, and religiosity can also be explored with the context of children's play, particularly imaginative or make-believe play (see Taylor & Carlson, 2000).

Regarding the recent movement of positive psychology (Rich, 2003), the theme of this new approach to adolescent development includes the investigation of positive characteristics of human nature and our social worlds. Seligman and Csikszentmihalyi (2000) describe the movement as a response to psychology's history of focusing on pathology and health problems only. In contrast to this negative focus, positive psychology aims to examine the positive features of human life that make our life meaningful, including the study of such topics as future-mindedness, hope, wisdom, creativity, spirituality, responsibility, and perseverance, amongst others. Given that spirituality is listed in the mandate for this new research movement in psychology, the focus on both initiative (a characteristic that is associated with individualism and autonomy) and social connectedness could help to promote spiritual development in children and adolescents, and extend to research on play and flow (e.g., Csikszentmihalyi, 1990).

As collaborative, transcultural applied research that entails spirituality from cognitive science, positive psychology would help to prevent mental illness by recognizing and developing sets of strengths, competencies, and virtues in young children, such as future-mindedness, hope, interpersonal and intrapersonal skills, the capacity for playfulness, faith, and a positive or optimistic work ethic. Building these strengths as a buffer is alien to the disease or deficit model that focuses on remedying deficits; the application of such research to educational and clinical settings would promote changes in both mind and behaviour. According to Seligman (2002), to promote authentic happiness, a renovated science of prevention needs courageous researchers who are willing to address issues of the mind, morals, and the meaning of life to help create a better society.

The second main area of psychological research that may provide particular insight into the silence experiences of adolescents involves the theory-of-mind research within the larger frame of social cognitive research and cognitive neuroscience. As previously explained, as cognitive neuroscience gains increased understanding of the cognitive and neural processes that underlay spiritual awareness (or Hay and Nye's [1998] term of relational consciousness), it may become clear which brain processes help adolescents to think in ways that are in tune with themselves, others, nature, and beyond. However, as Bruner (1996) cautions, we need to remain "perspectival" in that the two visions of the mind as either humanistic or naturalistic remain different yet complementary.

The application of the two new areas of research mentioned above include multidisciplinary, holistic, therapeutic and educational programs that draw on other cultures for their sources of expertise. An integrated, transformational learning model that connects education to therapy could provide a useful foundation within which holistic educational and therapeutic programs can be developed. Research findings from the areas of both cognitive science and positive psychology could be used to help create developmentally appropriate educational and clinical programs. For example, findings from applied developmental cognitive science research such as theory-of-mind work in children and adolescents could be used to help create a developmentally appropriate curriculum that aims to promote both interpersonal and intrapersonal competence.

I knew when I began this book that I could not—and did not plan to—provide answers. The issues around silence will continue to be "silenced" until researchers and educators decide to take the risk to address and deal with such sensitive issues. The conversation cannot begin until people are willing to break the silence around silence and agree to listen with open minds and hearts. Throughout this book, I have highlighted possible issues surrounding the notion of silence and the inner world of the adolescent, but the connections among these constructs and issues have yet to be made in any coherent manner. It is my hope that after reading this book, the reader will leave with sense of hopefulness; I hope I have inspired some new questions that will lead to new possibilities.

Consistent with Flanagan's (2002) sentiments that purport mind, morals, and the meaning of life to be paramount in our human life, timeless key questions—such as "who are we, what is the way to meaning and goodness, and what makes us human?"—cannot be addressed effectively until the conflict between the humanistic/perennial philosophy of the "ensouled" person and the scientific image of the person as devoid of soul is reconciled. If happiness is the key to life's purpose, the conversations between the scientists and the scientists of "ought" or mystics must begin to de/re-construct the connections between the mind, body, and soul.

If we are, as Dewey (1938) claims, active participants in the construction of knowledge and making meaning, then both fields of psychology and education need to promote a community of enquiry that addresses the definition of human nature in general. In line with humanistic educational thinkers and developmentalists (Haynes, 2002; Myers, 1997), communities of schools and academic disciplines need to engage in an intersubjective dialogue, not only with others but also to engage in private speech. In collaboration with social conversations, private, internal dialogue will strengthen one's connections to self, community, and beyond. Such openness and connection is necessary if we are to engage in the richness multiculturalism provides us when working with children and youth.

In short, as educators and researchers who work and care about youth, we need to awaken adolescents' appetite for learning and life. We cannot allow them to become disengaged from others around them or bored with life. Psychological isolation and the feeling of being silenced (either by yourself or by others) is the most terrifying experience that humans can endure. Educational programs and educators that promote "spiritual or emotional literacy" are perhaps the best coping strategies we can offer that will help to protect our youth from becoming psychological isolates. Such holistic programs can thus help to ensure that children develop into resilient adults. As cautioned by other holistic educators (Glazer, 1999), in the midst of this technological boom, we cannot forget that our purpose as educators is to assist in the formation of better people, not higher achievement scores. The enrichment of the human spirit is something that cannot be measured by a computer or test score.

As we embark upon the 21st century, the need is great for educators to co-create a "curriculum of caring and hope" that teaches youth to learn to listen, love, and accept not only themselves but also life itself. Such a curriculum will put an end to being "silenced about silence." That is, such a positive approach to education may encourage others and ourselves to be silent no longer about the meaning and functions of silences in today's schools. Thus, I agree with Sternberg's notion that to promote happiness, we need to teach for wisdom. Academic excellence will not guarantee happiness. To conclude, the ultimate goal of all holistic educators and developmentalists should be to foster spiritual literacy within the context of self-fulfillment. By acknowledging the spiritual or the "silent" human aspect of education, educators can foster and maintain both their own and their students' appetite for learning and life. In the end, if the reader finishes my book remembering the paradoxical message "silence speaks," then my task has been accomplished.

APPENDIX A

Interpersonal Understanding Interview: Story 1

Kenny and Mark are co-captains of the soccer team. They have one person left to choose for the team. Without saying anything, Mark winks at Kenny and looks at Tom who is one of the remaining children left to be chosen for the team. Mark looks back at Kenny and smiles. Kenny nods and chooses Tom to be on their team. Tom sees Mark and Kenny winking and smiling at each other. Tom, who is usually one of the last to be picked for team sports, wonders why Kenny wants him to be on his team.

Comprehension Questions
1. Does Tom see Mark and Kenny winking and smiling at each other? Yes/No
2. Is Tom usually the first person to be picked for team sports? Yes/No

A. Third Order Theory of Mind Questions
1. Why did Mark smile at Kenny?
2. Why did Kenny nod?
3. Why did Kenny choose Tom to be on the team? Why do you think this/How do you know this?
4. a) Do you think that Tom has any idea of why Kenny chose him to be on the team? Yes/No
   b) How do you know that Tom either has or doesn't have any idea of why Kenny chose him?

B. Empathetic Sensitivity
5. How do you think Tom feels? Why? Does he feel anything else? Why?

C. Person Perception
  Choose a character in the story and describe him.
  What kind of things can you think of to describe him?
  What kind of person do you think he is?

D. Alternative Explanations
  Is there another way that you can think about this story? Yes/No
  If so, how?

Note. This measure was designed by the author (Bosacki, 1998).

APPENDIX B

Interpersonal Understanding Interview: Story 2

Nancy and Margie are watching the children in the playground. Without saying a word, Nancy nudges Margie and looks across the playground at the new girl swinging on the swing set. Then Nancy looks back at Margie and smiles. Margie nods, and the two of them start off toward the girl at the swing set. The new girl sees the strange girls walk towards her. She'd seen them nudging and smiling at each other. Although they are in her class, she has never spoken to them before. The new girl wonders what they could want.

Comprehension Questions
1. Does the new girl see Nancy and Margie nudging and smiling at each other? Yes/No
2. Has the new girl ever spoken to Nancy and Margie before? Yes/No

A. Third Order Theory of Mind Questions
1. Why did Nancy smile at Margie?
2. Why did Margie nod?
3. a) Why did Nancy and Margie move off together in the direction of the new girl? Why do you think this/ How do you know this?
4. a) Does the new girl have any idea of why Nancy and Margie are walking towards her? Yes /No
   b) How do you know that the new girl has or doesn't have any idea of why Nancy and Margie are walking towards her?

B. Empathetic Sensitivity
5. How do you think the new girl feels? Why? Does she feel anything else?

Why?

C. Person Perception
Choose a character in the story and describe her.
What kind of things can you think of to describe her?
What kind of person do you think she is?

D. Alternative Explanations
Is there another way that you can think about this story? Yes/No
If so, how?

Note. This measure was designed by the author (Bosacki, 1998).

REFERENCES

Abrams, C. (1989). Differential association: Social developments in gender identity and intergroup relations during adolescence. In S. Skevington & D. Baker (Eds.), *The social identity of women* (pp. 59–83). London, UK: Sage Publications.

Acker, S. (1994). *Gendered education: sociological reflections on woman, teaching and feminism.* Toronto, ON: OISE Press.

Ackerman, B., Brown, E., & Izard, C. (2004). The relations between contextual risk, earned income, and the school adjustment of children from economically disadvantaged families. *Developmental Psychology, 40,* 204–216.

Adams, G., & Berzonsky, M. (Eds.) (2003). *Blackwell handbook of adolescence.* Malden, MA: Blackwell.

Adato, A (1998, Dec./1999, Jan.) Choosing my religion. *Teen People Magazine,* 138–144.

Almeida, A. (1999). Portugal. In P. Smith et al. (Eds.), *The nature of school bullying* (pp. 174–186). London: Routledge.

Alsaker, F. (1995). Is puberty a critical period for socialization? *Journal of Adolescence, 18,* 427–444.

Anderson, K., & Leaper, C. (1998). Emotion talk between same- and mixed-gender friends: Form and functions. *Journal of Language and Social Psychology, 17,* 421–450.

Andresen, J. (2001). Introduction: Towards a cognitive science of religion. In J. Andresen (Ed.), *Religion in mind: Cognitive perspectives on religious belief, ritual, and experience* (pp. 1–44). Cambridge: Cambridge University Press.

Aptheker, B. (1989). *Tapestries of life: Women's work, women's consciousness and the meaning of daily experience.* Amherst: University of Massachusetts Press.

Argyle, M. (2000). *Psychology and religion: An introduction.* London, UK: Routledge.

Aronson, E. (2004). Reducing hostility and building compassion: Lessons from the jigsaw classroom. In A. Miller (Ed.), *The social psychology of good and evil* (pp. 469–488). New York: Guilford Press.

Asher, S., & Coie, J. (Eds.). (1990). *Peer rejection in childhood.* New York: Cambridge University Press.

Astington, J. (1988). Children's understanding of the speech act of promising. *Journal of Child Language, 15,* 157–173.

Astington, J. (1993). *The child's discovery of the mind.* Cambridge, MA: Harvard University Press.

Astington, J. (1996). What is theoretical about the child's theory of mind? A Vygotskian view of its development. In P. Carruthers & P. Smith (Eds.), *Theories of theory of mind* (pp. 184–199). Cambridge: Cambridge University Press.

Astington, J., & Jenkins, J. (1995). Theory of mind development and social understanding. *Cognition and Emotion, 9,* 151–165.

Astington, J., & Olson, D. (1995). The cognitive revolution in children's understanding of mind. *Human Development, 38,* 179–189.

Astington, J., & Pelletier, J. (1996). The language of mind: Its role in teaching and learning. In D. Olson & N. Torrance (Eds.), *Handbook of education and human development: New models of learning, teaching, and schooling* (pp. 593–619). Oxford, UK: Blackwell.

Astington, J., & Pelletier, J. (1997, April). *Young children's theory of mind and its relation to their success in school. Paper presented at the biennial meeting of the Society for Research in Child Development,* Washington, DC.

Atwood, M. (1988). *Cat's eye.* New York: McClelland-Bantam.

Austin, J. (1962). *How to do things with words.* Cambridge, MA: Harvard University Press.

Baker, C., & Luke, A. (1991). *Toward a critical sociology of reading pedagogy.* Amsterdam: John Benjamins.

Bakhtin, M. (1981). *The dialogic imagination.* (C. Emerson & M. Holquist, Trans.). Austin: University of Texas Press.

Baladerian, M. (1994). Intervention and treatment of children with severe disabilities who become victims of abuse. *Developmental Disabilities Bulletin, 22,* 93–99.

Baldwin, J. (1902). *Social and ethical interpretations in mental life.* New York: Macmillan.

Baldwin, J. (1913). *History of psychology.* London, UK: Watts.

Banerjee, R., & Yuill, N. (1999). Children's understanding of self-presentational display rules: Associations with mental-state understanding. *British Journal of Developmental Psychology, 17,* 111–124.

Barbieri, M. (1995). *Sounds from the heart: Learning to listen to girls.* Portsmouth, NH: Hernemann.

Barenboim, C. (1981). The development of person perception in childhood and adolescence: From behavioral comparisons to psychological constructs to psychological comparisons. *Child Development, 52,* 129–144.

Barner-Barry, C. (1986). Rob: Children's tacit use of peer ostracism to control aggressive behavior. *Ethology and Sociobiology, 7,* 281–293.

Baron, R., & Kenny, D. (1986). The moderator-mediator variable distinction in social psychological research: Conceptual, strategic, and statistical considerations. *Journal of Personality and Social Psychology, 51,* 1173–1182.

Baron-Cohen, S. (1995). *Mindblindness.* Cambridge, MA: Bradford/MIT.

Barresi, J., & Moore, C. (1995). Intentional relations and social understanding. *Behavioral and Brain Sciences, 18,* 256–279.

Bartsch, K., & Wellman, H. (1995). *Children talk about the mind.* New York: Oxford University Press.

Basso, K. (1970). "To give up on words": Silence in Western Apache culture. *Southwestern Journal of Anthropology, 26,* 213–230.

Baumrind, D. (1991). Effective parenting during the early adolescent transition. In P. Cowan & M. Hetherington (Eds.), *Family transitions* (pp. 111–163). Mahwah, NJ: Lawrence Erlbaum Associates.

Bayer, G. (1982). *The relationship between religious orientation and sex-role identity.* Unpublished doctoral dissertation, Rosemead Graduate School of Professional Psychology.

Beatty, B. (1996). Rethinking the historical role of psychology in educational reform. In D. Olson, & N. Torrance (Eds.), *Handbook of education and human development: New models of learning, teaching, and schooling* (pp. 100–116). Oxford, UK: Blackwell.

Behrens, K. (2004). A multifaceted view of the concept of *amae:* Reconsidering the indigenous Japanese concept of relatedness. *Human Development, 47,* 1–27.

Belenky, M., Clinchy, B., Goldberger, N., & Tarule, J. (1986). *Women's ways of knowing.* New York: Basic Books.

Bellah, R., Madsen, R., Sullivan, M., Swider, A., & Tipton, S. (1985). *Habits of the heart: Individualism and commitment in American life.* Berkeley: University of California Press.

Bennett, M. (Ed.) (1993). *The child as psychologist: An introduction to the development of social cognition.* New York: Harvester Wheatsheaf.

Benson, P., Donahue, M., & Erickson, J. (1989). Adolescence and religion: A review of the literature from 1970 to 1986. *Research in the Social Scientific Study of Religion, 1,* 153–181.

Ben-Zur, H. (2003). Happy adolescents: The link between subjective well-being, internal resources, and parental factors. *Journal of Youth and Adolescence, 32,* 67–79.

Berger, P., & Luckmann, T. (1967). *The social construction of reality: A treatment in the sociology of knowledge.* Garden City, NY: Anchor.

Berryman, J. (2001). The nonverbal nature of spirituality and religious language. In J. Erricker, C. Ota, & C. Erricker (Eds.), *Spiritual education: Cultural, religious, and social differences: New perspectives for the 21st century* (pp. 9–33). Brighton, UK: Sussex Academic Press.

Best, D., & Thomas, J. (2004). Cultural diversity and cross-cultural perspectives. In A. Eagley, A. Beall, & R. Sternberg, R. (Eds.), *The psychology of gender* (pp. 296–327). New York: Guilford Press.

Bhatnager, P., & Rastogi, M. (1986). Cognitive style and basis ideal disparity in males and females. *Indian Journal of Current Psychological Research, 1,* 36–40.

Block, J., Gjerde, P., & Block, J. H. (1991). Personality antecedents of depressive tendencies in 18-year-olds: A prospective study. *Journal of Personality and Social Psychology, 60,* 726–738.

Bloom, M. (2000). The uses of theory in primary prevention practice: Evolving thoughts on sports and after-school activities as influences of social competence. In S. Danish & T. Gullotta (Eds.), *Developing competent youth and strong communities through after-school programming* (pp. 17–66). Washington, DC: CWLA Press.

Blos, J. (1979). *The adolescent passage: Developmental issues.* New York: International Universities Press.

Blume, J. (1972). *Tales of a fourth-grade nothing.* New York: Yearling.

Boivin, M., & Hymel, S. (1997). Peer experiences and social self-perceptions: A sequential model. *Developmental Psychology, 33,* 135–145.

Bolger, K., & Patterson, C. (2001). Pathways from child maltreatment to internalizing problems: Perceptions of control as mediators and moderators. *Development and Psychopathology, 3,* 913–940.

Bolger, K., Patterson, C., Thompson, W., & Kupersmidt, J. (1995). Psychosocial adjustment among children experiencing persistent and intermittent family economic hardship, *Child Development, 5,* 1107–1129.

Bosacki, S. (1995). Promoting positive attitudes towards aboriginal elementary students. *Canadian Social Studies, 30,* 19–23.

Bosacki, S. (1997, June). *Theory of mind, self-concept and social competence in preadolescence.* Paper presented at the 58th annual convention of the Canadian Psychological Association, Toronto, Ontario.

Bosacki, S. (1998). *Theory of mind in preadolescence: Connections among social understanding, self-concept, and social relations.* Unpublished doctoral dissertation, University of Toronto, Toronto, Ontario.

Bosacki, S. (2000). Theory of mind and self-concept in preadolescents: Links with gender and language. *Journal of Educational Psychology, 92,* 709–717.

Bosacki, S. (2001). "Theory of mind" or "Theory of soul"?: The role of spirituality in children's understanding of minds and emotions. In J. Erricker, C. Ota., & C. Erricker (Eds.), *Spiritual education: Cultural, religious, and social differences: New perspectives for the 21st century* (pp. 156–169). Brighton, UK: Sussex Academic Press.

Bosacki, S. (2003). Psychological pragmatics in preadolescents: Sociomoral understanding, self-worth, and school behavior. *Journal of Youth and Adolescence, 32,* 141–155.

Bosacki, S. (2004, April). *Psychological understanding, self-concept, and social competencies in school-age children.* Poster session presented at the annual meeting of the American Educational Research Association, San Diego, CA.

Bosacki, S., & Astington, J. (1999). Theory of mind in preadolescence: Relations between social understanding and social competence. *Social Development, 8,* 237–255.

Bosacki, S., & Moore, C. (2004). Preschoolers' understanding of simple and complex emotions: Links with gender and language. *Sex Roles: A Journal of Research, 50,* 659–675.

Bosacki, S., Innerd, W., & Towson, S. (1997). Field independence-dependence and self-esteem: Does gender make a difference? *Journal of Youth and Adolescence, 26,* 691–703.

Bosacki, S., Pelletier, J., & Astington, J. (1997, April). "She's such a shy child": Metacognitive underpinnings and teachers' perceptions of shyness in young girls and boys. Poster session presented at the annual meeting of the American Educational Research Association, San Diego, CA.

Boyes, M., & Chandler, M. (1992). Cognitive development, epistemic doubt, and identity formation in adolescence. *Journal of Youth and Adolescence, 21,* 277–304.

Braham, J. (1995). *Crucial conversations: Interpreting contemporary American literary autobiography by women*. New York: Teachers College Press.

Brennan, P., Hall, J., Bor, W., Najman, J., & Williams, G. (2003). Integrating biological and social processes in relations of early-onset persistent aggression in boys and girls. *Developmental Psychology, 1*, 309–323.

Briggs, J. (1970). *Never in anger*. Cambridge, MA: Harvard University Press.

Briggs, J. (1995). The study of Inuit emotions: Lessons from a personal retrospective. In J. Russell, J. Fernandez-Dols, A. Manstead, and J. Wellencamp (Eds.), *Everyday conceptions of emotion* (pp. 203–220). Dordrecht, Netherlands: Kluwer Academic Publishers.

Brinton, B., & Fujiki, M. (2002). Social development in children with specific language impairment and profound hearing loss. In P. Smith & C. Hart (Eds.), *Blackwell handbook of childhood social development* (pp. 588–603). Oxford, UK: Blackwell.

Britton, J. (1970). *Language and learning*. London: Penguin Books.

Brody, L. (2001). *Gender emotion and the family*. Cambridge, MA: Harvard University Press.

Brody, L., & Hall, J. (1993). Gender and emotion. In M. Lewis & J. Haviland (Eds.), *Handbook of emotions* (pp. 447–460). New York: Guilford.

Bronfenbrenner, U. (1977). Toward an experimental ecology of human development. *American Psychologist, 32*, 513–531.

Brooks-Gunn, J.(1989). Pubertal processes and the early adolescent tradition. In W. Damon (Eds.), *Child development today and tomorrow* (pp. 155–176). San Francisco CA: Jossey-Bass.

Brophy, J. (1983). Research on the self-fulfilling prophecy and teacher expectations. *Journal of Educational Psychology, 75*, 631–661.

Brown, J., Donelan-McCall, N., & Dunn, J. (1996). Why talk about mental states? The significance of children's conversations with friends, siblings, and mothers. *Child Development, 67*, 836–849.

Brown, L., & Gilligan, C. (1992). *Meeting at the crossroads*. New York: Ballantine.

Bruce, P. (1958). Relationship of self-acceptance to other variables with sixth-grade children oriented in self-understanding. *Journal of Educational Psychology, 49*, 229–237.

Bruchkowsky, M. (1992). The development of empathic cognition in middle and early childhood. In R. Case (Ed.), *The mind's staircase: Exploring the conceptual underpinnings of children's thought and knowledge*. (pp. 153–170). Mahwah, NJ: Lawrence Erlbaum Associates.

Bruner, J. (1986). *Actual minds, possible worlds*. Cambridge, MA: Harvard University Press.

Bruner, J. (1990). Acts of meaning. Cambridge, MA: Harvard University Press.

Bruner, J. (1996). *The culture of education*. Cambridge, MA: Harvard University Press.

Bruner, J., & Kalmar, D. (1997). Narrative and metanarrative in the construction of self. In M. Ferrari & R. Sternberg (Eds.), *Self-awareness: Its nature and development* (pp. 1–52). New York: Guilford.

Buber, M. (1970). *I and thou*. (W. Kaufmann, Trans.). New York: Charles Scribner's Sons.

Burke, K. (1990). Language and symbolic action. In P. Bizzell & B. Herzberg (Eds.), *The rhetorical tradition: Reading from classical times to the present* (pp. 1034–1041). Boston: Bedford Books of Martin's Press.

Buss, A. (1980). *Self-consciousness and social anxiety.* San Francisco: Freeman.

Bussey, K., & Bandura, A. (1999). Social cognitive theory of gender development and differentiation. *Psychological Review, 106,* 676–713.

Bybee, J. (1998). The emergence of gender differences in guilt during adolescence. In J. Bybee (Ed.), *Guilt and children* (pp. 114–122). San Diego, CA: Academic Press.

Cahan, E. (1997). John Dewey and human development. *Developmental Psychology, 28,* 205–214.

Caine, R. (2003). Eco-spirituality. *Encounter: Education for meaning and social justice, 16,* 48–51.

Cairns, R., Cairns, B., Neckerman, H., Ferguson, L., & Gariepy, J. (1989). Growth and aggression: 1. Childhood to early adolescence. *Developmental Psychology, 23,* 320–330.

Cajete, G. (1994). *Look to the mountain: An ecology of indigenous education.* Skyland, NC: Kivaki Press.

Capaldi, D., & Shortt, J. (2003). Understanding conduct problems in adolescence from a lifespan perspective. In G. Adams & M. Berzonsky (Eds.), *Blackwell handbook of adolescence* (pp. 470–493). Malden, MA: Blackwell.

Capps, L., Yirmiya, N., & Sigman, M. (1992). Understanding of simple and complex emotions in non-retarded children with autism. *Journal of Child Psychology and Psychiatry, 33,* 1169–1182.

Capra, F. (1996). *The web of life.* New York: Anchor.

Carpendale, J., & Shelton, C. (1999, April). *"Two kinds of happiness": Relations between interpretive theory of mind and ambivalent emotion understanding.* Poster presented at the Biennial Meeting of the Society for Research in Child Development, Albuquerque, NM.

Case, R., Okamoto, Y., Griffin, S., McKeough, A., Bleiker, C., Henderson, B., & Stephenson, K. (1996). The role of central conceptual structures in the development of children's thought. *Monographs of the Society for Research in Child Development, 61*(1–2, Serial No. 246).

Cederblom, J. (1989). Willingness to reason and the identification of the self. In E. Maimon, B. Nodine, & F. O'Connor (Eds.), *Thinking, reasoning, and writing* (pp. 147–159). New York: Longman.

Chandler, M. (1987). The Othello effect: Essay on the emergence and eclipse of sceptical doubt. *Human Development, 30,* 137–159.

Chen, X., Rubin, K., & Li, Z. (1995). Social functioning and adjustment in Chinese children. *Developmental Psychology, 31,* 531–539.

Chernin, K. (1985). *The hungry self: Women, eating, and identity.* New York: Harper & Row.

Children and the Internet: A parents' guide. (1999). *Time, 153* (18), 22–28.

Chodorow, N. (1978). *The reproduction of mothering.* Berkeley: University of California Press.

Cohen, J. (1999). Social and emotional learning past and present: A psychoeducational dialogue. In J. Cohen (Ed.), *Educating minds and hearts* (pp. 3–23). New York: Teachers College Press.

Coie, J., & Dorval, B. (1973). Sex differences in the intellectual structure of social interaction skills. *Developmental Psychology, 8,* 261–267.

Cole, D. (1989). Validation of the reasons for living inventory in general and delinquent adolescent samples. *Journal of Abnormal Child Psychology, 17,* 13–27.

Coles, R. (1990). *The spiritual life of children.* Boston: Houghton Mifflin.

Coles, R. (1997). *The moral intelligence of children: How to raise a moral child.* New York: Plume.

Collin, A. (1996). Re-thinking the relationship between theory and practice: practioners as map-readers, map-makers—or jazz players? *British Journal of Guidance and Counselling, 24,* 67–81.

Comer, J. P., Haynes, N., Joyner, E., & Ben-Avie, M. (1996). *Rallying the whole village: The Comer process for reforming education.* New York: Teachers College Press.

Coole, D. (1995). The gendered self. In D. Bakhurts & C. Sypnowich, *The social self* (pp. 123–139). London, UK: Sage.

Cooley, C. (1912). *Human nature and social order.* New York: Scribner.

Coopersmith, S. (1967). *The antecedents of self-esteem.* San Francisco: Freeman.

Corwyn, R., & Benda, B. (2000). Religiosity and church attendance: The effects on use of "hard drugs" controlling for sociodemographic and theoretical factors. *International Journal for the Psychology of Religion, 10,* 241–258.

Cowley, G., & Springen, K. (1995, April 17). Rewriting life stories. *Newsweek,* 70–74.

Cremin, L. (1976). *Public education.* New York, NY: Basic Books.

Creswell, J. W. (2002). *Educational research: Planning, conducting, and evaluating quantitative and qualitative research.* Upper Saddle River, NJ: Merrill/Prentice Hall.

Crick, N., & Dodge, K. (1994). A review and reformulation of social information-processing mechanisms in children's social adjustment. *Psychological Bulletin, 115,* 74–101.

Crick, N., Nelson, D., Morales, J., Cullerton-Sen, C., Casas, J., & Hickman, S. (2001). Relational victimization in childhood and adolescence: I hurt you through the grapevine. In J. Juvonen & S. Graham (Eds.), *School-based peer harassment: The plight of the vulnerable and victimized* (pp. 196–214). New York: Guilford Press.

Cronin, D. (2003). *Diary of a worm.* New York: Joanna Cotler Books.

Csikszentmihalyi, M. (1990). *Flow.* New York: Harper and Row.

Csikszentmihalyi, M ., Rathunde, K., & Whalen, S. (1993). *Talented teenagers: The roots of success and failure.* Cambridge, UK: Cambridge University Press.

Cutting, A., & Dunn, J. (1999). Theory of mind, emotion understanding, language, and family background: Individual differences. *Child Development, 70,* 853–865.

D'Andrade, R. (1984). Cultural meaning systems. In R. Shweder & R. LeVine (Eds.), *Culture theory: Essays on mind, self, and emotion* (pp. 92–108). Cambridge: Cambridge University Press.

Dabrowski, K. (1967). *Personality shaping through positive disintegration.* Boston: Little, Brown.

Daley, M., Diakiw, J., McLeod, P., Pitcairn, S., Scrimger, N., & Sumner, D. (1994). *The girl child: An investment in the future.* Toronto, ON: UNICEF.

Damasio, A. *The feeling of what happens: Body and emotion in the making of consciousness.* New York: Harcourt.

Damon, W., & Hart, D. (1988). *Self-understanding in childhood and adolescence.* New York: Cambridge University Press.

Danish, S., Taylor, T., & Fazio, R. (2003). Enhancing adolescent development through sports and leisure. In G. Adams, & M. Berzonsky (Eds.), *Blackwell handbook of adolescence* (pp. 92–108). Malden, MA: Blackwell.

Davis, M. (1980). Measuring individual differences in empathy: Evidence for a multidimensional approach. *Journal of Personality and Social Psychology, 44,* 113–126.

Davis, R., & Phillips, W. (1994). *Turning points: A psychoeducational program for overcoming an eating disorder.* Unpublished manuscript.

Davis, G., & Rimm, S. (1998). *Education of the gifted and talented* (4th ed.). Needham Heights, MA: Allyn & Bacon.

Debold, E., Tolman, D., & Brown, L. (1996). Embodying knowledge, knowing desire: Authority and split subjectives in girls' epistemological development. In N. Goldberger J., Tarule, B., Clinchy & M. Belenky (Eds.), *Knowledge, difference and power* (pp. 85–125). New York: Basic Books.

Delagado-Gaitan, C. (1994). Socializing young children in Mexican-American families: An intergenerational perspective. In P. Greenfield & R. Cocking (Eds.), *Cross-cultural roots of minority child development* (pp. 55–86). Mahwah, NJ: Lawrence Erlbaum Associates.

Denham, S. (1998). *Emotional development in young children.* New York: Guilford Press.

Denham, S., Cook, M., & Zoller, D. (1992). Baby looks very sad: Implications of conversations about feelings between mother and preschooler. *British Journal of Developmental Psychology, 10,* 301–315.

Denham, S., von Salisch, M., Olthof, T., Kochanoff, A., & Caverly, S. (2002). Emotional and social development in childhood. In P. Smith & C. Hart (Eds.), *Blackwell handbook of childhood social development* (pp. 307–328). Oxford, UK: Blackwell.

Denham, S., Blair, K., DeMulder, E., Levitas, J., Sawyer, K., Auerbach-Major, S., & Queenan, P. (2003). Preschool emotional competence: Pathway to social competence? *Child Development, 74,* 238–256.

De Villiers, P. (1999, April). *Language and thought: False complements and false beliefs.* Paper presented at the biennial meeting of the Society for Research in Child Development, Albuquerque, NM.

Dewey, J. (1897). My pedagogic creed. In J. Boydston (Ed.), *The early works of John Dewey, 1892–1898 (1967–1972), Vol., 5* (pp. 84–95). Chicago, IL: Chicago University Press.

Dewey, J. (1902/1966). *The child and the curriculum.* Chicago, IL: University of Chicago Press.

Dewey, J. (1933/1966). *How we think: A restatement of the relation of reflective thinking to the educative process.* Boston: D.C. Heath.

Dewey, J. (1938). *Experience and education.* New York: Collier Books.

Diamond, K. (2002). The development of social competence in children with disabilities. In P. Smith & C. Hart (Eds.), *Blackwell handbook of childhood social development* (pp. 571–587). Oxford, UK: Blackwell.

Dickenson, J., & Emler, N. (1996). Developing ideas about distribution of wealth. In P. Lunt & Furnham (Eds.), *Economic socialization* (pp. 47–68). Cheltenham, UK: Edward Elgar.

Dockett, S. (1997, April). *Young children's peer popularity and theories of mind.* Poster presented at the Biennial Meeting of the Society for Research in Child Development, Washington, DC.

Dodge, K., & Feldman, E. (1990). Issues in social cognition and sociometric status. In S. Asher & J. Coie (Eds.), *Peer rejection in childhood* (pp. 119–155). New York: Cambridge University Press.

Dodge, K., & Frame, C. (1982). Social cognitive biases and deficits in aggressive boys. *Child Development, 53*, 620–635.

Donald, M. (2004). The virtues of rigorous interdisciplinarity. In J. Lucariello, J. Hudson, R. Fivush & P. Bauer (Eds.), *The development of the mediated mind: Sociocultural context and cognitive development* (pp. 245–256). Mahwah, NJ: Lawrence Erlbaum Associates.

Donaldson, M. (1992). *Human minds: An exploration.* Harmondsworth, UK: Allen Lane.

Donelan-McCall, N., & Dunn, J. (1996). School work, teachers, and peers: The world of first grade. *International Journal of Behavioral Development, 21*, 155–178.

Doren, B., Bullis, M., & Benz, M. (1996). Predictors of victimization experiences of adolescents with disabilities in transition. *Exceptional Children, 63*, 7–18.

Drake, S. (1998). *Creating integrated curriculum: Proven ways to increase student learning.* Thousand Oaks, CA: Corwin Press.

Dunn, J. (1988). *The beginning of social understanding.* Oxford, UK: Blackwell.

Dunn, J. (1995). Children as psychologists: The later correlates of individual differences in understanding of emotions and other minds. *Emotion and Cognition, 9*, 187–201.

Dunn, J. (2000). Mind-reading, emotion understanding, and relationships. *International Journal of Behavioral Development, 24*, 142–144.

Eccles, J. & Roeser, R. (2003). Schools as developmental contexts. In G. Adams, & M. Berzonsky (Eds.), *Blackwell handbook of adolescence* (pp. 129–148). Malden, MA: Blackwell.

Edwards, D., & Potter, J. (1995). Attribution. In R. Harré & P. Stearns (Eds.), *Discursive psychology in practice* (pp. 87–119). London, England: Sage Publications.

Eisenberg, N., & Mussen, P. (1989). *The roots of prosocial behavior in children.* New York: Cambridge University Press.

Elbow, P. (1973). *Writing without teachers.* London, UK: University Oxford Press.

Elkind, D. (1967). Egocentrism in adolescence. *Child Development, 3*, 1025–1034.

Elliott, A., Woloshyn, V., Richards, M., Bosacki, S., & Golden, L. (2002, April). *Grade six students' experiences with traditional and interactive technological media.* Paper based on a larger study by Elliott A., Bosacki, S., Murray, N., Richards, M., Woloshyn, V.,

Mindorff, D., Golden, L., & Pollon, D., presented at the annual meeting of the American Educational Research Association, New Orleans, LA.

Ellis, A. (1980). Psychotherapy and aesthetic values: A response to A. Eg. Bergins "Psychotherapy and religious values." *Journal of Consulting and Clinical Psychology*, *48*, 635–639.

Erikson, E. (1968). *Identity, youth, and crisis*. New York: Norton.

Erwin, P. (1993). *Friendship and peer relations in children*. Chichester, UK: Wiley.

Evans, E. (2000). Beyond scopes: Why creationism is here to stay. In K. Rosengren, C. Johnson, & P. Harris (Eds.), *Imagining the impossible: The development of magical, scientific, and religious thinking in contemporary society* (pp. 305–333). Cambridge: Cambridge University Press.

Everitt, A. (2003). *Cicero: The life and times of Rome's greatest politician*. New York: Random House.

Farber, B. (1989). Psychological mindedness: Can there be too much of a good thing? *Psychotherapy*, *26*, 210–217.

Feldman, C. (1992). The new theory of theory of mind. *Human Development*, *35*, 107–117.

Ferguson, T., Stegge, H., & Damhuis, I. (1991). Children's understanding of guilt and shame. *Child Development*, *62*, 827–839.

Feuerverger, G. (1995). Oasis of peace: A community of moral education in Israel. *Journal of Moral Education*, *24*, 113–141.

Feuerverger, G. (2001). *Oasis of dreams: Teaching and learning peace in a Jewish-Palestinian village in Israel*. New York: Routledge Falmer.

Field, A., Camargo, C. Taylor, C., Berkey, C., & Colditz, G. (1999). Relation of peers and media influence to the development of purging behaviors among preadolescents and adolescent girls. *Archives of Pediatrics & Adolescent Medicine*, *153*, 1184–1189.

Finders, M. (1997). *Just girls: Hidden literacies and life in junior high*. New York: Teachers College Press.

Finn, J. (1989). Withdrawing from school. *Review of Educational Research*, *59*, 117–142.

Fiske, A., Kitayama, S., Markus, H., & Nisbett, R. (1998). The cultural matrix of social psychology. In D. Gilbert, A. Fiske, & G. Lindzey (Eds.), *The handbook for social psychology* (Vol. 2, pp. 915–981). New York: McGraw Hill.

Fivush, R. (1989). Exploring sex differences in the emotional content of mother-child conversations about the past. *Sex Roles*, *20*, 675–691.

Fivush, R. (2000). Accuracy, authority, and voice: Feminist perspectives on autobiographical memory. In P. Miller & E. Scholnick (Eds.), *Toward a feminist developmental psychology* (pp. 85–106). New York: Routledge.

Fivush, R. (2004). Voice and silence: A feminist model of autobiographical memory. In J. Lucariello, J. Hudson, R. Fivush & P. Bauer (Eds.), *The development of the mediated mind: Sociocultural context and cognitive development* (pp. 79–100). Mahwah, NJ: Lawrence Erlbaum Associates.

Flanagan, O. (2002). *The problem of the soul: Two visions of mind and how to reconcile them*. New York: Basic Books.

Flapan, D. (1968). *Children's understanding of social interaction*. New York: Teachers College Press.

Flavell, J., & Miller, P. (1998). Social cognition. In W. Damon (Series Ed.) & D. Kuhn & R. Siegler (Vol. Eds.), *Handbook of child psychology: Vol. 2. Cognition, perception and language development* (5th ed., pp. 851–898). New York: Wiley.

Flavell, J., Botkin, P., Fry, C., Wright, J., & Jarvis, D. (1968). *The development of role-taking and communication skills in children.* New York: Wiley.

Florian, V., & Har-Even, D. (1983). Fear of personal death: The effects of sex and religious beliefs. *Omega: Journal of Death and Dying, 14,* 83–91.

Flory, R. (2000). Toward a theory of Generation X religion. In R. Flory & D. Miller (Eds.), *Gen X religion* (pp. 231–250). New York: Routledge.

Ford, M. (1982). Social cognition and social competence in adolescence. *Developmental Psychology, 18,* 323–340.

Fordham, S. (1988). Those loud black girls: Women, silence, and gender "passing" in the academy. *Anthropology and Education Quarterly, 24,* 3–22.

Fordham, S. (1996). *Blacked out: Dilemmas of race, ethnicity, and success at capital high.* Chicago: University of Chicago Press.

Fordham, S., & Ogbu, J. (1986). Black students' school success: Coping with the "burden of acting white." *Urban Review, 18,* 176–206.

Fowler, J. (1981). *Stages of faith: The psychology of human development and the quest for Meaning.* New York: Harper and Row.

Fox, R. (1991). Developing awareness of mind reflected in children's narrative writing. *British Journal of Developmental Psychology, 9,* 281–298.

Fraser, S., & Strayer, J. (1997). *Guilt and shame in middle childhood: Relationships with empathetic responsiveness.* Poster presented at the biennial meeting of the Society for Research in Child Development, Washington, DC.

Freedman, J., & Combs, G. (1996). *Narrative therapy: The social construction of preferred realities.* New York: Norton.

Freud, S. (1918). *Totem and taboo: Resemblances between the psychic lives of savages and neurotics.* New York: Moffat, Yard, & Company.

Freymann, S., & Elffers, J. (1999). *How are you peeling? Foods with moods.* New York: Arthur S. Levine Books.

Fridja, N. (1986). *The emotions.* Cambridge, UK: Cambridge University Press.

Fujiki, M., Brinton, B., Robinson, L., & Watson, V. (1997). The ability of children with specific language impairment to participate in a group decision task. *Journal of Children's Communication Development, 18,* 1–10.

Fuligni, A. (1998). Authority, autonomy, and parent-adolescent conflict and cohesion: A study of adolescents from Mexican, Chinese, Filipino, and European backgrounds. *Developmental Psychology, 34,* 782–797.

Gardner, H. (1985). *Frames of mind.* New York: Basic Books.

Gardner, H. (1991). *The unschooled mind.* New York: Basic Books.

Gardner, H., Csikszentmihalyi, M., & Damon, W. (2001). *Good work: When excellence and ethics meet.* New York: Basic Books.

Garrod, A., & Larimore, C. (1997). *First person, first peoples: Native American college graduates tell their life stories.* Ithaca, NY: Cornell University Press.

Garrod, A., Robinson, T., & Kilkenny, R. (1999). *Souls looking back: Life stories of growing up black. New York:* Routledge.

Geary, D. (1998). *Male, female: The evolution of human sex differences*. Washington, DC: APA.

Geertz, C. (1973). *The interpretation of cultures*. New York: Basic Books.

Gergen, K., & Walhrus, L. (2001). *Social construction in context*. London: Sage Publications.

Gertner, B., Rice, M., & Hadley, P. (1994). Influence of communicative competence on peer preferences in a preschool classroom. *Journal of Speech and Hearing Research, 37,* 913–923.

Gilligan, C. (1982). *In a different voice: Psychological theory and women's development*. Cambridge, MA: Harvard University Press.

Gilligan, C. (1993). Adolescent development rediscovered. In A. Garrod (Ed.), *Approaches to moral development* (pp. 103–132). New York: Teachers College Press.

Giroux, H., & Penna, A. (1979). Social education in the classroom: The dynamics of the hidden curriculum. *Theory and Research in Social Education, 7,* 21–22.

Gjerde, P. (1995). Alternative pathways to chronic depressive symptoms in young adults: Gender differences in developmental trajectories. *Child Development, 66,* 1277–1300.

Gjerde. P., & Block, J. (1991). Preadolescent antecedents of depressive symptomatology in late adolescence: A prospective study. *Journal of Youth and Adolescence, 20,* 215–230.

Glazer, S. (Ed.). (1999). *The heart of learning: Spirituality in education*. New York: Penguin Putnam.

Goffman, I. (1959). *The presentation of self in everyday life*. New York: Doubleday.

Goldberg, M. (1997). *Arts and learning: An integrated approach to teaching and learning in multicultural and multilingual settings*. New York: Longman.

Goldberger, N. (1996). Cultural imperatives and diversity in ways of knowing. In N. Goldberger, J. Tarule, B. Clinchy, & M. Belenky (Eds.), *Knowledge, differences, and power: Essays inspired by women's ways of knowing* (pp. 335–371). New York: Basic Books.

Goldberger, N., Tarule, J., Clinchy, B., & Belenky, M. (1996). *Knowledge, differences, and powers: Essays inspired by women's ways of knowing*. New York: Basic Books.

Goldman, R. (1964). *Religious thinking from childhood to adolescence*. London: Routledge & Kegan Paul.

Goldstein, L. (1997). *Teaching with love: A feminist approach to early childhood*. New York: Peter Lang.

Goleman, D. (1995). *Emotional intelligence*. New York: Bantam Books.

Gollnick, D., & Chinn, P. (2002). *Multicultural education in a pluralistic society* (6th ed.). Upper Saddle River, NJ: Merrill/Prentice Hall.

Goodwin, M. (2003). Exclusion in girls' peer groups: Ethnographic analysis of language practices on the playground. *Human Development, 45,* 392–415.

Gopnik, A. (1993). How we know our minds: The illusion of first-person knowledge of intentionality. *Behavioural and Brain Sciences, 16,* 1–14.

Gopnik, A., & Astington, J. (1988). Children's understanding of representational change and its relation to the understanding of false belief and the appearance-reality distinction. *Child Development, 58,* 26–37.

Graber, J. (2003). Puberty in context. In C. Hayward (Ed.), *Gender differences at puberty* (pp. 307–325). Cambridge: Cambridge University Press.

Grant, C., & Gomez, M. (2001). *Campus and classroom: Making schooling multicultural* (2nd ed.). Upper Saddle River, NJ: Merrill/Prentice Hall.

Greer, J. (1972). Sixth form religion in Northern Ireland, Social Studies. *Irish Journal of Sociology, 1,* 325–340.

Gresham, F., & MacMillan, D. (1997). Autistic recovery? An analysis and critique of the empirical evidence on the early intervention project. *Behavioral Disorders, 22,* 185–201.

Grice, H. (1968). Utterer's meaning, sentence-meaning and word-meaning. *Foundations of Language, 4,* 1–18.

Griffin, S. (1995). A cognitive-developmental analysis of pride, shame, and embarrassment in middle childhood. In J. Tangney & K. Fischer (Eds.), *Self-conscious emotions: The psychology of shame, guilt, embarrassment, and pride* (pp. 219–236). New York: Guilford.

Griffith, J., & Griffith, M. (1994). *The body speaks: Therapeutic dialogues for mind-body problems.* New York: Basic Books.

Grossman, L. (2003, November, 24). Old school, new tricks, *Time Magazine* (Canadian edition), pp. 36–40.

Group for the Advancement of Psychiatry, Committee on Adolescents. (1996). *Adolescent suicide* (Report No. 140). Washington, DC: American Psychiatric Press.

Gruter, M., & Masters, R. (1986). Ostracism as a social and biological phenomenon: An introduction. *Ethology and Sociobiology, 7,* 149–158.

Guralnick, M. (1999). Family and child influences on the peer-related social competence of young children with developmental delays. *Mental Retardation and Developmental Disabilities Research Reviews, 5,* 31–29.

Guralnick, M., Connor, R., Hammond, M., Gottman, J., & Kinnish, K. (1996). The peer relations of preschool children with communication disorders. *Child Development, 67,* 471–489.

Guralnick, M., & Neville, B. (1997). Designing early intervention programs to promote children's social competence. In M. Guralnick (Ed.), *The effectiveness of early intervention* (pp. 579–610). Baltimore: Paul H. Brookes.

Gutierrez, K., & Rogoff, B. (2003). Cultural ways of learning: Individual traits or repertoires of practice. *Educational Researcher, 32,* 19–25.

Haden, C., Haine, R., & Fivush, R. (1997). Developing narrative structure in parent-child reminiscing across the preschool years. *Developmental Psychology, 33,* 295–307.

Haines, B., & Bartels, F. (1997, April). *Shyness and academic performance: Mediating or moderating roles of self-esteem, attributional style, and ethnicity.* Poster session presented at the biennial meeting of the Society for Research in Child Development, Washington, DC.

Hall, N. (1980). *The moon and the virgin.* New York: Harper and Row.

Hall, R. (1986). What nursery school teachers ask us about: Psychoanalytic consultations in preschools: Living with Spiderman et al.: Mastering aggression and excitement. *Emotions and Behavior Monographs* (Monograph No. 5), 89–99.

Hall, S. (1904). *Adolescence, its psychology, and its relations to physiology, anthropology, sociology, sex, crime, religion, and education* (Vol. 2). New York: D. Appleton & Co.

Halpern, D. (1992). *Sex differences in cognitive abilities* (2nd ed.). Hillsdale, NJ: Lawrence Erlbaum Associates.

Happé, F. (1993). Communicative competence and theory of mind in autism: A test of relevance theory. *Cognition, 48*, 101–119.

Hardy, A. (1966). *The divine flame*. London: Collins.

Harkness, S. (2002). Culture and social development: Explanations and evidence. In P. Smith & C. Hart (Eds.), *Blackwell handbook of childhood social development* (pp. 60–77). Oxford, UK: Blackwell.

Harre, R. (1986). *The social construction of emotions*. Oxford, UK: Blackwell.

Harris, P. (1989). *Children and emotion*. Cambridge, MA: Basil Blackwell.

Harris, P. (2000). On not falling down to earth: Children's metaphysical questions. In K. Rosengren, C. Johnson, & P. Harris (Eds.), *Imagining the impossible: The development of magical, scientific, and religious thinking in contemporary society* (pp. 157–178). Cambridge: Cambridge University Press.

Harris, P., Johnson, C., Hutton, D., Andrews, G., & Cooke, T. (1989). Young children's theory of mind and emotion. *Cognition and Emotion, 3*, 379–400.

Harry, B., Rueda, R., & Kalyanpur, M. (1999). Cultural reciprocity in sociocultural perspective: Adapting the normalization principles for family collaboration. *Exceptional Children, 66*, 123–136.

Hart, D., & Fegley, S. (1995). Prosocial behavior and caring in adolescence: Relations to self-understanding and social judgement. *Child Development, 66*, 1346–1359.

Harter, S. (1999). *The construction of the self: A developmental perspective*. New York: Guilford Press.

Harter, S., & Buddin, B. (1987). Children's understanding of the simultaneity of two emotions: A five-stage developmental acquisition sequence. *Developmental Psychology, 23*, 388–399.

Harter, S., Waters, P., Whitesell, N., & Kastelic, D. (1997, April). *Predictors of level of voice among high school females and males: Relational context, support, and gender orientation*. Paper presented at the biennial meeting of the Society for Research in Child Development, Washington, DC.

Harvey, P. (1996). *An introduction to Buddhism*. Cambridge: Cambridge University Press.

Hatcher, R., & Hatcher, S. (1997). Assessing the psychological mindedness of children and adolescents. In M. McCallum & W. Piper (Eds.), *Psychological mindedness: A contemporary understanding* (pp. 59–75). Mahwah, NJ: Lawrence Erlbaum Associates.

Hatcher, R., Hatcher, S., Berlin, M., Okla, K., & Richards, J. (1990). Psychological mindedness and abstract reasoning in late childhood and adolescence: An exploration using new instruments. *Journal of Youth and Adolescence, 19*, 307–325.

Hay, D. (2001). Spirituality versus individualism: The challenge of relational consciousness . In J. Erricker, C. Ota., & C. Erricker (Eds.), *Spiritual education: Cultural, religious, and social differences: New perspectives for the 21st century* (pp. 104–117). Brighton, UK: Sussex Academic Press.

Hay, D. (1990). *Religious experiences today*. London: Fount.

Hay, D., & Nye, R. (1998). *The spirit of the child*. London: Fount.

Haynes, J. (2002). *Children as philosophers: Learning through enquiry and dialogue in the primary classroom*. London: Routledge Falmer.

Haynes, N., & Marans, S. (1999). The cognitive, emotional, and behavioral (CEB) framework for promoting acceptance of diversity. In J. Cohen (Ed.), *Educating minds and hearts: Social emotional learning and the passage into adolescence* (pp. 158–170). New York: Teachers College Press.

Heke, I. (2001). *The Hokowhitu Program: Designing a sporting intervention to address alcohol and substance abuse in adolescent Maori*. Unpublished manuscript, University of Otago, Dunedin, New Zealand.

Helwig, C. (1997). The role of agent and social context in judgements of freedom of speech and religion. *Child Development, 66,* 152–166.

Hill, J., & Lynch, M. (1983). The intensification of gender-related role expectations during early adolescence. In J Brooks-Gunn, & A. Peterson (Eds.), *Girls at puberty: Biological and psychosocial perspectives* (pp. 201–228). New York: Plenum.

Hill, P., & Pargament, K. (2003). Advance in the conceptualization and measurement of religion and spirituality: Implications for physical and mental health research, *American Psychologist, 58,* 64–74.

Hinde, R. (1997, December). *Religion and Darwinism: The Voltaire Lecture, 9.* London: British Humanist Association.

Ho, W. (2001). The prospects of spirituality in a globalized, technologized world. In J. Erricker, A. Ota, & C. Erricker (Eds.), *Spiritual education: Cultural, religious, and social differences: New perspectives for the 21st century* (pp. 170–183). Brighton, UK: Sussex Academic Press.

Hobson, P. (1991). Against the theory of 'Theory of Mind'. *British Journal of Developmental Psychology, 9,* 33–51.

Hoffman, M. (1984). Interaction of affect and cognition in empathy. In C. Izard, J. Kaagn, & R. Zajonc (Eds.), *Emotions, cognitions and behavior* (pp. 103–121). New York: Cambridge University Press.

Honess, T. (1981). Girls' and boys' perceptions of their peers: Peripheral versus central and objective versus interpretive aspects of free descriptions. *British Journal of Psychology, 70,* 485–497.

Howlin, P., Mawhood, L., & Rutter, M. (2000). Autism and developmental receptive language disorder—A comparative follow-up in early adult life. II: Social, behavioural, and psychiatric outcomes. *Journal of Child Psychology and Psychiatry, 14,* 561–578.

Hughes, F. (1999). *Children, play, and development*. Boston, MA: Allyn & Bacon.

Hughes, C., & Dunn, J. (1998). Theory of mind and emotion understanding: Longitudinal associations with mental-state talk between young friends. *Developmental Psychology, 34,* 1026–1037.

Hughes, C., Dunn, J., & White, A. (1998). Trick or treat? Uneven understanding of mind and emotion and executive dysfunction in "hard-to-manage" preschoolers. *Journal of Child Psychology and Psychiatry, 39,* 981–994.

Hughes, C., Deater-Deckard, K., & Cutting, A. (1999). "Speak roughly to your little boy"? Sex differences in the relations between parenting and preschoolers' understanding of mind. *Social Development, 8*, 143–160.

Hurtado, A. (1996). Strategic suspensions: Women of color theorize the production of knowledge. In N. Goldberger, J. Tarule, B. Clinchy, and M. Belenky, *Knowledge, difference, and power* (pp. 372–392). New York: Basic Books.

Hutchison, D. (1998). *Growing up green: Education for ecological renewal.* New York: Teachers College Press.

Hyde, K. (1990). *Religion in childhood and adolescence.* Birmingham, AL: Religious Education Press.

Jack, D. (1991). *Silencing the self: Women and depression.* New York: Harper Collins.

Jack, D. (1999). *Behind the mask: Destruction and creativity in women's aggression.* Cambridge, MA: Harvard University Press.

Jackson, A., & Davis, G. (2000). *Turning points 2000: Educating adolescents in the 21st century.* New York: Teachers College Press.

Jacobsen, T., Edelstein, W., & Hofmann, V. (1995). A longitudinal study of the relation between representations of attachment in childhood and cognitive functioning in childhood and adolescence. *Developmental Psychology, 30,* 112–124.

Jahnke, H., & Blanchard-Fields, F. (1993). A test of two models of adolescent egocentrism. *Journal of Youth and Adolescence, 22,* 313–327.

Jahoda, G. (1959). The development of children's ideas about country and nationality, Pt. I: The conceptual framework. *British Journal of Educational Psychology, 33,* 47–60.

James, W. (1890). *Principles of psychology* (Vol. 1). New York: Dover.

Jenkins, J., & Astington, J. (1996). Cognitive factors and family structure associated with theory of mind development in young children. *Developmental Psychology, 32,* 70–78.

Jeynes, W. (2002). A meta-analysis of the effects of attending religious schools and religiosity on black and Hispanic academic achievement. *Education and Urban Society, 35,* 27–49.

Jimerson, S., Egeland, B. & Teo, A. (1999). A longitudinal study of achievement trajectories: Factors associated with change. *Journal of Educational Psychology, 91,* 116–126.

Johnson, E. (1997). Children's understanding of epistemic conduct in self-deception and other false belief stories. *Child Development, 68,* 1117–1132.

Jones, M., & Gerig, T. (1994). Silent sixth-grade students: Characteristics, achievement and teacher expectations. *The Elementary School Journal, 2,* 169–182.

Junger-Tas, J. (1999). The Netherlands. In P. Smith et al. (Eds.), *The nature of school bullying* (pp. 205–223). London: Routledge.

Juvonen, J., & Bear, G. (1992). Social adjustment of children with and without learning disabilities in integrated classrooms. *Journal of Educational Psychology, 84,* 322–330.

Kagan, J. (1984). *The nature of the child.* New York: Basic Books.

Kaiser Family Foundation (1999). *Kids and media at the new millenium.* Menlo Park: CA: Author.

Kashima, Y., Yamaguchi, S., Kim, U., Choi, S., Gelfand, M., & Yuki, M. (1995). Culture, gender, and self: A perspective from individualism-collectivism research. *Journal of Personality and Social Psychology, 69,* 925–937.

Keating, D. (1990). Adolescent thinking. In S. Feldman & G. Elliott (Eds.), *At the threshold: The developing adolescent* (pp. 56–89). Cambridge, MA: Harvard University Press.

Keenan, T. (1995). *The role of echoic information in young children's comprehension of sarcasm.* Unpublished doctoral dissertation, University of Toronto, Toronto, Ontario.

Kegan, R. (1994). *In over our heads: The mental demands of modern life.* Cambridge, MA: Harvard University Press.

Kelly, G. (1969). *A theory of personality: The psychology of personal constructs.* New York: W. W. Norton.

Kerr, B. (1994). *Smart girls two: A new psychology of girls, women and giftedness.* Dayton, OH: Ohio Psychology Press.

Kessler, R. (2000). *The soul of education: Helping students find connection, compassion, and character at school.* Alexandria, VA: ASCD.

King, C., Akiyama, M., & Elling, K. (1996). Self-perceived competencies and depression among middle school students in Japan and the United States. *Journal of Early Adolescence, 16,* 192–210.

Kirkpatrick, L. (1997). A longitudinal study of changes in religious belief and behavior as a function of individual differences in adult attachment style. *Journal for the Scientific Study of Religion, 36,* 207–217.

Kitayama, S., Markus, H., & Matsumoto, H. (1995). Culture, self, and emotion: A cultural perspective on "self-conscious" emotions. In J. Tangney & K. Fischer (Eds.), *Self-conscious emotions: The psychology of shame, guilt, embarrassment, and pride* (pp. 439–464). New York: Guilford.

Kitchener, K., & King, K. (1981). Reflective judgement: Concepts of justification and their relationship to age and education. *Journal of Applied Psychology, 2,* 89–116.

Kochanska, G. (1994). Maternal reports of conscience development and temperament in young children. *Child Development, 65,* 852–868.

Kopp, C. (1989). Regulation of distress and negative emotions: A developmental review. *Developmental Psychology, 25,* 343–354.

Kraut, R., Patterson, M., Lundmark, V., Kiesler, S., Mukopahdyay, T., & Scherlis, W. (1998). Internet paradox: A social technology that reduces social involvement and psychological well-being? *American Psychologist, 53,* 1017–1031.

Kroger, J. (1996). *Identity in adolescence: The balance between self and other.* London: Routledge.

Kruger, A. (1992). The effect of peer and adult-child transactive discussions on moral reasoning. *Merrill-Palmer Quarterly, 38,* 191–211.

Kuhn, D. (1989). Making cognitive development research relevant to education. In W. Damon (Ed.), *Child development today and tomorrow* (pp. 261–287). San Francisco: Jossey-Bass.

Kuhn, D., Nash, D., & Brucken, L. (1978). Sex-role concepts of two- and three-year-olds. *Child Development, 49,* 445–451.

Kumar, R., & Mitchell, C. (2003, July). *Silencing within the academy: Pressures to conform.* Paper presented at the biennial conference of the International Study Association for Teachers and Teaching, Leiden, Holland.

Laible, D., & Thompson, R. (1998). Attachment and emotional understanding in pre-school. *Developmental Psychology, 34*, 1038–1045.

Laing, R. (1961). *Self and others*. London: Penguin Books.

Lalonde, C., & Chandler, M. (1995). False belief understanding goes to school: On the social-emotional consequences of coming early or late to a first theory of mind. *Cognition and Emotion, 9*, 167–185.

Lalonde, C., & Chandler, M. (1997, April). *The development of an interpretive theory of mind*. Paper presented at the biennial meeting of the Society for Research in Child Development, Washington, DC.

Lamb, S. (2001). *The secret lives of girls: What good girls really do—Sex play, aggression, and their guilt*. New York: Free Press.

Lantieri, L. (2001). A vision of schools with spirit. In L. Lantieri (Ed.), *Schools with spirit: Nurturing the inner lives of children and teachers* (pp. 7–20). Boston: Beacon Press.

Lather, P. (1986). Issues of validity in openly ideological research: Between a rock and a soft place. *Interchange, 17*, 63–84.

Lather, P. (1991). *Getting smart: Feminist research and pedagogy with/in the postmodern*. New York: Routledge.

Leahy, R. (1981). Development of the conception of economic inequality: I. Descriptions and comparisons of rich and poor people. *Child Development, 52*, 523–532.

Leaper, C. (2000). The social construction and socialization of gender during development. In P. Miller & E. Scholnick (Eds.), *Toward a feminist developmental psychology* (pp. 127–152). New York: Routledge.

Lee, C. (2003). Why we need to re-think race and ethnicity in educational research. *Educational Researcher, 32*, 3–5.

Leech, G. (1980). *Explorations in semantics and pragmatics*. Amsterdam: Johns Benjamins B. V.

Leekam. S. (1993). *Children's understanding of mind. In M. Bennett (Ed.), The child as psychologist: An introduction to the development of social cognition* (pp. 26–61). New York: Harvester Wheatsheaf.

Leiser, D., Sevon, G., & Levy, D (1990). Children's economic socialization: Summarizing the cross-cultural comparison of ten countries. *Journal of Economic Psychology, 11*, 591–614.

Levin, J., Taylor, R., & Chatters, L. (1994). Race and gender differences in religiosity among older adults: Findings from four national surveys. *Journal of Gerontology, 49*, 137–145.

Levinas, E. (1989). Ethics as first philosophy. In S. Hand (Ed.), *The Levinas reader* (pp. 31–54). Oxford, UK: Blackwell.

Levine, S. (1999). Children's cognitive capacities: The foundation for creative healing. *Journal of Poetry Therapy, 12*, 135–153.

Levinson, S. (1995). Interactional biases in human thinking. In E. Goody (Ed.), *Social intelligence and interaction* (pp. 221–260). New York: Cambridge University Press.

Lewis, M. (1995). Embarrassment: The emotion of self-exposure and evaluation. In J. Tangney & K. Fischer (Eds.), *Self-conscious emotions: The psychology of shame, guilt, embarrassment, and pride* (pp. 198–218). New York: Guilford Press.

Lewis, M., Sullivan, M., Stanger, C., & Weiss, M. (1989). Self-development and self-conscious emotions. *Child Development, 60,* 146–156.

Lightfoot, C. (1997). *The culture of adolescent risk-taking.* New York: Guilford Press.

Lillard, A. (1997). Other folks' theories of mind and behavior. *Psychological Science, 8,* 268–274.

Lionni, L. (1970). *Fish is fish.* New York: Dragonfly Books.

Lips, H. (1997). *Sex and gender: An introduction* (3rd ed.). Mountain View, CA: Mayfield Publishing.

Litchfield, A., Thomas, D., & Li, B. (1997). Dimensions of religiosity as mediators of the relations between parenting and adolescent deviant behavior. *Journal of Adolescent Research, 12,* 199–226.

Livesley, W., & Bromley, D. (1973). *Person perception in childhood and adolescence.* London: Wiley.

Lloyd, G. (1998). Rationality. In A. Jagger & I. Young (Eds.), *A companion to feminist philosophy* (pp. 165–172). Oxford, UK: Blackwell.

Loeb, R., & Sarigiani, P. (1986). The impact of hearing impairment on self-perceptions of children. *The Volta Review, 88,* 89–100.

Loewenthal, K. (2000). *The psychology of religion: A short introduction.* Oxford, UK: Oneworld.

Lomawaima, K. (1995). Educating Native Americans. In J. Banks & C. Banks (Eds.), *Handbook of research on multicultural education* (pp. 45–67). New York: Macmillan.

Lopez, A. (2003). Mixed-race school age children: A summary of census 2000 data. *Educational Researcher, 32,* 25–37.

Lord, C., & Magill-Evans, J. (1995). Peer interactions of autistic children and adolescents. *Development and Psychopathology, 7,* 611–626.

Lovecky, D. (2004). *Different minds: Gifted children with AD/HD, Asperger Syndrome, and Other Learning Deficits.* London: Jessica Kingsley Publishers.

Luttrell, W. (1993). "The teachers, they all had their pets": Concepts of gender, knowledge, and power. *Signs: Journal of Women in Culture and Society, 18,* 505–546.

Lutz, C. (1988). *Unnatural emotions: Everyday sentiments on a Micronesian atoll and their challenge to Western theory.* Chicago: University of Chicago Press.

Lutz, C., & White, G. (1986). The anthropology of emotions. *Annual Reviews in Anthropology, 15,* 405–435.

Maccoby, E. (1998). Gender and relationships: A developmental account. *American Psychologist, 45,* 513–520.

Mallick, J., & Watts, M. (2001). Spirituality and drugs education: A study in parent/child communication. *International Journal of Children's Spirituality, 6,* 67–83.

Mansfield, A., & Clinchy, B. (1997, April). *Toward the integration of objectivity and subjectivity: A longitudinal study of epistemological development between the ages of 9 and 13.* Poster presented at the biennial meeting of the Society for Research in Child Development, Washington, DC.

Mant, C., & Perner, J. (1988). The child's understanding of commitment. *Developmental Psychology, 24,* 343–351.

Marcia, J. (1980). Identity in adolescence: In J. Adelson (Ed.), *Handbook of adolescent psychology* (pp. 159–187). New York: Wiley.

Mares, M., & Woodward, E. (2001). Prosocial effects on children's social interactions. In D. Singer & J. Singer (Eds.), *Handbook of children and the media* (pp. 183–205). Thousand Oaks, CA: Sage Publications.

Marini, Z., Dane, A., Bosacki, S., & YLC-CURA (2002, August). *The intrapersonal adjustment of adolescent bullies, victims and bully/victims.* Poster session presented at the biennial meeting of the International Society for the Study of Behavioral Development, Ottawa, Ontario, Canada.

Marini, Z., Fairbairn, L., & Zuber, R. (2001). Peer harassment in individuals with developmental disabilities: Towards the development of a multidimensional bullying identification model. *Developmental Disabilities Bulletin, 29,* 170–195.

Marini, Z., Spear, S., & Bombay, K. (1999). Peer victimization in middle childhood: Characterizations, causes and consequences of school bullying. *Brock Education, 9,* 32–47.

Markus, H., & Kitayama, S. (1994). The cultural construction of self and emotion: Implications for social behavior. In S. Kitayama & H. Markus (Eds.), *Emotion and culture: Empirical studies of mutual influence* (pp. 89–132). Washington, DC: APA.

Markus, H., & Wurf, E. (1987). The dynamic self-concept: A social psychological perspective. *Annual Review of Psychology, 38,* 299–337.

Marsh, H., & Shavelson, R. (1985). Self-concept: Its multifaceted, hierarchical, structure. *Educational Psychologist, 20,* 107–125.

Martin, K. (1996). *Puberty, sexuality, and the self: Girls and boys at adolescence.* New York Routledge.

Martlew, M., & Hodson, J. (1991). Children with mild learning difficulties in an integrated and in a special school: Comparisons of behaviour, teasing and teachers' attitudes. *British Journal of Special Education, 22,* 24–27.

Maslow, A. (1971). *The farther reaches of human nature.* New York: Viking.

Matousek, M. (1998, July–Aug.) Should you design your own religion? *UTNE Reader,* 44–48.

Matthews, G., Zeidner, M., & Roberts, R. (2002). *Emotional intelligence: Science and myth.* Cambridge, MA: MIT Press.

Matthews, D., & Keating, D. (1995). Domain specificity and habits of mind: An investigation of patterns of high-level development. *Journal of Early Adolescence, 15,* 319–343.

McCree, D. H., Wingood, G. M, & DiClemente, R., Davies, S., & Harrington, K. F. (2003). Religiosity and risky sexual behavior in African-American adolescent females. *Journal of Adolescent Health, 33,* 2–8.

McCormick, P. (1994). *Children's understanding of mind: A case for cultural diversity.* Unpublished doctoral dissertation, University of Toronto, Toronto, Ont.

McDevitt, T., & Ormrod, J. (2004). *Child Development: Educating and working with children and adolescents* (2nd ed.) Upper Saddle River, NJ: Merrill/Prentice Hall.

McGinn, M., & Bosacki, S. (2004, March). Research ethics and practitioners: Concerns and strategies for novice researchers engaged in graduate education. *Forum Qaulitaive Sozialforschung/Forum: Qualitative Social Research, 5*(2). Retrieved March 16, 2004, from http://www.Qualitative-research.net/fqs-texte/2-04/2-04mcginnbosacki-e. html

McGrath, E., Keita, G., Strickland, B., & Russo, N. (1990). *Women and depression.* Washington, DC: American Psychological Association.

McKeough, A. (1992). A neo-structural analysis of children's narrative and its development. In R. Case (Ed.), *The mind's staircase: Exploring the conceptual underpinnings of children's thought and knowledge* (pp. 171–188). Mahwah, NJ: Lawrence Erlbaum Associates.

McKeough, A., Templeton, L., & Marini, A. (1995). Conceptual change in narrative knowledge. Psychological understandings for low-literacy and literate adults. *Journal of Narrative and Life History, 5,* 21–49.

McLaughlin, T., O'Keefe, J., & O'Keefe, B. (1996). *The contemporary Catholic school: Context, identity and diversity.* London: Falmer Press.

Mead, G. (1934). *Mind, self and society.* Chicago: Chicago University Press.

Meehan, C. (2002, March). Promoting spiritual developing in the curriculum. *Pastoral Care,* 16–24.

Menyuk, P., & Menyuk, D. (1988). Communicative competence: A historical and cultural perspective. In J. Wurzel (Ed.), *Toward multiculturalism: A reader in multicultural education* (pp. 131–152). Yarmouth, ME: Intercultural Press.

Miller, A. (1997). *The drama of the gifted child: The search for the true self (Rev. ed.).* New York: Basic Books.

Miller, J. (1993). *The holistic curriculum.* Toronto, ON: OISE Press.

Miller, J. (2000). *Education and the soul: Toward a spiritual curriculum.* New York: State University of New York Press.

Miller, L., Davies, M., & Greenwald, S. (2000). Religiosity and substance use and abuse among adolescents in the National Comorbidity Survey. *Journal of the American Academy of Child & Adolescent Psychiatry, 39,* 1190–1197.

Miller, P., & Scholnick, E. (2000). Introduction: Beyond gender as a variable. In P. Miller & E. Scholnick (Eds.), *Toward a feminist developmental psychology* (pp. 3–10). New York: Routledge.

Miller, P., Kessel, F., & Flavell, J. (1970). Thinking about people thinking about people thinking about. . . : A study of social cognitive development. *Child Development, 41,* 613–623.

Moore, T. (1992). *Care of the soul: A guide for cultivating depth and sacredness in everyday life.* New York: Harper Collins.

Moore, C. (1996). Theories of mind in infancy. *British Journal of Developmental Psychology, 14,* 19–40.

Morrison, T. (1994). *The bluest eye.* New York: Plume.

Muller, R. (1984). *New genesis: Shaping a global spirituality.* Garden City, NY: Doubleday.

Myers, B. (1997). *Young children and spirituality.* New York: Routledge.

Myers, D. (2000). *The American paradox: Spiritual hunger in an age of plenty.* New Haven, CT: Yale University Press.

Nagel, T. (1986). *The view from nowhere.* New York: Oxford University Press.

Nakashima, C. (1992). An invisible monster: The creation and denial of mixed-race people in America. In M. P. Root (Ed.), *Racially mixed people in America* (pp. 162–178). Newbury Park, CA: Sage.

Nasir, N., & Saxe, G. (2003). Ethnic and academic identities: A cultural practice perspective on emerging tensions and their management in the lives of minority students. *Educational Researcher, 32*, 14–18.

Neisser, U. (1988). Five kinds of self-knowledge. *Philosophical Psychology, 1*, 35–39.

Nelson, K. (1996). *Language in cognitive development: Emergence of the mediated mind*. New York: Cambridge University Press.

Nelson, K., Henseler, S., & Plesa, D. (2000). Entering a community of minds: Theory of mind from a feminist standpoint. In P. Miller & E. Scholnick (Eds.), *Toward a feminist developmental psychology* (pp. 61–83). New York: Routledge.

Nesbitt, E. (1998). British, Asian, and Hindu: Identity, Self-narration and the ethnographic interview. *Journal of Beliefs and Values, 19*, 189–200.

Nesbitt, E. (2001). Religious nurture and young people's spirituality: Reflections on research at the university of Warwick. In J. Erricker, C. Ota, & C. Erricker (Eds.), *Spiritual education: Cultural religious, and social differences: New perspectives for the 21st century* (pp. 130–142). Brighton, UK: Sussex University Press.

Noddings, N. (1984). *Caring: A feminine approach to ethnic and moral education*. Berkeley, CA: University of California.

Noddings, N. (2003). *Happiness and education*. Cambridge: Cambridge University Press.

Nucci, L. (2001). *Education in the moral domain*. New York: Cambridge University Press.

Nussbaum, M. (2000). Emotions and social norms. In L. Nucci, G. Saxe, & E. Turiel (Eds.), *Culture, thought, and development* (pp. 41–63). Mahwah, NJ: Lawrence Erlbaum Associates.

Nye, R., & Hay, D. (1996). Identifying children's spirituality: How do you start without a starting point? *British Journal of Religious Education, 18*, 144–154.

Oatley, K., & Duncan, E. (1994). The experience of emotions in everyday life. *Cognition and Emotion, 8*, 369–381.

Ochoa, S., & Palmer, D. (1995). Comparison of the peer status of Mexican-American students with learning disabilities and non-disabled students. *Learning Disability Quarterly, 18*, 57–63.

Ochs, E., & Schieffelin, B. (1984). Language acquisition and socialization: Three developmental stories. In R. Shweder & R. LeVine (Eds.), *Culture theory: Mind, self and emotion* (pp. 276–320). Cambridge, UK: Cambridge University Press.

Offer, D., Ostrov, E., Howard, K., & Atkinson, R. (1988). *The teenage world: Adolescents' self-image in ten countries*. New York: Plenum.

Okely, J. (1987). Privileged, schooled and finished: Boarding education for girls. In G. Werner and M. Arnot (Eds.), *Gender under scrutiny* (pp. 101–113). London, UK: Hutchison.

Olson, D. (1997). Critical thinking: Learning to talk about talk and text. In G. Phye (Ed.), *Handbook of academic learning* (pp. 493–510). New York: Academic Press.

Olson, D., & Bruner, J. (1996). Folk psychology and folk pedagogy. In D. Olson & N. Torrance (Eds.), *Handbook of education and human development: New models of learning, teaching and schooling* (pp 9–27). Oxford, UK: Blackwell.

Olweus, D. (1993). *Bullying at school.* Cambridge, MA: Blackwell.

Ontario Ministry of Education and Training (1997). *The Ontario Curriculum, Grades 1–8, Language.* Toronto, ON: Ministry of Education.

Oser, F., & Scarlett, G. (1991). (Eds.). Religious development in childhood and adolescence. *New Directions for Child Development, 52.*

Oyserman, D., & Markus, H. (1993). The sociocultural self. In J. Suls (Ed.), *Psychological perspectives on the self* (Vol. 4, pp. 187–220).

Paechter, C. (2000). *Changing school subjects: Power, gender, and curriculum.* Buckingham, UK: Open University Press.

Paik, H. (2001). The history of children's use of electronic media. In D. Ginger & J. Singer (Eds.), *Handbook of children and the media* (pp. 7–27). Thousand Oaks, CA: Sage.

Pajares, F., Miller, D., & Johnson, M. (1999). Gender differences in writing self-beliefs of elementary school students. *Journal of Educational Psychology, 91,* 50–61.

Paley, V. (1999). *The kindness of children.* Cambridge, MA: Harvard University Press.

Palmer, P. (1999, January). Evoking the spirit. *Educational Leadership, 6–11.*

Parent, S., Normandeau, S., Cossett-Richard, M., & Letarte, M. (1999, April). *Preschoolers' emotional competence and social behavior within the family: May gender differences be in the eye of the beholder?* Poster session presented at the biennial meeting of the Society for Research in Child Development, Albuquerque, NM.

Parkhurst, J., & Asher, S. (1992). Peer rejection in middle school: Subgroup differences in behavior, loneliness, and interpersonal concerns. *Developmental Psychology, 28,* 231–241.

Park, L., & Park, T. (1997). Personal intelligence. In M. McCallum & W. Pipher (Eds.), *Psychological mindedness: A contemporary understanding* (pp. 133–168). Mahwah, NJ: Lawrence Erlbaum Associates.

Patterson, C., Kupersmidt, J., & Griesler, P. (1990). Children's perceptions of self and of relationships with others as a function of sociometric status. *Child Development, 61,* 1335–1349.

Peevers, F., & Secord, P. (1973). Developmental changes in attribution of descriptive concepts of persons. *Journal of Personality and Social Psychology, 27,* 120–128.

Pekrun, R. (1990). Social support, achievement evaluations, and self-concepts in adolescence. In L. Oppenheimer (Ed.), *The self-concept: European perspectives on its development, aspects and applications* (pp. 107–119). Berlin, Germany: Springer.

Pellegrini, D. (1985). Social cognition and competence in middle childhood. *Child Development, 56,* 253–264.

Pepler, D., & Craig, W. (1995). A peek behind the fence: Naturalistic observations of aggressive children with remote audiovisual recording, *Developmental Psychology, 31,* 348–553.

Perner, J. (1991). *Understanding the representational mind.* Cambridge, MA: Bradford/MIT.

Perry, W. (1970). *Forms of intellectual and ethical development in the college years*. New York: Holt, Rinehart & Winston.

Peshkin, A. (1988). In search of subjectivity—one's own. *Educational Researcher, 14*, 17–22.

Peterson, G., & Leigh, G. (1990). The family and social competence in adolescence. In T. Gullotta, G. Adams, & R. Montemayor (Eds.), *Developing social competency in adolescence* (pp. 97–138). Newbury Park, CA: Sage Publications.

Phinney, J. (1990). Ethnic identity in adolescents and adults: A review of the research. *Psychological Bulletin, 108*, 499–514.

Piaget, J. (1963). *The origins of intelligence in children*. New York, NY: Norton.

Piaget, J. (1965). *The moral judgement of the child*. New York: Free Press.

Piaget, J. (1981). *Intelligence and affectivity: Their relationship during children development*. Palo Alto, CA: Annual Reviews.

Piaget, J., & Inhelder, B. (1956). *The child's conception of space*. London, UK: Routledge & Kegan Paul.

Pinker, S. (1994). *The language instinct*. New York: W. Morrow.

Pipher, M. (1994). *Reviving Ophelia: Saving the selves of adolescent girls*. New York: Ballantine Books.

Plath, S. (1996). *The it-doesn't-matter suit*. New York: St. Martin's Press.

Pope, C. (2001). *"Doing school." How are we creating a generation of stressed out, materialistic, and miseducated students*. London: Yale University Press.

Postman, N. (1995). *The end of education: Redefining the value of school*. New York: Vintage Books.

Postman, N. (1999). *Building a bridge to the 18th century: How the past can improve our future*. New York: Vintage Books.

Powlishta, K. (1995). Gender bias in children's perceptions of personality traits. *Sex Roles, 32*, 17–28.

Pratt, C., & Bryant, P. (1990). Young children understand that looking leads to knowing (So long as they are looking into a single barrel). *Child Development, 61*, 973–982.

Randall, T., & Desrosiers, M. (1980). Measurement of supernatural beliefs: sex difference and locus of control. *Journal of Personality Assessment, 44*, 493–498.

Razack, S. (1998). *Looking white people in the eye: Gender, race, and culture in courtrooms and classrooms*. Toronto, ON: University of Toronto Press.

Ream, G., & Savin-Williams, R. (2003). Religious development in adolescence. In G. Adams & M. Berzonsky (Eds.), *Blackwell handbook of adolescence* (pp. 51–59). Malden, MA: Blackwell.

Regnerus, M. (2003). Religion and positive adolescent outcomes: A review of research and theory. *Review of Religious Research, 44*, 394–413.

Reid, S. (1995). Why teach music? *Federation of Women Teachers Association, 13*, 12–13.

Reinsmith, W. (1989). The whole in every part: Steiner and Waldorf schooling. *The Education Forum, 54*, 79–91.

Rhedding-Jones, J. (2000). The other girls: Culture, psychoanalytic theories and writing. *International Journal of Qualitative Studies in Education, 13*, 263–280.

Rich, G. (2003). The positive psychology of youth and adolescence. *Journal of Youth and Adolescence, 32,* 1–3.

Richards, M. (1980). *Toward wholeness: Rudolf Steiner education in America.* Middletown, CT: Wesleyan University.

Richardson, R., & Evans, E. (1997). *Connecting with others: Lessons for teaching social and emotional competence.* Waterloo, ON: Colwell Systems/Research Press.

Rigby, K. (2002). Bullying in childhood. In P. Smith & C. Hart (Eds.), *Blackwell handbook of childhood social development* (pp. 549–568). Oxford, UK: Blackwell.

Rintel, E., & Pittam, J. (1997). Strangers in a strange land: Interaction management on Internet relay chat. *Human Communication Research, 23,* 507–534.

Robbins, P. (1998). *Adolescent suicide.* Jefferson, NC: McFarland.

Roeser, R., & Eccles, J. (1998). Adolescents' perceptions of middle school: Relation to longitudinal changes in academic and psychological adjustment. *Journal of Research on Adolescence, 88,* 123–158.

Rogers, A. (1993). Voice, play, and practice of courage in girls and women's lives. *Harvard Educational Review, 63,* 265–295.

Rogoff, B. (1990). *Apprenticeship in thinking: Cognitive development in social context.* New York: Oxford University Press.

Rosenberg, M. (1989). *Society and the adolescent self-image* (Rev. ed.). Middletown, CT: Wesleyan University Press.

Rossiter, G. (1999). The shaping influence of film and television on the spirituality and identity of children and adolescents: An educational response—part 3. *International Journal of Children's Spirituality, 4,* 207–224.

Rozak, T. (1992). *The voices of the earth.* New York: Simon & Schuster.

Rubin, K. (1972). Relationship between egocentric communication and popularity among peers. *Developmental Psychology, 7,* 364.

Rubin, K., & Asendorpf, J. (1993). Social withdrawal, inhibition, and shyness in childhood: Conceptual and definitional issues. In K. Rubin & J. Asendorf, J. (Eds.), *Social withdrawal, inhibition and shyness in childhood* (pp. 3–17). Mahwah, NJ: Lawrence Erlbaum Associates.

Rubin, K., LeMare, L., & Lollis, S. (1990). Social withdrawal in childhood: Developmental pathways to peer rejection. In S. Asher & J. Coie (Eds.), *Peer rejection in childhood* (pp. 217–249). Cambridge: Cambridge University Press.

Rubin, K., Burgess, K., & Coplan, R. (2002). Social withdrawal and shyness. In P. Smith & Hart (Eds.), *Blackwell handbook of childhood social development* (pp. 329–352). Oxford, UK: Blackwell.

Rubin, K., & Burgess, K. (2001). Social withdrawal and anxiety. In M. Vasey & M. Dadds (Eds.), *The developmental psychopathology of anxiety* (pp. 407–434). New York: Oxford University Press.

Saarni, C. (1999). *The development of emotional competence.* New York: Guilford Press.

Sabornie, E. (1994). Social-affective characteristics in early adolescents identified as learning disabled and nondisabled. *Learning Disabilities Quarterly, 17,* 268–279.

Sadker, M., & Sadker, D. (1994). *Failing at fairness: How America's schools cheat girls.* New York: Charles Scribner.

Salovey, P., & Sluyter, D. (1997). *Emotional development and emotional intelligence: Educational implications.* New York: Basic Books.

Sangster, J. (2002). *Girl trouble: Female delinquency in English Canada.* Toronto, ON: Between the Lines.

Santrock, J. (1993). *Adolescence: An introduction.* Dubuque, IA: Brown & Benchmark.

Schaffer, R. (1996). *Social development.* Oxford, UK: Blackwell.

Schank, R., & Cleary, C. (1995). Making machines creative. In S. Smith, T. Ward, & R. Finke (Eds.), *The creative cognitive approach* (pp.229–247). Cambridge, MA: MIT Press.

Schultz, L., & Selman, R. (1989). Bridging the gap between interpersonal thought and action in early adolescence: The role of psychodynamic processes. *Development and Psychopathology, 1,* 133–152.

Schuster, B. (1996). Rejection, exclusion, and harassment at work and in schools: An integration of results from research on mobbing, bullying, and peer rejection. *European Psychologist, 1,* 293–317.

Schweichart, P. (1996). Speech is silver, silence is golden: The asymmetrical intersubjectivity of communication action. In N. Goldberger, J. Tarule, B. Clinchy, M. Belenky (Eds.), *Knowledge, difference, and power: Essays inspired by women's ways of knowing* (pp. 305–331). New York: Basic Books.

Searle, J. (1969). *Speech acts: An essay in the philosophy of language.* Cambridge: Cambridge University Press.

Seligman, M. (2002). *Authentic happiness: Using the new positive psychology to realize your potential for lasting fulfillment.* New York: Free Press.

Seligman, M., & Csikszentmihalyi, M. (2000). Positive psychology: An introduction. *American Psychologist, 55,* 5–15.

Selman, R. (1980). *The growth of interpersonal understanding.* New York: Academic Press.

Selman, R. (2003). *The promotion of social awareness: Powerful lessons from the partnership of developmental theory and classroom practice.* New York: Russell Sage Foundation.

Shantz, C. (1983). Social cognition. In P. Mussen (Eds.), *Handbook of child psychology: Vol. 3* (pp. 495–555). New York: Wiley.

Sheridan, S., Kratochwill, T., & Elliott, S. (1990). Behavioral consultation with parents and teachers: Delivering treatment for socially withdrawn children at home and school. *School Psychology Review, 19,* 33–52.

Shields, S. (2002). *Speaking from the heart: Gender and the social meaning of emotion.* Cambridge: Cambridge University Press.

Shilling, A. (1986). *The Ojibway dream.* Montreal, QE: Tundra.

Shweder, R. (1990). In defense of moral realism: Reply to Gabennesch. *Child Development, 61,* 2060–2067.

Shweder, R. (1991). *Thinking through cultures: Expeditions in cultural psychology.* Cambridge, MA: Harvard University Press.

Silverman, L. (1989). Invisible gifts, invisible handicaps. *Roeper Review, 12,* 37–42.

Silverstein, B., & Perlick, D. (1995). *The cost of competence: Why inequality causes depression, eating disorders, and illness in women.* New York: Oxford University Press.

Simmons, E., & Blyth, D. (1987). *Moving into adolescence: The impact of pubertal change and the school context.* Hawthorn, NY: Aldine de Gruyter.

Simmons, R., Rosenberg, F., & Rosenberg, H. (1973). Disturbance in the self-image at adolescence. *American Sociological Review, 38,* 535–568.

Simon, W., & Gagnon, J. (1986). Sexual scripts: Permanence and change. *Archives of Sexual Behavior, 15,* 97–120.

Slomkowski, C., & Dunn, J. (1996). Young children's understanding of other people's beliefs and feelings and their connected communication with friends. *Developmental Psychology, 32,* 442–447.

Smith, C. (1982). *God-concept, sex role perceptions, and religious experience.* Unpublished doctoral dissertation, Fuller Theological Seminary, School of Psychology.

Smith, F., & Smoll, R. (1996). *Children and youth in sport: A biopsychological perspective.* Madison, WI: Brown & Benchmark.

Sobsey, D., & Mansell, S. (1997). Teaching people with disabilities to be abused and exploited: The special educator as accomplice. *Developmental Disabilities Bulletin, 25,* 77–93.

Spatz, J., & Wright Cassidy, K. (1999). *Theory of mind and prosocial behavior in preschool children.* Poster session presented at the biennial meeting of the Society for Research in Child Development, Albuquerque, NM.

Sperber, D., & Wilson, D. (1986). *Relevance: Communication and cognition.* Cambridge, MA: Harvard University Press.

Spilka, B., Hood, R., Hunsberger, B., & Gorsuch, R. (2003). *The psychology of religion* (3rd ed.). New York: Guildford.

Stanton, A. (1995). Reconfiguring teaching and knowing in the college classroom. In N. Goldberger, J. Tarule, B. Clincky & M. Belenky (Eds.), *Knowledge difference and power* (pp. 25–56). New York: Basic Books.

Staub, D., Schwartz, I., Gallucci, C., & Peck, C. (1994). Four portraits of friendship at an inclusive school. *Journal of the Association for Persons with Severe Handicaps, 19,* 314–326.

Steeves, D. (2003, December 8). God and the brain. *Globe and Mail,* p. A16.

Steinberg, L., & Silverberg, S. (1986). The vicissitudes of autonomy in early adolescence. *Child Development, 57,* 841–851.

Steiner, R. (1976). *Education of the child in the light of anthroposophy.* (G. Adams & M. Adams, Trans.). London: Rudolph Steiner Press.

Sternberg, R. (2003). What is an "expert student?" *Educational Researcher, 32,* 5–9.

Stipek, D., Recchia, S., & McClintic, S. (1992). Self-evaluation in young children. *Monographs of the Society for Research in Child Development, 57* (1, Serial No. 226), 1–84.

Strasburger, V., & Wilson, B. (2002). *Children, adolescents, and the media.* Thousand Oaks, CA: Sage Publications.

Strauss, S., & Shiloney, T. (1994). Teachers' models of children's minds and learning. In L. Hirschfield & S. Gelman (Eds.), *Mapping the mind: Domain specificity in cognition and culture* (pp. 455–473). New York: Cambridge University Press.

Sullivan, H. (1953). *The interpersonal theory of psychiatry.* New York: Norton.

Sullivan, K., Zaitchik, D., & Tager-Flusberg, H. (1994). Preschoolers can attribute second-order beliefs. *Developmental Psychology, 30*, 395–402.

Sulloway, F. (1996). *Born to rebel: Birth order, family dynamics and creative lives.* New York: Vintage Books.

Super, C., & Harkness, S. (1997). The cultural structuring of child development. In J. Berry, P. Dasen, & T. Saraswathi (Eds.), *Handbook of cross-cultural psychology: Vol. 2. Basic processes and human development* (pp. 1–39). Boston: Allyn & Bacon.

Swanson, H. (2000). Issues facing the field of learning disabilities. *Learning Disabilities Quarterly, 23*, 37–49.

Sweet, L. (1997). *God in the classroom: The controversial issue of religion in Canada's schools.* Toronto, ON: McClelland & Stewart.

Tager-Flusberg, H., Sullivan, K., Barker, J., Harris, A., & Boshart, J. (1997, April). *Theory of mind and language acquisition: The development of cognition verbs.* Poster presented at the biennial meeting of the Society for Research in Child Development, Washington, DC.

Tamminen, K. (1994). Religious experiences in childhood and adolescence: A viewpoint of religious development between the ages of 7 and 20. *International Journal for the Psychology of Religion, 4*, 51–85.

Tangney, J. (1991). Moral affect: The good, the bad and the ugly. *Journal of Personality and Social Psychology, 61*, 598–607.

Tannen, D. (1994). *Gender and discourse.* New York: Oxford University Press.

Tarpley, T. (2001). Children, the Internet, and other new technologies. In D. Singer & J. Singer (Eds.), *Handbook of children and media* (pp. 547–556). Thousand Oaks, CA: Sage Publications.

Tatum, B. (2003). *Why are all the black kids sitting together in the cafeteria: And other conversations about race.* New York: Basic Books.

Tavris, C. (1992). *The mismeasure of women.* New York: Simon & Schuster.

Taylor, M., & Carlson, S. (2000). The influence of religious beliefs on parental attitudes about children's fantasy behavior. In K. Rosengren, C. Johnson, & P. Harris (Eds.), *Imagining the impossible: The development of magical, scientific, and religious thinking in contemporary society* (pp. 247–268). Cambridge: Cambridge University Press.

Teen trouble: Drugs, sex, depression: Canadian experts on how to help kids survive trying times. (2004, March 1). *Maclean's: Canada's Weekly Magazine*, 26–33.

Teen Vogue (2003, Dec./2004, Jan.). Make me over: 50 ways to rethink your clothes, bedroom, makeup, hair, workout. Cover page title.

The new lexicon Webster's dictionary of the English language: Encyclopedic edition. (1989). New York: Lexicon Publications Inc.

Thomas, D., & Carver, C. (1990). Religion and adolescent social competence. In T. Gullota and G. Adams (Eds.), *Developing social competency in adolescence: Advances in adolescent development* (pp. 195–219). Newbury Park, CA: Sage.

Tilley, S. (1998). Conducting respectful research: A critique of practice. *Canadian Journal of Education, 23*, 316–328.

Tomasello, M. (1999). *The cultural origins of human cognition.* Cambridge, MA: Harvard University Press.

Tomasello, M., Kruger, A., & Ratner, H. (1993). *Cultural learning. Behavioral and Brain Sciences, 16*, 495–511.

Torrance, D. (1997). "Do you want to be in my gang?" A study of the existence and effects of bullying in a primary school class. *British Journal of Special Education, 24*, 158–162.

Trawick-Smith, J. (2003). *Early childhood development: A multicultural perspective* (3rd ed.). Upper Saddle River, NJ: Merrill-Prentice Hall.

Tremblay, R. (2000). The development of aggressive behaviours during childhood: What have we learned in the past century? *International Journal of Behavioural Development, 24*, 129–141.

Trulear, H. (2000). *Faith-based institutions and high-risk youth: First report to the field.* Philadelphia, PA: Public/Private Ventures.

Underwood, M. (2002). Sticks and stones and social exclusion: Aggression among boys and girls. In P. Smith & C. Hart (Eds.), *Blackwell handbook of childhood social development* (pp. 533–348). Oxford, UK: Blackwell.

Underwood, M., Galen, B., & Paquette, J. (2001). Top ten methodological challenges for understanding gender and aggression: Why can't we all just get along? *Social Development, 10*, 248–267.

Urberg, K. (1982). The development of the concepts of masculinity and femininity in young children. *Sex Roles, 8*, 659–668.

Veith, D. (1980). Recursive thinking and the self-concepts of preadolescents. *The Journal of Genetic Psychology, 137*, 233–246.

Vernon, A. (1997). *Thinking, feeling and behaving: An emotional education curriculum for adolescents.* Waterloo, ON: Colwell Systems/Research Press.

Vygotsky, L. (1978). *Mind in society: The development of higher psychological processes.* Cambridge, MA: Harvard University Press.

Wallander, J., & Varni, J. (1998). Effects of pediatric chronic physical disorders on child and family adjustment. *Journal of Child Psychology and Psychiatry, 39*, 29–46.

Wang, Q. (2004). The emergence of cultural self-constructs: Autobiographical memory and self-description in European American and Chinese children. *Developmental Psychology, 40*, 3–15.

Ward, M. (2004). Wading through stereotypes: Positive and negative associations between media use and black adolescents' conceptions of self. *Developmental Psychology, 40*, 284–294.

Warren, D. (1994). *Blindness and children: An individual differences approach.* New York: Cambridge University Press.

Watson, J. (2000). Whose model of spirituality should be used in the spiritual development of school children? *International Journal of Children's Spirituality, 5*, 91–101.

Watts, F., & Williams, M. (1988). *The psychology of religious knowing.* Cambridge, UK: Cambridge University Press.

Watson, A., Nixon, C., Wilson, A., & Capage, L. (1999). Social interaction skills and theory of mind in young children. *Developmental Psychology, 35*, 386–391.

Weaver-Hightower, M. (2003). The "boy turn" in research on gender and education. *Review of Educational Research, 73*, 471–498.

Wellman, H. (1990). *The child's theory of mind*. Cambridge, MA: MIT Press.

Wentzel, K., & Asher, S. (1995). The academic lives of neglected, and rejected, popular, and controversial children. *Child Development, 66*, 754–763.

Werner, H. (1948). *Comparative psychology of mental development*. New York: The Free Press.

Werner, R., & Cassidy, K. (1997, April). *Children's psychological understanding and its relationship to social information processing and social competence*. Poster session presented at the biennial meeting of the Society for Research in Child Development, Washington, DC.

Wertsch, J. (1989). A sociocultural approach to mind. In W. Damon (Ed.), *Child development today and tomorrow* (pp. 14–33). San Francisco: Jossey Bass.

Whitney, I., & Smith, P. (1993). A survey of the nature and extent of bullying in junior/middle and secondary schools. *Educational Research, 35*, 3–25.

Wierzbicka, A. (1989). Soul and mind: Linguistic evidence for ethnopsychology and cultural history. *American Anthropologist, 91*, 41–58.

Wilgosh, L. (1994). The underachievement of girls: A societal rather than a gender issue. *Education in Canada, Spring*, 18–23.

Williams, K. (2001). *Ostracism: The power of silence*. New York: Guilford Press.

Wiltshire, D. (1989). The uses of myth, image, and the female body in revisioning knowledge. In A. Jagger & S. Bordo (Eds.), *Gender/body/knowldege: Feminist reconstructions of being and knowledge* (pp. 92–114). New Brunswick, NJ: Rutgers University Press.

Wimmer, H., & Hartl, M. (1991). Against the Cartesian view on mind: Young children's difficulty with own false beliefs. *British Journal of Developmental Psychology, 9*, 125–138.

Wimmer, H., & Perner, J. (1983). Beliefs about beliefs: Representation and constraining function of wrong beliefs in young children's understanding of deception. *Cognition, 13*, 103–128.

Wineburg, S. (1991). Historical problem solving: A study of the cognitive processes used in the evaluation of documentary and pictorial evidence. *Journal of Educational Psychology, 83*, 73–87.

Winner, E. (2000). The origins and ends of giftedness. *American Psychologist, 55*, 159–169.

Winner, E., & Leedam, S. (1991). Distinguishing irony from deception: Understanding the speaker's second-order intention. *British Journal of Developmental Psychology, 9*, 257–270.

Winston, J. (2002). Drama, spirituality and the curriculum. *International Journal of Children's Spirituality, 7*, 241–255.

Wolfendale, S. (Ed.). (2000). *Special needs in the early years: Snapshots of practice*. New York: Routledge Falmer.

World Health Organization (1999). *WHO Statistical Information System*. Geneva, Switzerland.

Yon, D. (2000). *Elusive culture: Schooling, race, and identity in global times*. New York: State of University of New York Press.

Young, E. (1992). *Seven blind mice*. New York: Philomel Books.

Youniss, J., McLellan, J., & Yates, M. (1999). Religion, community service, and identity in American youth. *Journal of Adolescence, 22*, 243–253.

Yuill, N. (1993). Understanding of personality and dispositions. In M. Bennett (Ed.), *The child as psychologist: An introduction to the development of social cognition* (pp. 87–110). New York: Harvester Wheatsheaf.

Zahn-Waxler, C., & Robinson, J. (1995). Empathy and guild: Early origins of feelings of responsibility. In J. Tangney & K. Fischer (Eds.), *Self-consciousness emotions: The psychology of shame, guilt, embarrassment, and pride* (pp. 143–173). New York: Guilford Press.

Zimmer-Gembeck, M., & Collins, W. (2003). Autonomy development during adolescence. In G. Adams & M. Berzonsky (Eds.), *Blackwell handbook of adolescence* (pp. 175–204). Malden, MA: Blackwell.

Zippelius, R. (1986). Exclusion and shunning as legal and social sanctions. *Ethology and Sociobiology, 7*, 159–166.

INDEX

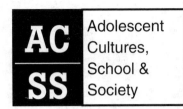

Joseph L. DeVitis & Linda Irwin-DeVitis
GENERAL EDITORS

As schools struggle to redefine and restructure themselves, they need to be cognizant of the new realities of adolescents. Thus, this series of monographs and textbooks is committed to depicting the variety of adolescent cultures that exist in today's post-industrial societies. It is intended to be a primarily qualitative research, practice, and policy series devoted to contextual interpretation and analysis that encompasses a broad range of interdisciplinary critique. In addition, this series will seek to provide a pragmatic, pro-active response to the current backlash of conservatism that continues to dominate political discourse, practice, and policy. This series seeks to address issues of curriculum theory and practice; multicultural education; aggression and violence; the media and arts; school dropouts; homeless and runaway youth; alienated youth; at-risk adolescent populations; family structures and parental involvement; and race, ethnicity, class, and gender studies.

Send proposals and manuscripts to the general editors at:

  Joseph L. DeVitis & Linda Irwin-DeVitis
  College of Education and Human Development
  University of Louisville
  Louisville, KY 40292-0001

To order other books in this series, please contact our Customer Service Department at:

  (800) 770-LANG (within the U.S.)
  (212) 647-7706 (outside the U.S.)
  (212) 647-7707 FAX

or browse online by series at:

  WWW.PETERLANGUSA.COM